DIRECTORS IN PERSPECTIVE

General editor: C. D. Innes

Joseph Chaikin

DIRECTORS IN PERSPECTIVE

What characterizes modern theater above all is continual stylistic innovation, in which theory and presentation have combined to create a wealth of new forms – naturalism, expressionism, epic theater, etc. – in a way that has made directors the leading figures rather than dramatists. To a greater extent than is perhaps generally realized, it has been directors who have provided dramatic models for playwrights, though of course there are many variations in this relationship. In some cases a dramatist's themes challenge a director to create new performance conditions (Stanislavski and Chekhov), or a dramatist turns director to formulate an appropriate style for his work (Brecht); alternatively a director writes plays to correspond with his theory (Artaud), or creates communal scripts out of exploratory work with actors (Chaikin, Grotowski). Some directors are identified with a single theory (Craig), others gave definitive shape to a range of styles (Reinhardt); the work of some has an ideological basis (Stein), while others work more pragmatically (Bergman).

   Generally speaking, those directors who have contributed to what is distinctly "modern" in today's theater stand in much the same relationship to the dramatic texts they work with as composers do to librettists in opera. However, since theatrical performance is the most ephemeral of the arts and the only easily reproducible element is the text, critical attention has tended to focus on the playwright. This series is designed to redress the balance by providing an overview of selected directors' stage work: those who helped to formulate modern theories of drama. Their key productions have been reconstructed from promptbooks, reviews, scene-designs, photographs, diaries, correspondence and – where these productions are contemporary – documented by first-hand description, interviews with the director, etc. Apart from its intrinsic interest, this record allows a critical perspective, testing ideas against practical problems and achievements. In each case, too, the director's work is set in context by indicating the source of his ideas and their influence, the organization of his acting company and his relationship to the theatrical or political establishment, so as to bring out wider issues: the way theater both reflects and influences assumptions about the nature of man and his social role.

C. D. *Innes*

TITLES IN THIS SERIES:

Ingmar Bergman: Lise-Lone and Frederick J. Marker
Peter Stein: Michael Patterson
Max Reinhardt: J. L. Styan
Edward Gordon Craig: Christopher Innes

Future titles in this series:

Adolphe Appia: Richard Beacham
Bertolt Brecht: John Fuegi
Peter Brook: Albert Hunt and Geoffrey Reeves
Jerzy Grotowski   Nicholas Sales
Constantin Stanislavski: Peter Holland

Chaikin with actress Brenda Dixon in an Open Theater workshop, 1967. Photograph by Hope Herman Wurmfeld.

Joseph Chaikin

Exploring at the Boundaries of Theater

EILEEN BLUMENTHAL
Rutgers University

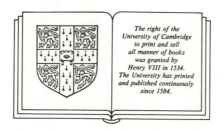

The right of the
University of Cambridge
to print and sell
all manner of books
was granted by
Henry VIII in 1534.
The University has printed
and published continuously
since 1584.

CAMBRIDGE UNIVERSITY PRESS

CAMBRIDGE

LONDON   NEW YORK   NEW ROCHELLE

MELBOURNE   SYDNEY

PN
2287
C46
B58
1984

Rev

Published by the Press Syndicate of the University of Cambridge
The Pitt Building, Trumpington Street, Cambridge CB2 1RP
32 East 57th Street, New York, NY 10022, USA
296 Beaconsfield Parade, Middle Park, Melbourne 3206, Australia

First published 1984

Printed in the United States of America

Material from "Chaikin and Shepard Speak in Tongues" by Eileen Blumenthal, *Village Voice*, Nov. 26, 1979, pp. 103ff., and from "Joseph Chaikin: An Open Theory of Acting" by Eileen Blumenthal, *yale/theatre* 8, nos.
2–3, pp. 112–33, is used by permission.

Library of Congress Cataloging in Publication Data

Blumenthal, Eileen, 1948–
Joseph Chaikin: exploring at the boundaries of theater.
(Directors in Perspective)
Bibliography: p.
Includes index.
1. Chaikin, Joseph, 1935–   . 2. Theater –
Production and direction. 3. Experimental theater –
United States. I. Title. II. Series.
PN2287.C46B58   1984   792'.0233'0924   84-12707
ISBN 0 521 24298 3 hardcovers
ISBN 0 521 28589 5 paperback

FOR DIANE, PHILIP, AND JUDITH BLUMENTHAL

Contents

List of illustrations		*page* xi
Preface		xv
1.	Overview	1
	The theater scene	1
	The formative years	5
	The Open Theater	14
	After the Open Theater	27
	The Winter Project	31
2.	An open theory	38
	The purpose of theater	38
	The languages of theater	44
	The actor and the character	50
	The communities of theater	56
	The politics and economics of theater	62
	Openness	65
3.	The workshop investigations	67
	Underscoring presence	71
	Finding new theater languages	83
	Thematic investigations	101
4.	Early collaborative play making: *The Serpent*	104
	The beginnings of collaborative play making	104
	The Serpent	106
5.	The growth of ensemble playwriting	140
	The process – and the problems	140
	The Mutation Show: playwriting without a playwright	148
	Tongues and *Savage/Love:* ensemble creation without an ensemble	171
6.	Directing plays: going from the part to the person	185
7.	Afterword	208
Chronology		212
Notes		226
Bibliography		250
Index		256

Illustrations

Chaikin with actress Brenda Dixon in an Open Theater
workshop, 1967 *frontispiece*
Chaikin during a rehearsal of *Endgame* *page* 2
The Chaikin family, New York, 1936 7
Chaikin, circa 1954, Des Moines, Iowa 9
Chaikin as Galy Gay in the Living Theater production of
Man Is Man, New York, 1962 13
Chaikin with actors in an Open Theater workshop, New
York, 1967 16
Chaikin in the Open Theater production of *Keep Tightly
Closed in a Cool Dry Place*, New York, 1966 18
Scene from *The Serpent* at Washington Square Methodist
Church, New York, 1970 19
Scene from *Terminal*, New York, 1971 20
Scene from *Terminal*, New York, 1971 21
Scene from *The Mutation Show* at St. Clement's Church,
New York, 1973 22
Scene from *Nightwalk* at the Space for Innovative Develop-
ment, New York, 1973 23
The two journeyers in *Nightwalk* at the Space for Innovative
Development, New York, 1973 24
Scene from *The Sea Gull* at the Manhattan Theatre Club,
New York, 1975 31
Chaikin in *Tongues* at the New York Shakespeare Festival
Public Theater, 1979 32
Chaikin in *Texts* at the New York Shakespeare Festival Pub-
lic Theater, 1981 33
A group of faceless refugees in *Tourists and Refugees* at La-
Mama, New York, 1980 35
A refugee "testimony" scene from *Tourists and Refugees* at
LaMama, New York, 1980 36
Chaikin in an Open Theater workshop, 1966 40
Beggars scavenging for food in *The Dybbuk* at the New York
Shakespeare Festival Public Theater, 1977 43
Comic "bums" in *Tourists and Refugees* at LaMama, New
York, 1980 49

xi

Chaikin works with Winter Project actress Tina Shepard,
        New York, 1980   55
Chaikin in an Open Theater workshop with Tina Shepard,
        New York, 1973   68
A journeyer observes the "sleep world" in *Nightwalk* at the
        Space for Innovative Development, New York, 1973   72
An Open Theater "chord" exercise in workshop, New
        York, 1968   73
"Jamming" with movement in *The Mutation Show* at St. Cle-
        ment's Church, New York, 1973   75
Two born-again Christians sing their religious ecstasy in
        Tourists and Refugees at LaMama, New York, 1980   80
An "interview" scene in *Re-Arrangements* at LaMama, New
        York, 1979   82
A refugee-condition image being developed in a Winter
        Project workshop, New York, 1980   84
The same refugee-condition image in performance in *Tour-
        ists and Refugees* at LaMama, New York, 1980   85
"Perfect" dinner guests are observed by the two journeyers
        in *Nightwalk* at the Space for Innovative Develop-
        ment, New York, 1973   88
"Perfect" tourists encounter a pair of multinational-corpo-
        rate wives in *Tourists and Refugees*, in rehearsal,
        New York, 1980   89
A distilled image of a domestic moment in *Re-Arrangements*
        at LaMama, New York, 1979   94
A distilled image showing two couples in *Re-Arrangements*
        at LaMama, New York, 1979   95
The "men's world" from *Nightwalk* at the Space for Innova-
        tive Development, New York, 1973   96
The "dance on the graves of the dead" in *Terminal*, New
        York, 1971   102
A dying woman and her attendant in *Trespassing* at La-
        Mama, New York, 1982   103
The serpent forms in the garden in *The Serpent* in work-
        shop, New York, 1967   113
The temptation of Eve by the tree-serpent in *The Serpent* in
        workshop, New York, 1967   114
The temptation of Eve in *The Serpent* in workshop, New
        York, 1967   115
The curses of God in *The Serpent* in workshop, New York,
        1967   121

Abel and Cain in *The Serpent* in workshop, New York,
    1967   123

Cain and Abel in *The Serpent* in workshop, New York, 1967   124

The chorus of women in *The Serpent* in workshop, New
    York, 1967   127

The "begatting" in *The Serpent* in performance at Washing-
    ton Square Methodist Church, New York, 1970   128

The "first birth" in *The Serpent* in workshop, New York,
    1967   130

The Kennedy assassination scene in *The Serpent* in perfor-
    mance at Washington Square Methodist Church,
    New York, 1970   132

Chaikin (with JoAnn Schmidman) in an Open Theater
    workshop, 1973   141

The Open Theater *Nightwalk* workshop, New York, 1973   144

A hunter and the wolf-girl in *The Mutation Show* at St. Cle-
    ment's Church, New York, 1973   154

The wolf-girl being roped in *The Mutation Show* at St. Cle-
    ment's Church, New York, 1973   155

"The boy in the box" in *The Mutation Show*   156

Caspar's journey in *The Mutation Show* at St. Clement's
    Church, New York, 1973   157

The boy who breaks out from the box in *The Mutation Show*
    at St. Clement's Church, New York, 1973   159

The "human gallery" in *The Mutation Show* at St. Clement's
    Church, New York, 1973   163

The barker presents "the man who smiles" in *The Mutation
    Show*   167

A mutated reprise of Caspar's journey in *The Mutation Show*
    at St. Clement's Church, New York, 1973   168

Chaikin and Sam Shepard during a rehearsal break at the
    Eureka Theater, San Francisco, 1979   175

Chaikin and Sam Shepard jamming during a rehearsal of
    Tongues at the Eureka Theater, San Francisco, 1979   177

Chaikin and Shepard in *Tongues* at the Magic Theater, San
    Francisco, 1978   178

Chaikin in *Savage/Love* at the New York Shakespeare Festi-
    val Public Theater, 1979   181

Scene from *Interview* from *America Hurrah*, at the Pocket
    Theater, New York, 1966   186

Scene from *The Dybbuk* at the New York Shakespeare Festi-
    val Public Theater, 1977   187

Chaikin as Hamm and Peter Maloney as Clov in the Open
    Theater production of *Endgame*, New York, 1969   189
Chaikin working with actors on "filled" versus "unfilled"
    modes in *Endgame*   193
Hamm and Clov are again a vaudeville team in the Manhat-
    tan Theatre Club production of *Endgame*, New
    York, 1979   198
Nagg and Nell in *Endgame* at the Manhattan Theatre Club,
    New York, 1979   200
Hamm prepares to fling away his dog in *Endgame* at the
    Manhattan Theatre Club, New York, 1979   202
Clov launches *Endgame* with a lively flourish at the Manhat-
    tan Theatre Club, New York, 1979   203
Hamm and Clov in a moment of active waiting in *Endgame*
    at the Manhattan Theatre Club, New York, 1979   204
Chaikin, New York, 1983   210

Preface

Occasionally a work of art changes everything, breaks through the boundaries of one's vision and imagination. Joseph Chaikin's theater has unsettled me in that way. And over the years it has done much to reshape my values and thoughts. To write about work that one finds so exhilarating is a particular kind of good fortune.

I have been multiply blessed in this project by the support and cooperation of many generous, intelligent, and talented people. Dean Keller and, especially, Alex Gildzen of the Kent State University Library assisted me in all sorts of ways, from ferreting out information, to allowing me to sift through cartons of uncatalogued material, to offering me hospitality in Kent. Jane Yockel of Artservices, Serge Mogilat at the New York Shakespeare Festival, Andy Hamner at the Eureka Theater, and the research librarians at the Lincoln Center Library of the Performing Arts were among the people who pored through old files to help pin down the chronology of Chaikin's work; Barry Daniels gave me access to an Open Theater chronology that he had compiled independently. Michael Feingold let me use unpublished portions of an interview with Chaikin, and Sara Laschever lent a tape recording from Chaikin's stint in Princeton. The Rutgers University Research Council provided generous and patient support. And Alois M. Nagler gave his open-minded assistance and encouragement to my work on Chaikin from the beginning—and has my special and affectionate thanks.

I have benefited greatly from the comments of friends and colleagues who read early drafts of this study. Gordon Braden, David Cole, M. E. Comtois, and Erika Munk offered extremely useful perspectives. M. Mark's editorial guidance in shaping an earlier version of the *Tongues* section for the *Village Voice* has been carried over to the revised version here. Robert Massa repeatedly came through for me with his fine copy-editing advice (and typing). And Christopher Innes's suggestions all along the way have been invaluable.

The photographers whose pictures enrich my book have been generous in allowing the use of their work—and in some cases have gone to considerable effort to locate old, buried material. For the use of photos, I wish to thank Karl Bissinger, Ron Blanchette, Claude Furones and Hank Gans, Carol Greunkie of the Max Waldman Ar-

xv

chives, James Lapine, Mary Ellen Mark, Inge Morath, Phill Niblock, Sylvia Plachy, Ricki Rosen, Nat Tileston, and Hope Herman Wurmfeld. I am grateful also to Steven Gomer for making available stills from his film on Chaikin, to Joel Schechter for supplying a print from *Theater* magazine, and to Shami Chaikin and Roberta Sklar for providing photographs from their personal collections.

The active cooperation of many of Chaikin's colleagues has yielded information and insights to me that I could not otherwise have gotten. Joyce Aaron, James Barbosa, Shami Chaikin, Steven Gomer, Ellen Maddow, Judith Malina, Peter Maloney, Sam Shepard, Tina Shepard, Roberta Sklar, Jean-Claude van Itallie, Barbara Vann, Susan Yankowitz, and Paul Zimet spoke with me at length, on tape, about their work with Chaikin. Mark Kaminsky, Ellen Maddow, Peter Maloney, the late Daniel Seltzer, Tina Shepard, Roberta Sklar, Susan Yankowitz, and Paul Zimet gave me access to their private – and sometimes intensely personal – work notes. For conversations that helped to flesh out my portrait and/or permission to quote from private correspondence, I am obliged to most of the people already listed and many others, including Ronnie Gilbert, Richard Gilman, Fred Katz, Harry Mann, Mira Rafalowicz, Gordon Rogoff, Ellen Sandler (Schindler), and Lee Worley.

Most important of all, of course, has been Chaikin's assistance. His concrete help – consisting of hours and hours of taped interviews, hundreds of conversations, access to his notes, and permission to attend his private workshops and rehearsals during the past ten years – has made this project not only possible but nourishing and exciting.

This book is intended as a work portrait, not a biography. It does, however, contain some elements of personal history that I felt were germane. Although most of this information came to me off the record, Chaikin has given me carte blanche in using it, as well as in drawing on the wealth of behind-the-scenes material to which I have been privy. As I trust that I have not abused my insider's privilege, I hope that it has not impaired my critical perspective. Still, I would be disappointed if the reader did not catch some of my enthusiasm about Chaikin's theater, which is what launched this project in the first place.

1   Overview

"To express the extreme joy of being alive at a certain moment is practically impossible – and really worth trying." Offering this challenge to his theater workshop, Joseph Chaikin was also revealing the values that have charged his work. He has searched for ways to transmit conditions that have no adequate expression in life or art: feelings too extreme or elusive to have a vocabulary, too complex or subversive to have a forum. Fascinated by problems that seem unsolvable, he has tried to extend the boundaries of what we can communicate. While much of his work has addressed the darker regions of experience, behind his obsession with these questions – and his engagement with the theater medium itself – is a startling alertness to the thrill of being alive.

Through his investigations in the Open Theater and after, Chaikin has probably done more than anyone to shake American theater loose from its nineteenth-century roots in naturalism and psychology. He has found new ways to develop nonliterary languages and nonnarrative structures for the stage and, in the shadow of films and television, to affirm the special energy of its liveness. His example, moreover, has inspired the growth of experimental workshops and ensemble creations, and has nourished resistance to commercialism. Although he has kept out of the limelight, most theater in America and much abroad have been touched by his innovations in stage aesthetics, values, and training.

THE THEATER SCENE

Chaikin came to New York to break into theater in 1955, just as the first rumblings of off-off-Broadway were getting started. He became one of a growing number of artists who, over the next several years, turned away from the established stage to experiment in lofts and cafés. Their questioning reached into nearly every facet of performance: the relationship between theater forms and observable reality; the connection between the actor and the character; the role of the audience; the responsibility of art to address social issues; and the economic structure of the industry itself.

The notion of an alternative American theater was not new, of

1

Chaikin during a rehearsal of *Endgame*. Photograph by Gomer/Heller
Productions.

course. There had been the Washington Square Players, Provincetown Players, and Neighborhood Playhouse, all founded in 1915
(and all closed before 1930), then the Civic Repertory Theater,
Group Theater, and Federal Theater Project in the late twenties and
thirties. But their momentum toward a noncommercial and, in some
cases, socially activist theater had not outlived them. And while
several of these earlier companies had been artistically innovative,
the only one to have a lasting effect on the mainstream was the
Group Theater, which had reinforced, even cemented, naturalism as
the mode of serious American drama.

Indeed, it was partly the legacy of the Group Theater that many of the new artists were opposing in their discontent with the strangle-hold of naturalism. Apart from musical comedy or old classics, realism was the only acceptable form in commercial theater. The few off-Broadway productions of Brecht, Beckett, Ionesco, and Genet in the fifties offered glimpses of a greater range of expression but did little to expand the field in general.

Perhaps the strongest single influence was Artaud, whose *Theater and Its Double* appeared in English in 1958. In revolt against prosaic, self-centered art, Artaud demanded that the stage create "a blood-stream of images, a bleeding spurt of images in the poet's head and in the spectator's as well." Theater, he insisted, must become directly, sensually expressive rather than merely realistic; the audience must be engulfed, attacked, and changed by the spectacle, rather than politely entertained. Amid the epidemic pedestrianism of the late Eisenhower years, his ideas came as an explosion of possibilities.

Some of the impetus for the experiments was political. Never radical to begin with, Broadway had retreated – with the help of congres-sional anti-Communist witchhunts and competition from television – into particular benignity. Now, as the sixties brought a surge of civil rights activism and then disillusionment and rage over Vietnam, com-mitted theater artists grew determined to include a social dimension in their work. The escapist musicals and Neil Simon–type comedies that dominated the stage seemed narcotic and reactionary; the preoc-cupation with personal crises that typified "serious" dramatists like Williams and Inge now seemed self-indulgent. Brecht's epic theater of engagement became a political inspiration, as well as an aesthetic model.

The antiestablishment bent turned, too, against the theater indus-try. The commercial stage was a business, and production costs had reached the point where artistic innovation was an unaffordable risk. Moreover, the rich producers and investors who largely fi-nanced Broadway seemed to be part of the ruling class rather than kindred spirits resisting it. Off-Broadway, a handful of small houses that began to thrive in the fifties, mostly in and around Greenwich Village, was less conservative politically and artistically; but still, it was more a scaled-down copy of the commercial system than a regular forum for alternative work.

The desire to disentangle art from moneymaking also spawned a movement toward antiprofessionalism. Amateurism, moreover, suited the super-democratic, communal ethos of the time, because it made everyone equal. And since Method-schooled actors were not necessarily more qualified than beginners to handle nonnaturalistic plays, there was some justification for challenging professional theater instruction. Happenings and other performance art forms designed for untrained actors grew from and supported this trend.

Meanwhile, the various explorations gradually began to have an outlet. In 1958, Joe Cino opened a Greenwich Village coffeehouse, the Caffe Cino, which presented theatrical productions, poetry readings, and art exhibitions. A handful of similar establishments opened over the next few years, presenting tiny-budget productions, mostly of original plays exploring new forms. The most important of these was the LaMama Experimental Theatre Club, launched in 1961 by Ellen Stewart. Individual productions and ongoing groups also began to find homes in local churches, including the Judson Memorial Church on Washington Square and St. Marks in the Bowery.

Perhaps the major force in early off-off-Broadway was the Living Theater, which established itself on Fourteenth Street in 1959. Formed in 1946 by Judith Malina and her husband, Julian Beck, to work on poetic drama, the company already had a reputation for innovation. It had presented Nō dramas, medieval miracle plays, and works by Paul Goodman, Alfred Jarry, Jean Cocteau, William Carlos Williams, August Strindberg, and Jean Racine. Intensely political (professed anarchists), the directors of the Living Theater set out in the late fifties to integrate their social conviction with their art. Their repertory focused on works like Jack Gelber's *The Connection*, Brecht's *Man Is Man*, and Kenneth Brown's *The Brig*. The company began to take public stands on social issues, including U.S. involvement in Southeast Asia, and to engage in civil disobedience. Brashly antiestablishment, the Living Theater was important in opening ground for theater outside bourgeois respectability and "high culture" and in drawing public attention to the alternative New York stage. And it was instrumental in shaping Joseph Chaikin's values and sensibilities.

Chaikin is not only a child – and pioneer – of off-off-Broadway. He is, in addition, part of an international network of theater experiment. After World War II, much of Western theater was straining against its seams. Jerzy Grotowski in Poland and Peter Brook in England were the dominant figures in a widespread attempt to find new forms beyond naturalism, beyond innocuous entertainment. Brook, in the sixties, was directly influenced by Artaud and by Happenings: He was exploring ways for the stage to cut through polite facades of traditional drama (and society) to transmit the vital core; he was trying to break through conventional forms to discover which were truly theatrical. Grotowski's passion was to strip the stage to its essential, holy center: Theater should be "poor," he felt, purged of extraneous scenic trappings; training should be a *via negativa*, a process of breaking down physical and psychic barriers so that the actor can offer a purified, sacred self to the audience. Although Chaikin began his explorations independently of these European directors, he has come to know Grotowski, Brook, and others, and they have exchanged encouragement and inspiration.

Chaikin's theater also connects – though this has not generally been recognized – with American values and traditions from long before the 1960s. For all his affinity with European movements, and his sense of alienation from mainstream U.S. culture, Chaikin's work is very deeply American. His use of the body to locate and express emotions and, especially, his focus on breathing are at least as much in a line with the dance innovations of Loïe Fuller, Isadora Duncan, and Martha Graham as with Grotowski's *plastiques* or Artaud's *gestes*. His stress on the emotive power of sounds reflects back *through* Artaud and the French symbolists to their ancestor, Edgar Allan Poe.

Moreover, the basic spirit behind Chaikin's theater is American. He is the rebel, the iconoclast, the lone troubleshooter. His stance is closer to that of Twain or Thoreau, to Bartleby the Scrivener's "I prefer not to," than to Brook, directing at the Royal Shakespeare Company and under the aegis of the French government, or Grotowski, who operated for nearly twenty-five years within a stable institutional framework and with government subsidies. And the work has a kind of Transcendentalist wonder that is distinctly native. His insistence on theater's living "presence" rings with a Transcendentalist passion to experience the life force in each moment, and is perhaps, even, tinged with a typically American refusal of history. Certainly Chaikin is more the son of Emerson and Whitman, of a sensibility that sees the whole world contained in each person, each blade of grass, than of Artaud or Genet, with their visions of poison and pus. While Grotowski's work is shaped by the ascetic, mortifying passion of his Polish Catholic background, Chaikin's is infused with an idealistic, left-wing activism that is part of the heritage of twentieth-century American Jews.

THE FORMATIVE YEARS

Indeed, a great deal of Chaikin's sensibility and perspective trace back to his early life. He was born in Brooklyn in 1935, the youngest child of Russian–Jewish immigrants. He described his parents (years after their death) as "traumatized, crazy people, who were running away" and could not rebuild their torn-up lives. His father, a Hebrew scholar, barely supported the family doing factory work; at home, he was cold and distant. Chaikin recalls his mother as having a kind of charisma and a beautiful singing voice; but she became bitter, trapped by a horrible marriage and poverty that forced her to clean other people's houses. The Borough Park neighborhood where the family lived was "a kind of Jewish ghetto with a few Italians, who were the only thing that made it possible to respirate." As for his early cultural life, Chaikin says, "My father was very learned and extremely pedantic. His greatest pleasure was in reading and studying. None of us could share it with him."

The extreme life/death issues that have dominated Chaikin's work entered his life early: At the age of six, he became critically ill with rheumatic heart disease. The family could not afford hospital care, so "Yuss," as he was called, was kept at home in bed for a year and a half, then "around the bed" for another year. He remembers not only the physical pain but the social and psychological trauma; when he became well enough to leave the apartment, the family used to wheel him around in a baby carriage: "I was seven or eight years old at this point; I remember it was very humiliating."

Although his heart was permanently damaged, Chaikin was able for a while to resume moderately normal activity, and during this time, quite by chance, he was introduced to the theater. An older sister and brother had become active on the fringes of the Jewish stage, and one afternoon the whole family packed off to Madison Square Garden to see a production in which Yuss's brother Ben was an understudy – and which, as it happened, was directed by Max Reinhardt. Chaikin was captivated. Thirty-five years later, he recalled the experience in detail – and with so strong a sense of having been an outsider that it is clear he wanted in:

They were doing *The Flag Is Born*, by Ben Hecht. It was about the founding of Israel, and it starred Celia Adler, Paul Muni, and Marlon Brando. I remember there was an old couple in it, refugees – and then different biblical characters appeared behind a scrim. My parents and the kids were in the very top row, in the cheapest seats, this ghetto family in the middle of Madison Square Garden. And my mother had brought a paper bag with kosher food for us, because nothing you bought would be fit to eat.

Back home in Brooklyn, Chaikin set up his own little theater group with neighborhood friends. His favorite theme, which he staged again and again, was Tarzan in the jungle.

The Chaikin family, New York, 1936. Baby "Yuss" is on his father's lap. Photographer unknown. Print courtesy of Shami Chaikin.

When Chaikin was ten, his heart began to fail, and he was sent to a charity clinic in Florida for children with cardiac problems. He was not expected to live.

I begged my parents to let me stay at home. They sent me away because they couldn't afford me anymore. Medically I was very expensive. And I required a lot of attention, and they had four other kids to take care of. But also they couldn't stand it. I was this little kid dying, and they couldn't stand to have that around. So they sent me away to die.

At this unwelcome haven from his family, where he lived for two years, Chaikin got his first experience of mainstream America. And, also, he continued his involvement with theater. He wrote plays and organized performances for his fellow patients. Since learning lines seemed the hardest part of acting, he found excuses for the characters to be reading (e.g., looking at a newspaper) so that they could have their words in front of them. One time, though, he tried breaking away from realism and, instead, had one set of performers mime the action while others read the parts from the wings; that production, he says, was his most successful.

When Chaikin was discharged, he rejoined his family, who felt like complete strangers to him. They were settled now in Des Moines, where Chaikin's father had got a job teaching Hebrew, and Chaikin spent the rest of his youth, during the late forties and fifties, in Iowa, the heart of WASP middle America. He attended the public junior high school, made friends, and even learned how to ride a horse. He began to read a great deal, and he developed a passion for opera, which he would listen to on the family radio. By high school, he was acting in extracurricular and little community plays, mostly light comedies and musicals. He continued his theater studies on a scholarship at Drake University in Des Moines, working on the classics, including Shakespeare, and some contemporary drama.

Chaikin became expert, during this period, at maintaining the social mask. He concealed his unfashionable medical problems and, since Jews were considered an oddity (at best) among his peers, he hid his background. Meanwhile, he discovered that he was unacceptable to the mainstream in still another way: Chaikin disguised his bisexuality as well. Carefully navigating around these secrets, he passed himself off as the all-American teenager. Living at the cardiac clinic, he says, he "had to learn how to be lovable" in order to win affection or attention. Now, that skill, his basic generosity and sensitivity, his strong will, and his edited persona began to make him a focal person in Drake theater circles.

Chaikin, circa 1954, Des Moines, Iowa. Photographer unknown. Print courtesy of Shami Chaikin.

These early experiences affected Chaikin deeply and helped to shape his later work. His straddling of cultures and the disjointedness of his own family gave him keen perspectives on social myths and relationships. His intimacy with death made him determined to face the most extreme questions about living. His sense of always existing on borrowed time strengthened, eventually, an unwilling-ness to compromise.

Chaikin has a low threshold for institutions. After about three years of college, he moved to New York City to study acting and try to break into professional theater. Supporting himself by doing temporary office work and waiting on tables, he took as many classes as he could afford, with such teachers as Herbert Berghof, Nola Chilton, William Hickey, Peter Kass, Mira Rostova, Anthony Mannino, and, in Chicago one summer, Viola Spolin. Before long, he began to find acting work, including a part in a touring com-pany of *No Time for Sergeants* and a couple of roles in off-Broadway comedies. During this period, also, for about three seasons, Chai-kin worked as an extra at the Metropolitan Opera, earning two dollars a performance.

Meanwhile, Chaikin helped form the Harlequin Players, whose stated aim was "to share with the audiences the benefits of en-semble playing." He directed his first public production for this fledgling repertory company, a double bill of Sean O'Casey's *Bedtime Story* and Edna St. Vincent Millay's *Aria da Capo;* he also performed in the plays, a practice he has not continued. The work was enthusi-astically reviewed, with the company's ensemble work and Chai-kin's direction singled out for special praise.* The Harlequin Players disbanded after less than two years, but Chaikin's experience with the group helped to form his commitment to working with an ongo-ing company.

Despite his involvement with this ensemble, Chaikin's real goal during his first few years in New York was to become a big star: "I thought – along with the other actors I knew and the teachers I was studying with – that you apprentice for a while and go to classes, then you get small roles, and then you get larger roles, and then you're discovered. And when you're discovered, it's the beginning of the second life. You go into another orbit." His main ambition at the time was "to be important." A friend recalls:

He was very concerned with meeting the right sort of people. He was a

---

Village Voice critic Jerry Tallmer congratulated the Harlequin Players "for giving us as much brief pleasure as you will find on any stage in town this week" and said that Chaikin was "to be praised" for his direction. Ann Jezer wrote in the *New York East:* "It is the ensemble work that differentiates this group from many with similar aims and composition. Not the least of the credit for this accomplishment should go to Joseph Chakin [sic] whose direction of the production was fluid, gently paced, and dramatically precise."

person that was on the phone an awful lot, always making contacts, always expanding outward. He was the only person I ever met who could dial the telephone without looking at it; he would be able to carry on a conversation and dial the telephone.

In 1959 Chaikin auditioned for the Living Theater, thinking it would provide good exposure. He was cast as a replacement in William Carlos Williams's *Many Loves,* and got roles in a few new productions. Then, late in the season, he took over the lead for a while in *The Connection.* At the time, Chaikin was put off by the "unrelieved dread" he found in Jack Gelber's play about junkies waiting for a fix: "I felt that doing *The Connection* was a morbid experience. I didn't like it. Besides, the jazz-musicians in the play thought I was too square for Leach." After a few weeks in *The Connection,* Chaikin left the Living Theater for an off-Broadway job, but when that gig ended and he needed work, he again found himself playing Leach. Now something changed: "This time it was a whole different thing. My back was broken, I got another idea of myself. It wasn't just another job, it was a different relationship: I began to want to inhabit the world of *The Connection.* I became a part of it."

Chaikin was a principal actor in the Living Theater for the next three years. He appeared in several plays, including Brecht's *In the Jungle of the Cities,* and he toured Europe with the company.

In 1962 the Living Theater added Brecht's *Man Is Man* to its repertory with Chaikin as Galy Gay, the waterfront porter who sets out to buy a fish for dinner and ends up as "a human fighting machine." Playing this role was a turning point in Chaikin's career and life. When he first took the part, he still had his eye on Broadway stardom:

Now that I had this big role maybe I could be a big actor with a lot of attention, a lot of options – and even this other dimension that comes with being a special actor that I would enjoy. I got a couple of extremely good reviews for the part, and with the reviews came also a personal manager. I had then an agent and a personal manager. I was exhilarated to be so central. All I could see was that it could only go up. My career could only go up.

But as Chaikin got his first tastes of "success," and as he became involved with Brecht's message in *Man Is Man,* his ambitions began to change:

I got offers from various places and I actually did one television something or other with someone or other. The woman was extremely blond and the man was extremely tall, and I was in this party they were giving. He was running for senator of some state. It was so boring. And I had the feeling that even if I could play the senator, it would still be extremely boring. I was meanwhile going in the evenings to the Living Theater to perform. And it was very challenging playing that part. As I played it night after night, I got very involved wtih the questions that were brought up in it. And I had a kind of dismay, a disillusionment with the promises that I was hoping would become my life.

Chaikin started to see his own values as uncomfortably close to those Brecht exposed in the play: "There I was, night after night, giving all my attention to pleasing, seducing, and getting applause from the audience, which is the very process wherein Galy Gay allows himself to be transformed from an innocent and good man into a thing, a machine – all because of flattery, one flattery after another." This realization was sharpened by the form of Brecht's play, which required Chaikin to address the audience directly, "knowing that what I said to the audience I didn't believe, and then coming to believe what I was saying." Commitment began to re-place showmanship in his performance as he, in his words, "started cutting out a lot of my fancy stuff." He received his first *Village Voice* Obie award (the off-Broadway equivalent of a Tony) for Galy Gay.

Until that time, Chaikin had resisted the Living Theater's activ-ism. Although very drawn to the passion and defiance of it, he had found the company's political involvement "ridiculous and unnecessary":

The world didn't seem to me to be all that bad. I used to say to them again and again, "Are you a theater or are you a political movement? You can't be both." I was very determined to define my path, and it was their ambiva-lence about what they were doing that made my path appear clearer to me.

But now he became radicalized:

What Judith and Julian were saying and doing, the lines of Galy Gay which I was saying every night to the audience, and the conversations I got into at the time began to have an impact on me. I started getting involved in political things, and getting in demonstrations and getting arrested and going to jail. I was only there a couple of nights at a time, but it had a lasting effect on me. I began to feel that the political aspect of the Living Theatre, which had looked so ridiculous, was very necessary. And the fact that it *was* ridiculous didn't make it any less necessary.

Chaikin's aspirations began to change. Having joined the Living Theater with the idea that he "might really 'get somewhere,' " he found that his "idea of 'somewhere' became very confused." He wrote in a notebook early in 1963: "Perhaps if I only realized that I do not admire what everyone seems to admire, I would really begin

Chaikin as Galy Gay, the innocent, in the Living Theater production of *Man Is Man*, New York, 1962. Photograph by Karl Bissinger. Print courtesy of the Chaikin Papers, Kent State University Libraries.

to live after all. Why do we spend our lives striving for something that we would never want to be, if we only knew what we wanted?"

Meanwhile, he continued to act throughout the early sixties, with the Living Theater and other noncommercial companies in New York and, occasionally, out of town. He got a second Obie in 1965.

It was within the Living Theater in 1962 that Chaikin set up his first theater laboratory. He felt that although individual members of the company were very talented, "no one had the same assumptions" about acting, and performers often did not really connect on stage. He wanted to try "working out different ideas . . . about ensemble playing and different improvisational things." At first, most of the company, including Beck and Malina, and a few non–Living Theater people took part. Interest waned, though, as the group's political, financial, and legal crises mounted: "You never knew what you'd find when you got there– the whole place being auctioned off or the cops surrounding it . . . Gradually everyone dropped out [of the study group] and it was just the Becks and me, and then just Judith and me, and finally I was left alone."

About this time, in the first weeks of 1963, Chaikin was approached by a group of Nola Chilton's former acting students, who wanted to continue working together after her emigration to Israel. Chaikin joined them, and they began to meet in a small room in the back of the Living Theater. The following year, when the Living Theater went abroad into what became a four-year exile, Chaikin decided not to go along. In part, he was uneasy with their proposed communal living/working setup, and was afraid he would not be able to keep up physically with the peripatetic life they had ahead. But, finally, he wanted to remain in New York, because his interest now centered on the new workshop in which he was involved, the embryonic Open Theater.

THE OPEN THEATER

In its earliest days, the Open Theater was a loose association of actors, directors, playwrights, and critics, who met first weekly, then twice a week, to work on exercises, improvisations, and plays. Any member could initiate a project, and Chaikin immediately started a workshop to explore nonnaturalistic material. Though he began with Nola Chilton's departures from Method acting, his experiments soon took off in their own directions, and within weeks this workshop had become the core of the group.

The dominance of Chaikin's project precipitated a crisis: Claiming that Chaikin was violating the workshop's original intentions by steering into new areas, some Chilton devotees attempted to draw up a constitution. "People were into having copies of things written and passed out," one actress recalls; "They were always drafting bills of rights and artistic creeds." Finally, the people who wanted to restrict the work left, and it became a strong tenet of the company not to fix any structure or aesthetic principle: to allow the workshop to change, grow, and even completely transform itself, pursuing whatever directions seemed fertile. The members chose the name "Open Theater" because, Chaikin says, it "implied a susceptibility to continue to change" and "would serve to remind us of that early commitment to stay in process."

This openness was not a refusal to make artistic choices. The group had specific, if flexible, interests: They wanted to explore the nonbehavioristic–dream, myth, poetry–together with ensemble interaction and the actor–spectator relationship; they were looking for political and spiritual values that they could share with each other and their audiences. And they hoped, in Chaikin's words, "to find ways of presenting plays and improvisational programs without the pressures of money, real estate, and other commercial considerations which usurp creative energy." More fundamentally, the Open Theater's "aesthetic intention" was, Chaikin said, "to bring about a kind of theater immediacy–a presence, being present, in the theater. To explore those powers which the live theater possesses."

For the first seven of its ten years, the Open Theater remained a loose conglomerate of more or less discrete projects with Chaikin's laboratory at the center. Neither a class with a teacher nor a collection of co-equal creators, his workshop was an ensemble with a definite (if not always admitted) leader. While playwrights and actors often suggested extensions or modifications, the basic directions of the work were Chaikin's; although he sometimes joined in as an actor, for the most part he remained apart, observing and monitoring. And he charged the group with a passion and energy that fired the creativity of the others.

Chaikin invented thousands of exercises. Most of them were abandoned after five minutes, and some were developed and used over years. Rather than just seeking new techniques to perform existing plays, his experiments looked for new types of expression, for ways to say things that people "otherwise might not find a way to transmit to each other." Dissatisfied not only with naturalism and the Method, but with the psychological principles on which

Chaikin with actors in an Open Theater workshop, New York, 1967. Photograph by Hope Herman Wurmfeld.

they were based, he looked for alternative understandings of character as well as new ways to enter stage roles using somatic and musical methods. Constrained by conventional language, he made exercises both to try to revitalize spoken words and to discover ways of speaking without words. And he explored means to create more sensitive, alive interactions among actors on stage and with their audiences.

In some ways, this workshop was extremely trying for its members. Since Chaikin was not teaching something that he already knew, the actors often had little sense of where they were going. A playwright who was in the company for a short time recalled his frustration with Chaikin's methods:

Joe would offer his workshop fragmentary impulses, glimpses of ways to work, and the actors were remarkable in being able to do something with them. They'd get out on the floor and as soon as Joe saw a little bit of result, he was ready to move on to something else. To me the work was maddeningly inconclusive.

Another early member compared the workshop to "a musical world of unfinished symphonies."

Actors in the ensemble rarely even got clear feedback. This was partly because Chaikin was wary of short-circuiting potential:

I don't like to criticize work when it's in the early, forming stages. If I criticize it, the criteria for judging start to exist. Since I don't know what its possibilities are for expressing yet, I don't want to set up criteria.

But also, he was ambivalent about the role of leader and reluctant to assume its prerogatives. When asked once to offer more comment, he evaded the issue, saying, "I always feel that most of you are developed enough to know as you work whether or not you are working from your own nature."

For a while, Chaikin recalls, "people quit right and left." But for those who thrived on its uncharted explorations, the research was rich and rewarding. One actor noted, "The time at work is absolutely timeless," and another, "Everything has opened for us."

Apart from Chaikin's workshop, the Open Theater had dozens of other projects over the years – some lasting, by intention or abortion, only a few weeks, some a season, and a few longer. From the beginning, there were playwrights' readings and workshops involving Megan Terry, Maria Irene Fornes, and others; Jean-Claude van Itallie, the writer most central to the Open Theater, usually worked directly with Chaikin. From 1963 through 1970, Living Theater veteran Peter Feldman headed a workshop that was a kind of second company; although he has described it as "a peripheral thing, which Joe never attended," in fact it was an important stabilizing force within the Open Theater. Each season, starting in 1964–5, there also were beginners' workshops, the most important of which, led by Lee Worley from 1966 through 1968, eventually supplied more than half the actors in Chaikin's own group. Jacques Levy ran a particularly interesting project in 1966–7, focusing mainly on assassination and violence, multimedia theater, and Brechtian alienation exercises. Other workshops actually were technique classes led by teachers – such as Kristin Linklator, Ze'eva Cohen, and Swami Satchinananda – whom the Open Theater hired with monthly dues and, later, grant moneys.

Many short-term projects were aimed specifically at performance, and the company gave limited public showings from its first season. While much of the work grew directly from Chaikin's explorations, ad hoc groups with various leaders also formed to prepare a particular script or try to develop a performance piece.

During 1963–4, the Open Theater presented two public programs of original work. The next year, the group performed on eight Mon-

Chaikin, with James Barbosa (*left*) and Ron Faber (*center*), in the Open Theater production of *Keep Tightly Closed in a Cool Dry Place*, New York, 1966. Photograph by Phill Niblock.

day nights at the off-Broadway Sheridan Square Playhouse, and the following season for one week a month at LaMama. In 1966–7, the Open Theater was involved in its only two commercial productions, both off-Broadway: *Viet Rock*, which had grown out of Megan Terry's playwrights' workshop; and Jean-Claude van Itallie's *America Hurrah*. From 1967 through 1970, the company had a repertory that included a variety of original works and, starting in 1969, two full-length scripted plays: Jarry's *Ubu Cocu*, directed by Feldman, and Beckett's *Endgame*, directed by Roberta Sklar.

Chaikin's own acting at the Open Theater was in the productions of scripted works. First, he was in *Keep Tightly Closed in a Cool Dry Place* (1966), which Megan Terry wrote for the Open Theater and which was structured around transformations, a technique Chaikin had worked on with his group. Then he played Hamm in the company's *Endgame*.

After several years of putting together small, original performance pieces, mainly from exercises and improvisations, in 1967 Chaikin began a season-long project to create a full-length play

Scene from *The Serpent* at Washington Square Methodist Church, New York, 1970. Five actors have woven themselves into a combined snake and tree of life for the temptation of Eve (Tina Shepard). Photograph by Karl Bissinger.

based on parts of the Bible. Using research as well as improvisation to enter the material, and working with van Itallie, his workshop counterpointed Genesis stories with modern images of violence and loss. The result was *The Serpent*, a moving expression of the state of regret that the company felt was our contemporary inheritance.

After a European tour performing *The Serpent* and a program of short works, followed by an unfruitful project on China that occupied several months, Chaikin's workshop began its next major study: an investigation of dying and death. The ensemble looked at

Scene from *Terminal*, New York, 1971. The dying (Tina Shepard, *right*, and JoAnn Schmidman) are already treated like carcasses by their attendant (Tom Lillard). Photograph by Max Waldman. © Max Waldman, Archives 1984.

the subject in social and psychological terms, examining taboos against seeing one's own or someone else's impending death; in physiological terms, researching the physical process of dying; and in mythic terms, seeking images for the passage between life and death, the interplay between the worlds of the living and the dead. This work, for which Susan Yankowitz was the final writer, led to *Terminal* (1970). Set in an unspecified institution that the group thought of as a terminal ward, the piece contrasted stark images of the loss of physical functions (sight, voice, and so forth) with live cartoons of the American way of death (embalming), with comic, brutal scenes of institutional life. Periodically, spirits of the dead possessed the dying, using their bodies and voices to articulate messages, some of them highly political, to the living. *Terminal* was performed, along with *The Serpent, Ubu Cocu,* and *Endgame,* on a European tour during the winter of 1969–70, then again back home in the Open Theater's loft. In the spring, prior to a run at Washington Square Methodist Church, the company took its work to New York state colleges and prisons – the beginning of a commitment to prison performances.

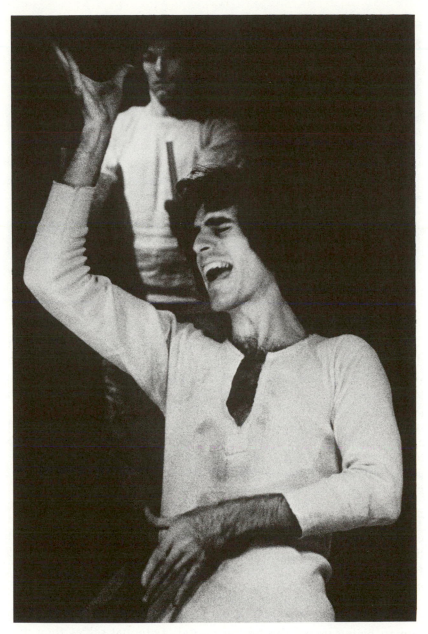

Scene from *Terminal*, New York, 1971. The spirit of a dead creole mystic "comes through" one of the dying (Paul Zimet). Photograph by Max Waldman. © Max Waldman, Archives 1984.

Scene from *The Mutation Show* at St. Clement's Church, New York, 1973. A musical interlude by the motley band of actor/"mutants." Photograph by Mary Ellen Mark/Archive.

But for all its success and its growing repertory, Chaikin thought that the Open Theater had become unwieldy. He felt, too, that the work was being hampered by growing pressure within the ensemble to become more of a political commune, and by some chronic interpersonal strains. During the preparation of *Terminal*, he had announced that he planned to work next "in a concentrated way and on a smaller scale." Now, he pruned his workshop from eighteen actors to six, and suggested that his group split off from the rest of the company. The Open Theater's financial resources were divided, half going to a new company, the Medicine Show, formed by several actors.

From the fall of 1970 until it disbanded three years later, the Open Theater was a simple, tight organization, consisting of Chaikin, an ensemble of six to eight actors, at times an assistant director, at times a dramaturge, and whatever writers, musicians, and designers were involved with a particular project. The company reworked *Terminal* for a smaller cast and created two new works.

The Mutation Show (1971) came from a study of change – of how relative and mutable the identities of people and objects are, and how human beings move among the various potential selves they contain. It was, finally, a zany, disturbing carnival of "freaks" frozen in one self-definition and of characters (based largely on Caspar

Scene from *Nightwalk* at the Space for Innovative Development, New York, 1973. The two journeyers (Tina Shepard and Paul Zimet) observe different "worlds." Photograph by Inge Morath/Magnum.

Hauser, the wolf-girl Kamala, and Open Theater actors) wrenched into change. The play, which had no writer but was shaped by Chaikin and Sklar, was shown on a Mideast tour, in New York, and in colleges and prisons around the United States.

The Open Theater began its final piece in December 1972. A journey by two not specifically human characters through terrain inhabited by people in different levels of sleep, *Nightwalk* was about one of Chaikin's main concerns in the theater: "presence" versus "absence," awareness versus not-quite-thereness. This time Chaikin drew on the work of several writers, including van Itallie, Terry, and Sam Shepard, and Mira Rafalowicz was dramaturge. The piece was performed in New York, Europe, and California from the spring through the fall of 1973.

During its ten years, the Open Theater had become recognized as the most important experimental company in America. From the London production of *America Hurrah* and from four European tours between 1968 and 1973, it also had earned a strong international reputation. Chaikin had spent part of one summer working with Grotowski and Brook in London, and part of another with Grotowski and Barba in Denmark; Grotowski had extended a New York trip to meet twice with Chaikin's ensemble. Former members of Chaikin's workshops were carrying on his approaches in theaters and schools in New York, Minneapolis, Boulder, London, and Amsterdam. The company had

The two journeyers in *Nightwalk* at the Space for Innovative Development, New York, 1973. Photograph by Inge Morath/Magnum.

been featured in international stage festivals and had collected prizes in the United States and abroad – including Drama Desk, Vernon Rice, and Brandeis awards, several Obies, and a first prize at the Belgrade International Theatre Festival. Chaikin's original desire to try "working out different ideas . . . about ensemble playing and different improvisational things" had flowered into a major force in modern theater.

But Chaikin thought that the Open Theater should disband. He had always intended the company to be "like a clearing in the woods" rather than a permanent shelter, and at the close of nearly every season had considered moving on. Now, in 1973, he was convinced that the time had come. He felt, first of all, that the group's success had begun to undermine its openness. The attention it received from the press discouraged risk taking. Its administrative and financial growth, despite Chaikin's pruning, had brought energy-draining responsibilities. And, while Chaikin had no illusions that he could manage without grants in the future, the company's total dependence on government and foundation money made him feel overly vulnerable to official disapproval.*

Chaikin saw the Open Theater starting to get "stuck . . . institutionalized in a way that we can't reverse." He felt that although the members were wonderfully gifted and could "go on and do ten plays which would be better than the ones we've done," the Open Theater was in danger of becoming "embalmed as an institution":

After you go on for a little while, you tend to see your own reflection in a way, you tend to get defined. And if you don't do it to yourself, the outside world helps you to do it . . . When that happens, very often the group freezes, the work freezes in a certain way.

Chaikin was also feeling personally drained by the pressures of heading the organization for so long. Until the last few seasons, in fact, he had avoided facing up to his leadership. In the early years, the extent of his power had been largely unrecognized within the company, though to an outsider who spent several months observing the work, it was obvious:

*From a tiny-budget group, meeting in a borrowed space, and supported by monthly dues of five dollars, the Open Theater had become a $100,000 a year organization, which leased its own loft, hired teachers, subsidized its own productions, and even bought health insurance and paid salaries of twenty to seventy-five dollars a week. (Most members, obviously, still supplemented their Open Theater income. Several, including Chaikin, taught in area colleges; others alternated odd jobs with unemployment insurance.)

There is a feeling of anarchic freedom: Chaikin has a knack for stepping off-center, especially at times of controversy, and people feel their influence within the group to be equal. This is an illusion . . . At the Open Theater . . . the members tend to be unaware of the fact that their will is a reflection of Chaikin's. Chaikin is the leader of the troupe but seems not to be; he controls practically everything while giving the impression of controlling practically nothing.

When Chaikin was away on tour with his workshop, the portion of the Open Theater left behind barely functioned; during his winter 1969–70 European trip, even the scheduling of garbage pickups was neglected, and the loft became infested with mice. At one point, Lee Worley tried to get Chaikin to recognize and accept his power in the company:

The O.T. is a dictatorship. Nothing gets done without you. We are as great as you and our future depends solely on what you care to focus on . . . You of course are the dictator and whether you believe in governing very little or a whole lot it amounts to the same thing.

In retrospect, Chaikin feels that he was not prepared to face the control that he exerted: "Because of my politics at the time, I wanted it to be a collective very much. And also because of my timidity. I was very worried about being the head of a group of that size." In a moment of less charitable self-judgment, he said: "I was a real imposter in the way that I chose to appear self-sacrificing toward the wishes of the group – which was not usually true, because I manipulated a lot in terms of my own wishes and interests, while appearing to think that the only thing I was concerned about was a strictly Maoist idea of The People."

In any case, by the last few years of the Open Theater, there was little equivocation about Chaikin's leadership, and the weight of that responsibility added to his desire to disband the company. Directing in the theater and leading a workshop, he says, one is constantly refining the ability to manipulate people, and that skill starts to invade even one's personal life. Heading the Open Theater was turning him into someone who expected, and was able, to manage people too well.

The Open Theater closed gradually. As the group began performing *Nightwalk*, they tapered off and wound down classes and workshops. But after the last performance, in December 1973, when the Open Theater was officially dissolved, they kept holding regular sessions. Even after those meetings ended, members continued working together and established new projects. Before long, though, with their heritage of openness, these offspring (including the Talking Band, the Quena Company, and Chaikin's various workshops) went off in their own directions and took on their own dynamics.

AFTER THE OPEN THEATER

The theater world Chaikin faced in 1974 was very different from the one in which the Open Theater had started. Alongside the Broadway and off-Broadway stages, nonprofit theater had come of age. Joseph Papp, who in 1963 had been doing only free Shakespeare in Central Park, now controlled a theater empire that sponsored dozens of projects each season. And there were several ongoing smaller-scale institutions in New York, such as Robert Kalfin's Chelsea Theater Company and the American Place Theater. Noncommercial stages were also thriving now in many other American cities, including New Haven, Hartford, Providence, Washington, Louisville, Dallas, Houston, Minneapolis, Los Angeles, San Francisco, and Seattle.

More immediately relevant for Chaikin was the growth of off-off-Broadway, partly through his contribution, into a major part of the New York scene. In addition to LaMama and the churches, there were scores of little theaters, often in lofts and storefronts, sponsoring or hosting shoestring productions. Several, including Lynne Meadow's Manhattan Theatre Club, which opened in 1970, and Theatre for the New City, founded by Crystal Field and George Bartenieff in 1969, had become well-established venues. When the Open Theater had begun work, there had been fewer than thirty off- and off-off-Broadway productions listed in a typical week's *Village Voice;* now there were nearly two hundred "off-off-" alone.

Moreover, there was now a flourishing community of experimental artists off-off-Broadway. Richard Schechner, who as editor of the *Drama Review* was a strong advocate for the avant-garde, was staging "environmental" productions in a remodeled garage. André Gregory, one of the earliest off-Broadway producers, had put on several Artaud-inspired pieces with his Manhattan Project, most notably a highly physical, group-created *Alice in Wonderland.* Meredith Monk, who had worked on developing new voice and movement vocabularies, was composing very personal image-collages that she performed with her company, The House. Richard Foreman and Robert Wilson were bringing a postmodern sensibility into the theater with their icy, visually elaborate works.

Noncommercial stages meanwhile had become a forum for non-establishment points of view. The Bread and Puppet Theater performed antiwar pieces, often in the streets; and two California-based companies – El Teatro Campesino, an outgrowth of the United Farm Workers Union, and the San Francisco Mime Troupe, which after 1966 concentrated on "guerrilla theater" – were spiritually, if not geographically, part of off-off-Broadway. The Living Theater had returned from Europe in 1968 as a group of radical messiahs and was at work on a cycle of political plays. There were several thriving black theaters, including the New Lafayette Theater, headed by Robert Macbeth, Barbara Ann Teer's Black Theater Workshop, and the Negro Ensemble Company, headed by Douglas Turner Ward and Robert Hooks. Gay drama had found a home downtown, and the "Ridiculous" flaming drag companies of Ron Tavel and Charles Ludlum had become avant-garde staples.

At the same time, as the Open Theater's experience testified, off-off-Broadway had become entangled in one of the very systems it had been designed to escape: establishment money. Feeding the hands that were biting them, the government and major foundations had undertaken a series of subsidies to noncommercial theaters unprecedented in American theater history. In 1962, the Ford Foundation allocated $6.1 million in special theater grants, and in the early seventies was giving out over $4 million each year. (The Open Theater had received $100,000 of Ford money.) The Rockefeller Foundation, by the sixties, was providing subsidies in five, six, and seven figures, though mostly to universities and mainstream institutions such as Lincoln Center. The temporary New York State Commission on the Arts, founded in 1960, was made into a permanent council in 1965, and gave grants to experimental as well as conventional work. The National Endowment for the Arts, begun with a modest budget in 1965, by 1971 was handing out $1.5 million in theater subsidies, and its contribution was still expanding. Smaller donors, including the Shubert and Peg Santvoord foundations, also helped to support the new theater.

While making it possible for the nonprofit stage to thrive, this funding also affected its character. Offending the powers now carried a potentially crippling price. And the freewheeling days of loose, easy organization off-off-Broadway were over, as noncommercial theater was caught in the elaborate system of grantsmanship. Although the money provided was at subsistence level, it was so needed, and required so much less compromise than did box office economics, that most artists, including Chaikin, eventually could not justify shunning it. But this meant shaping one's projects somewhat to the terms of available grants. A nearly universal feature of the grants was that they were given to institutions rather than to individual artists. And after the end of the Open Theater, Chaikin wanted precisely *not* to head an organization.*

For a while after 1973, Chaikin stayed shy of situations where he would have too much responsibility or control. He wanted not only a rest from leadership but also a period to float, to leave his work unstructured so that it could find its own direction. The first few years were difficult. Although he had no second thoughts about having disbanded the Open Theater, he experienced "a great sense of loss . . . like a death" from its ending. And while he knew that periods of floundering almost always precede finding a new path, he was a little afraid he would never again find as rich a working situation as the one he had dissolved. Moreover, Chaikin's uncertainty during this period was exacerbated by a series of medical crises, which culminated in two open-heart operations and long stretches of reduced energy and activity.

For three years, Chaikin worked in other people's frameworks and in ad hoc projects established for a single show. First, in the summer of 1974, he did a new *Electra* written by Robert Montgomery with some collaboration by Chaikin and the cast. Two of the actors were Open Theater veterans; the third, an actress Chaikin knew through Peter Brook. Their new version refined the Electra story into two-character encounters, climaxing with Electra briefly possessed by Agamemnon's spirit, and then with brother and sister rehearsing the matricide step by step. *Electra* had a week of public showings at St. Clement's Church, and then was revived two seasons later for a national tour.

In 1975 Chaikin directed a new ensemble creation, working with van Itallie, several Open Theater actors, and a number of people he knew from other places. *A Fable Telling about a Journey* used the form of traditional quest legends to address modern fears and aspirations. Like *Electra*, *A Fable* was more the work of the writer (as opposed to Chaikin or the cast) than any of the Open Theater's major pieces had been. Like the *Electra* ensemble, the *Fable* company was a tem-

---

*In order that Chaikin not be totally ineligible for grants, Artservices (the off-off-Broadway management agency that handles a number of experimental artists) set up the Other Theater as a nonprofit organizational umbrella for Chaikin's post–Open Theater work. In fact, though, he has managed since 1973 with levels of funding greatly reduced from those of the Open Theater's grants of the early seventies.

porary one assembled for a single work. After a five-week run at the Westbeth Theater in New York, the group dissolved.

In the fall of 1976, Chaikin directed the only new script he has ever done that was not connected to one of his workshops, Adrienne Kennedy's autobiographical *A Movie Star Has to Star in Black and White*. He was drawn to Kennedy's depiction of direct experience being redigested and reshaped to conform to popular culture models: A black woman playwright continually imagines episodes from her own life grafted onto familiar movie scenes. The production was done as a tiny-budget Public Theatre workshop.

During its last few seasons, the Open Theater had held regular sessions to explore the classics, and Chaikin continued to pursue this interest now. The *Electra* project had begun with Chaikin's desire to work on the Sophocles play. A few months after that production, he directed Chekhov's *The Sea Gull*, in a new translation by van Itallie, at the Manhattan Theater Club. He explored two other classic plays in depth through repeated productions: Beckett's *Endgame*, first at Princeton University (1977), then at the Manhattan Theatre Club (1980); and Ansky's *The Dybbuk* (in a new version) at the Public Theater (1977) and again, in Hebrew, at the Habimah Theater in Tel Aviv (1979), where it replaced the traditional Vakhtangov version in the company's repertory. He returned to the Greeks, then, with an adaptation of *Antigone* at the Public Theater (1982).

One of Chaikin's ambitions after the Open Theater was to perform again. In 1975 he arranged for a workshop production of Büchner's *Woyzeck* at the Public Theater, with himself in the title role, and Leonardo Shapiro directing. He next acted in two monologues-with-music that he created with Sam Shepard: *Tongues* (1978), a piece largely about dying; and *Savage/Love* (1979), about the posturing, self-consciousness, and anguish of love. In both cases, Chaikin and Shepard shared the writing and directing, and Chaikin was the sole actor. Each work was first shown in San Francisco; Chaikin then performed the double bill at the Public Theater and in Europe. His most ambitious acting project, though, was in a one-person stage adaptation of Beckett's *Texts for Nothing* and *How It Is*. Chaikin conceived the piece, obtained the author's blessings and some suggestions, and developed the work with director Steve Kent. *Texts* ran at the Public Theater in March 1981, then in London the following summer. In the fall of 1983, Chaikin played the title role in Chekhov's *Uncle Vanya*, directed by Andrei Serban at LaMama. And since 1981 he has talked about wanting to perform in Shakespeare, especially to play Macbeth and King Lear.

Scene from *The Sea Gull* at the Manhattan Theatre Club, New York, 1975, with (*left to right*) Tina Shepard as Nina, Ron Seka as Trigorin, Leueen MacGrath as Mme. Arkadina, Margo Lee Sherman as Masha, and Daniel Seltzer (foreground) as Sorin. Photograph by Inge Morath/Magnum.

THE WINTER PROJECT

Meanwhile, by 1976 Chaikin again felt ready to head an open-ended, presumably ongoing workshop. He assembled a group of about twenty actors, musicians, writers, and directors, and a dramaturge. Many, including Paul Zimet, Tina Shepard, and Mira Rafalowicz, were Open Theater veterans; some, such as Ronnie Gilbert and Joyce Aaron, came from its early phases. Nearly all had collaborated with Chaikin sometime before. He chose the name "Winter Project" partly because it was a simple descriptive title (the group met only during winters for its first three years because of limited funding), and it did not seem to overdefine the character of the work. But the name also *did* express the group's interest: The ensemble was looking into cold and dark regions of experience.

For its first two seasons, the Winter Project, like the early Open Theater, pursued various directions, continuing research begun in the Open Theater and exploring new questions. One extended study reexamined the basic elements of theater, looking at how dif-

Chaikin in *Tongues* at the New York Shakespeare Festival Public Theater, 1979. Photograph by Sylvia Plachy.

Chaikin in *Texts* at the New York Shakespeare Festival Public Theater, 1981. Photograph by Sylvia Plachy.

33

ferent types of vocal sounds, musical accompaniments, spatial arrangements, and lighting affect what is transmitted to the audience. Insofar as the Project had a focus, it was exploring contemporary modes of expressing feelings, trying to locate the taboos and limits, then seeking ways to give voice and body to the much larger store of full and extreme emotions that people possess. The group worked through improvisations, exercises, and written texts.

Chaikin was always the director and central influence in the Winter Project, but during the first two years, as in the early Open Theater, other members also initiated investigations, and Chaikin sometimes expanded on studies that other people had begun. He functioned as both an actor and a director and, comfortable with this sense of diffused leadership, often stayed on the sidelines.

Not until the final weeks of the second season were limited audiences admitted to observe the work; the press was not invited. Even so, some parts of the explorations that Chaikin considered the most vital were not shown. "It's not ready," he explained. "It's too embryonic. Some of the work we're showing the audience is quite developed and, in fact, will be performed other places, but what people are seeing this year is mainly little fragments of things. And yet some of the work that's unseeable is very much the context of our meetings."

In its third year, the Winter Project was reduced by funding cuts to a dozen people and a shorter season – and its grants were conditional now on public performances, which Chaikin would have liked to postpone one more year. Since there were just eight weeks of meetings before the first public showings, no new exploration was attempted. With Chaikin assuming much fuller leadership now, the company worked at drawing together the most performable of its past investigations, then seeing what sorts of themes and shapes suggested themselves, going with (and continually revising) those tentative bearings.

Re-Arrangements, the resulting piece, was shown at LaMama in 1979. A collage of images and little scenes, it focused on the adjustments people make to deal with, or avoid dealing with, others. The work connected directly to Chaikin's San Francisco collaborations. *Re-Arrangements* incorporated two sections of *Tongues,* and although the settings were different, the sensibility of the earlier piece flowed into the new one. When Shepard and Chaikin began discussing a second collaboration, Chaikin suggested the theme of love, following one major area of investigation that *Re-Arrangements* had begun.

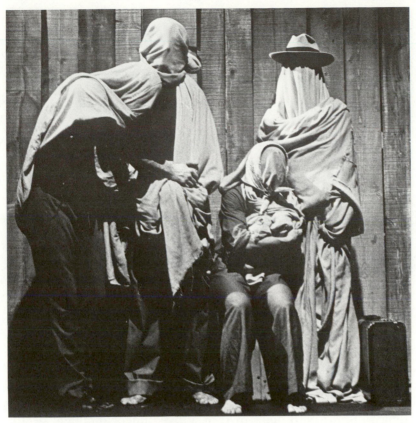

A group of faceless refugees in *Tourists and Refugees* at LaMama, New York, 1980. Photograph by Sylvia Plachy.

Meanwhile, Chaikin was gathering thoughts and notes for the Winter Project's first major piece, which he developed and presented at LaMama the following year. He wanted to explore the theme of home and homelessness: how populations are uprooted for power and profit; how people feel either housed or exiled in a foreign land, their native city, their own bodies. *Tourists and Refugees* (1980), performed by five actors and three musicians, was a shifting collage of urban cranks and misfits, tourists on out-of-town jaunts, caravans of faceless refugees, and intimate, fractured households. Chaikin was passionate about this piece as he had not been about any for years, and made reworking and expanding the study the focus of the Project's next season. *Tourists and Refugees No. 2* played

Scene from *Tourists and Refugees* at LaMama, New York, 1980. One refugee (Paul Zimet) gives "testimony" while another (Tina Shepard), in the distance, tries to manage her bundles. Photograph by Sylvia Plachy.

at LaMama in the spring of 1981 and at the Caracas Theater Festival the following summer.

For the company's main 1981–2 project, Chaikin tackled a subject that has haunted his work since the beginning of the Open Theater: coming to terms with one's own or a loved one's imminent death. *Trespassing,* which took place in the last moments of a woman's life after a stroke, was an internal monologue set in a whorl of surrounding people and events. Chaikin essentially wrote the script himself, though with constant feedback and some contributions from the ensemble. The work was shown at LaMama in the winter of 1982.

That summer, Chaikin also created an ensemble piece in Israel with a group of Jewish and Palestinian actors. *The Other,* a largely political play, opened in Tel Aviv, to general acclaim, in the middle of the Israeli invasion of Lebanon.

After this period of relatively heavy involvement with productions, Chaikin preserved most of the Winter Project's following season as workshop, with no specific performance goal. (There were several open showings of the work, publicized by word of mouth.) Then, in three weeks, he created a chamber piece with three performers. *Lies and Secrets* interspersed bits of well-known plays, comments on the actual show as it was going on, and political material, some of it recycled from *Tourists and Refugees*. It played at LaMama in March of 1983 and later that spring at the Riverside Studios in London. Then, with little fanfare or explanation, Chaikin ended the Winter Project.

Chaikin's next season – including a collaboration with Sam Shepard at the American Repertory Theater and an aborted production of *Waiting for Godot* in Stratford, Canada – was hampered by medical crises. But through the year, Chaikin was also incubating and preparing notions for a new workshop. In the course of an afternoon involved with something else, he would invariably jot down a few thoughts, ideas, well, semi-, or just barely defined, that he could not wait to try out in action. Always, he is possessed by the theater that does not yet exist.

2   An open theory

Chaikin's theories about theater change all the time. Ideas trigger experiments, which reshape the ideas and generate new ones. Although in the early months of the Open Theater, Chaikin helped to draw up "Principles of the Workshop," the main artistic principle was to avoid rigid artistic principles. Unlike much of the avant-garde, he does not pronounce manifestos and axioms that the work then illustrates. Nor, though, does he share the common American theater prejudice that too much thinking will strangle sub- or supra-rational artistic faculties. He calls that "a silly idea."

Chaikin's evolving thoughts about theater do not add up to a totally coherent poetics or theatrics. In fact, notions he has worked with over the years flatly contradict each other, and even ideas he is exploring at one time may be incompatible. Still, certain basic values and interests have consistently run through his thinking. He has always focused on theater's *liveness*, the special power of the present actor. He has viewed the stage as a forum for investigating *life* questions rather than abstract, aesthetic concepts, a place to find new languages to speak the nameless dimensions of experience. And he has considered and reconsidered art's place in the larger community, the role of the audience and the politics and economics of the stage.

THE PURPOSE OF THEATER

Theater's function, Chaikin says, is first of all to entertain.

You don't have to go there for instruction or scolding. People should go there for enjoyment, essentially. That doesn't mean enjoyment like some sitcom on television, but enjoyment in the sense of a nourishment. Brecht said that theater should entertain and it should instruct, and if it had to do one or the other then it should entertain. (This was after he was finger-wagging at everybody with his *Lehrstücke*.) I agree with that. Theater's first obligation is to entertain.

Chaikin wants each performance to be a "celebration" shared by those on stage and in the audience. Theater should create a community with a sense of occasion.

38

Beyond this, he believes that the purpose of theater is to give voice to the most powerful human forces and feelings. In times characterized by "a real momentum toward numbness," this becomes especially important:

I feel that theater is a place where you *can* express extreme emotions; from the time of the ancients, it has been a place where intense passions can be manifest. That's part of what theater is about, and I enjoy that. But I also feel that this question of expressing feelings in the theater is linked to something political. I sense that there's a kind of increasing need to repress emotions, to cancel and neutralize emotions. I'm very aware of certain emotions being forbidden little by little, more and more. Not all feelings are taboo. Anything in the range of anger is okay, for example. But I have the sense that if a person in a room with other people expresses real tenderness, or a certain kind of wonder, or mourning, that person usually is in the way. One can refer to mourning, or tenderness, or wonder. But certain kinds of direct, emotional expression have no place.

Chaikin sees this denial of passion reflected in the contemporary stage, especially in some experimental work: "It's true that these artists are addressing the numbness, and in some cases they are doing that very brilliantly; but they also are citizens of it." His interest is "to try to see if there's a way to give expression to feelings that are very much a part of our experience, but that are not permitted air very much." The stage should even find ways to rediscover and "give expression to the passions that we've lost."

Theater, in fact, can extend human understanding. Chaikin thinks of actors partly as detectives who work from the visible bits of experience to learn what is hidden underneath, as explorers who enter uncharted territory: "To me the glorious thing to do is to come to the point of the limit of what we can see, what we can imagine, and what we can understand, and to potchkey around at that limit, to play around at that point . . . – to me *that's* the exciting point to play at."

"Everything we do," Chaikin once said, "changes us a little, even when we purport to be indifferent to what we've done. And what we witness, we also do." Although he, like Brecht, hedges on the question, Chaikin finally thinks that theater *should* affect the lives of its spectators.

Part of any play's effect comes simply from its aliveness. In fact, whatever the subject matter, all theater for Chaikin is basically about *presence*. The "very essential heart" of it is the instant-to-instant awareness of shared moments between the actors and the audience:

Chaikin in an Open Theater workshop, 1966. Photograph by Phill Niblock.

"You're there in that particular space in that room, breathing in that room . . . That's what the theater is. It's this demonstration of presence on some human theme or other and in some form or other." This quality, the fundamental difference between the stage and film or television, involves a heightened "sense of being alive now in this room," even a "confrontation of all the live bodies in the room with the mortality which they share." Theater, finally, can help to create an "appreciation of being."

Such a reminder of our aliveness is desperately needed. Chaikin wrote in an early Open Theater notebook, "People don't know if they're watching TV or seeing an actual event"; he says that people no longer seem to know the difference between a person and a photograph of a person, between a voice and a recording of a voice. The failure to appreciate other people's aliveness precludes compassionate or even responsible social interaction. In an interview at the height of the Vietnam war, he said:

I think that people are very divided from a kind of reality, so that it's very easy for somebody in a plane to push a button and drop a bomb on a village because he has no relationship to the village at all, none; he sits on a plane. And in a sense I think that people have lost the sense of people being alive. They say: I am alive, but other people are projections of mine, they don't feel like me.

Theater's affirmation of being, therefore, has a vital social purpose.

Moreover, actors' presentation of the marvelous can become a foil to everyday reality and so, potentially, a force to change it. Every human creation, Chaikin says, reflects and so promotes a certain way of seeing the world. By showing alternative understandings, one "recommends" and, ultimately, strengthens them: "All entertainment becomes instructive. It instructs the sensibility. It needn't give information in order to instruct. In fact, the information can more easily be neglected than the ambiance of the entertainment."

Since the early sixties, Chaikin has also been interested in theater's potential for direct political use. He has been active in political and social causes: During the Vietnam war, he engaged in civil disobedience demonstrations, draft counseling, and fundraising; he has worked in prisons and with ex-offenders, has participated in U.S. civil rights efforts, has helped organize support for groups abroad, including Russian Jews and Southeast Asian "boat people," and has been active in the antinuclear movement.

For a time, he felt that his political and aesthetic concerns intersected in the theater. He believed that the communal nature of performance created the imperative that theater, of all the arts, address public issues, and he was critical of stage work that stayed within the confines of the personal:

We are political animals as well as private ones, and our mythical selves and dream selves are realms which are separate from but which cross each other and are interdependent, so that the emphasis on the inner self which bypasses the social self results in the discovery of one's deep sense of misery.

Although the Open Theater never had a rigid platform, it some-times took stands, and its members shared what Chaikin called a strong social conscience. He maintained that in addition to being "very gifted," a person needed to be "politically oriented" to come into the company, that although "a lot of it is naive and vague and unspecific, . . . the group shares a political attitude, unlike Lincoln Center, unlike the commercial theater." Much of the Open Theater's early work was directly activist in intent. In 1966, Chaikin described the group as "dedicated to the overthrow of public opinion," and early the following year he said that one of the group's two ambi-tions was to encourage "a certain kind of political honesty" doing frankly propagandist theater. He was attempting "to understand the stage as a weapon."

By late 1967, though, Chaikin had come to feel that the require-ment of direct usefulness was an unacceptable straitjacket, that art should not be policed in this way: "There is no need to demand that material we work on must have topical propaganda benefit any more than we would demand that every poem written should be against the State and every song sung should be a call to ac-tion." He had become uneasy, too, with agitprop's preachy, intimi-dating "rightness," its "missionary thing." Except, he said, where artists are performing out of personal experience and for an audi-ence that shares their situation (the case of some women's, black, and gay groups, or the Vietnam Veterans against the War), the work tends to polarize the theater community into a group of self-proclaimed enlightened performers playing "for the enemy, for the adversary . . . the unenlightened other." In any case, Chaikin felt, non–community-based agitprop accomplishes little, aside from making the artists feel virtuous and, therefore, less likely to engage in more effective types of action:

One of the major mistakes is that of the actor who believes that expressing his outrage is the same as doing something about it. It is doing something, of course, for the actor. It is release. Getting your rocks off is not at all necessarily a political action. Strategy is missing.

However significant the message and sincere the intention, the ex-perience for the audience is usually bland.

Still, Chaikin has never repudiated the notion of theater's social responsibility. He always monitors the message of his work. Discuss-ing possible types of couple relationships to show in *Re-Arrangements*, he rejected one suggestion about an emotionally savage pair, saying,

Beggars scavenging for food in a scene from *The Dybbuk* at the New York Shakespeare Festival Public Theater, 1977. Photograph by Inge Morath/Magnum.

"There's too much of that in the world already; I don't want to add any more." Despite, or because of, his own Eastern European Jewish heritage, he insisted that sexual and class repressions in *stetl* society be highlighted in his *Dybbuk*. *Terminal* included several very strong, angry speeches about blind obedience to authority and abuses of power. And in *Tourists and Refugees* the Winter Project tried to show the relationship between multinational economic interests and personal human upheaval.

In fact, Chaikin has not given up on the stage as a weapon. He was interested in making *The Other* in Israel "only for political reasons." And he once told a South African friend that he would like to go there to work "to make trouble any way I can." He is discouraged by the theater's movement away from political involvement, and dismayed that some of the most inspired artists stay aloof from social concerns. He said in 1980:

We used to say that we wished theater would be a place for ceremony. And it's happened. Sometimes what you wish for is the worst thing that could happen. Now Brook is using theater as ceremony. He and Grotowski both are using it for a kind of mystical thing. The terrible part of it is the otherworldliness of it, the retreat from the world.

THE LANGUAGES OF THEATER

Words. Chaikin's mistrust of conventional language comes partly from his politics. Like many modern playwrights, he feels that everyday speech is part of the social facade that systematically distorts and masks more than it communicates. Moreover, popular culture has so tightly bound a whole range of important phrases to make-believe values and social myths that they have become unusable for expressing real feelings. For example:

As [a person] says "I love you," all the movies he has ever seen come rushing between him and the other person. Immediately he starts to compare what is happening to him with a filmed romance. He experiences the hollowness of the words – there seems to be an absence and in fact, as he says, "I love you," he sneakily feels he lies.

In the sixties, Chaikin's wariness about language was exacerbated by the political climate, by the government's use of misleading vocabulary such as "incursion" and "antipersonnel" bomb, to manipulate popular thought. More recently, in 1973, Chaikin said, "We don't say what we mean, but we come to mean what we say. So one has to find a way to 'speak' in other ways."

After several years of largely nonverbal explorations, though, Chaikin came to feel that actors must work *through* language. "Only words," he said, "have such precise and focused meaning." Besides, to find other ways to "speak," "one has to know the conventional vocabulary pretty clearly as well." Rather than discarding the verbal, he wants "to see each play have its own code in the use of words, . . . its [own] special poetry."

Actors must learn also to reintegrate the information in words with the actual vowels, consonants, pitches, and timbres that constitute them:

The spoken word is too often simply giving sound to the printed word. We should want to find how to speak words, not simply as data, but using the sounds which make up the word to create the universe of the word. For example, if the word *radiance* can be spoken not simply to stand for the *idea* but to bring up "radiance," then the voice is creating through the word. The question is how to use the voice, not to refer to a condition, but to enter it.

When the impulse and the sound are integrated, language becomes alive: "Sometimes words merge with sounds. Then they are present."

Forms beyond naturalism. In any case, theater must expand beyond the skimpy vocabulary – verbal and nonverbal – of social discourse:

If you think about it, our repertory of actions is very, very limited. We sit or we stand or we lean or we lay down. That doesn't prepare the body for being expressive for other kinds of things. We talk – that's about all we do with our voices. We talk, sometimes a little louder, sometimes a little softer, and that's about it. Yet, the voice and body in fact are potentially very, very expressive . . . The actor expands his physical and vocal expressiveness so that he can find a way to give testimony to all kinds of things.

Chaikin's research is not merely to develop a new performance lexicon but to explore fundamental questions about behavior. Most naturalistic theater is rooted in a simplified version of the "scientific" view of character developed in the nineteenth and early twentieth centuries. To Chaikin, this approach is inadequate:

An actor-person who sees his life as being completely contained within the describable situations which move in and around him is necessarily an actor in the service of a limited idea. Thus, the psychological actor sees the space of a house as the full scope and vastness of experience, and when he inadvertently looks up and sees the sky he sees it as nothing more than a covering for the house.

For a while, Chaikin subscribed to a quasi-Marxist view that character is determined by economic and political forces, but he came to see that approach, too, as a reduction. Theater based on either the psychological or the political–economic theory of behavior assumes that people are shaped by wholly definable conditions and forces, either of one's individual past or of history: "Chayevsky and Inge make a theater out of circumstances. A woman is upset because she doesn't have a husband. If she gets one the situation is finished; she behaves differently because the circumstances are different." Such work, Chaikin feels, glosses over bewildering and important contradictions. Ultimately, it closes out the imagination.

Chaikin's rejection of naturalism, in fact, is directly entwined with his politics. "Natural" behavior includes a great deal of conditioning from social and even media models, which hardly reflect the most progressive values. In any case, to limit the actor's potential for articulation on stage to the range possible "over coffee and a danish" is to restrict stage action to the laws of society:

Just as good manners very often keep in check the violence in a situation, confining behavior on the stage to the simple social reality keeps concealed all that which is bewildering.

I think one of my reasons for rejecting naturalism is because it corresponds to social order, certain kinds of emphasis, and certain kinds of repression . . . The mode of behavior which a theater chooses to emphasize is a political choice, whatever the content. Naturalism corresponds to the programmed responses of our daily life – to a life style which is in accord with the political gestalt of the time. To accept naturalism is to collaborate, to accept society's limits.

Chaikin wants the theater to show new realms of human possibility, a different way of being:

We want to develop a theater style which has an implication of a whole other kind of species of people, to try to see what other kinds of voices, bodies, expressions we may be . . . When I go to a foreign city I feel I know nothing about the city unless I know its prisons and its temples, unless I go into the dungeons and I go into the shrine. We want to do this in the mind. To make a kind of theater which has to do with creatures, creatures that we see, that we agree as a group we can try to depict, monsters, angels, fairies.

This inner world, he says, involves a realm of shared humanness which transcends an individual person's life. Chaikin asks, "Where does the actor draw from in himself to play a role on stage very unlike his life-role? And where is this energy all the rest of the time?" And his answer is, "There are zones in us which know more than we think they do. The secret is in knowing how to listen to them." Chaikin believes that "the actor can find a way to report on experience which is not just the experience of that actor." The performer, in this way, gives expression not merely to personal memories, but to something larger, something akin to Jung's archetypes, Emerson's universal nature.

It is important, moreover, that this testimony confound tendencies to reduce it to "meanings." Chaikin noted, for example, during the work on *Nightwalk* that the travelers "need an identity which would short-circuit symbolism." And he told the actors: "When a piece is successful it evades the logic that some audience people want to impose on it. [They] can't package it." His dislike of facile systems and solutions is one of the areas in which Chaikin's politics and his aesthetics directly meet. In fact, actor Paul Zimet noted on the day Chaikin made this comment: "Joe's politics entering his theater. Against society of easily packaged commodities, emotions, dogmas."

Music. Rejecting realism, Chaikin has drawn inspiration from the art form that is least concrete and least mimetic of real-world models. While most Western theater has been a first cousin to literature, using linear, narrative structures and concentrating on text (which, indeed, is usually the only part noted and passed down), Chaikin's basic conception of theater is much more closely allied with music.

Chaikin's hobby and his greatest passion, apart from theater, is music. He has an enormous collection of records and tapes: classical (instrumental and vocal), jazz, folk, and non-Western. At home, he listens to music almost constantly, and he will not travel for more than a day or two without a cassette player and tapes. Indeed, once when he was critically ill, unsure if he would be alive in half an hour, he calmed himself by *mentally* listening to Mozart: connected to an IV, getting oxygen through a tube, he rhapsodized with a visitor about the exquisite bass line in one of the late symphonies.

Chaikin wants to explore dimensions in theater that function like music: The theater

exists not just to make a mirror of life, but to represent a kind of realm just as certainly as music is a realm. But because the theater involves behavior and language, it can't be completely separated from the situational world, as music can. But much passes between people in the theater which is intuitive and not at all concrete, having nothing to do with data.

His theater notebooks include thoughts about music's ability to convey things that cannot be captured in words and do not replicate outward reality:

Susanne Langer says: What is criticized as a weakness is really the strength of musical expressiveness: Music articulates forms which language cannot set forth.

All the ingredients of music are not *supplied* but merely inspired by sounds heard in nature . . . Art seeks to defy the model or dispense with it altogether, because it is a less literal description that it aspires to.

Theater, Chaikin feels, should similarly aim to express conditions that, although they may not have precise embodiments in the external world, are part of deep, shared experience. Stage artists must expand their goals beyond the literal. And music, he says, has the "most developed kind of vocabulary."

Chaikin also draws on musical prototypes for dramatic structure. Although there are formal similarities between his stage works and early expressionist theater and film, it is to music that Chaikin himself looks for a model. Plays, like abstract sound compositions, can be built through the development and interweaving of themes and motifs. It is possible in this way to draw connections more complex and fragile than those of narrative or logic. Chaikin speaks about the "overtones" as well as the "main pitch" in individual images, about interplays of rhythm and dynamics among actors or among moments of a play. His basic principle in assembling a performance piece is not to construct a coherent story, but to find "a shape that's musically tenable."

Chaikin feels that all theater affects its audiences through musical, as well as literary, vocabulary and syntax. The relationships among stage moments always involve mode and dynamics as well as story:

In Bach's St. Matthew's Passion, the narrative is the continuity and returning point, but within the narrative are stops where, for example, a violin comes in with a contralto voice singing contrapuntally about grief and sin. Then the narrative returns. During the duet between the violin and the contralto, the music calls on the listener with a special form of intimacy. One way we realize this realm is through contrast with the narrative.

. . . Structurally, this is clearer to understand in music, but it is no less present in acting.

Even Chaikin's emphasis on "presence," finally, shows his conception of theater as more allied to music or dance than to literature. Theater, for him, takes place in a series of immediate, disappearing instants; it can be remembered, but exists only for the moments when it is happening.

Humor. Another way to transcend the literal and the logical is through humor. Laughter, Chaikin says, is "a collapse of control in response to something which cannot be fitted into the file cabinet of the mind . . . , a form of ecstasy, a collapse of reason into a basic clarity." Although he is put off by cleverness for its own sake and warns against pandering for laughs that may distract from the point of a play, he thinks that complex, subtle connections can be highlighted through comedy. In *The Mutation Show* and *Tourists and Refugees*, for example, he used funny reprises of serious motifs, and serious echoes of funny moments, to make the audience grasp not only the agony in what seemed ridiculous, and the humor in what was barely endurable, but also very specific thematic implications.

He feels that comedy makes it possible for audiences to see and hear material that they might otherwise resist. It is not an escape, but a way of looking that "makes anything tolerable" and can often be "more powerful than serious statement." "It is felt," he once wrote, "that what is important must be serious. Humor can be a response to anything."

Spareness and precision. While experimenting with various kinds of nonnaturalistic performance, Chaikin has generally moved toward

Comic "bums" (Will Patton and Ronnie Gilbert) in *Tourists and Refugees* at LaMama, New York, 1980. Photograph by Ricki Rosen.

an aesthetic of extreme spareness. He has, first of all, deemphasized scenery, props, and, usually, costumes. This preference for "poor theater" is partly a function of economics, to be sure, but mostly it has come from a desire and a determination, like Grotowski's, "to make the actor *do* all he can do." The performer should not have to compete for attention with elaborate material trappings.

Beyond this Chaikin believes that the best way to create sharp images is through sensory focus, not overload, through rigorous editing. While much new American theater, mainstream and alternative, has been colored by the rock concert aesthetic of bombardment, Chaikin, like Brook and Barrault, has preferred increasingly distilled forms: "The most articulate performances are always those which have been pared away. All that's nonessential, all that's accessory, all that's indulgent, all that's outside the center has been dropped, and what remains is a spare language of tasks which speak of life and nature."

As he has worked more and more with carefully refined images, Chaikin has come to prefer very precisely fixed theater rather than improvisation. This represents a turnaround from his views of the early and mid-sixties, when his dream theater was one in which "certain things change nightly." Over the years, such "freedom" on stage came to seem more and more limiting. And Chaikin now feels that "the task is to find as much as possible a kind of inevitability" in a sequence of precise images. Having found it, "then you shouldn't just keep changing it." He was especially fond of *Terminal* partly because it came to be so exactly crafted, "so very definite, each movement of it," that it was "almost like a piece of sculpture." While sections of some later pieces were improvised in each performance, this was, according to Chaikin, only because the group had been unable to find the "inevitable" forms for what they wanted to express.

Still, even within the most precise images there should be a living flow. Without altering the shapes of the piece, the aliveness of the event should create differences from night to night:

Underneath, certain things really ought to change. If there is a kind of reciprocity between the audience and the action, a kind of respiration on that particular night, things do change in spite of the fact that the form doesn't change. There should be a certain feeling of the presence of the audience and there should be something moving within that.

THE ACTOR AND THE CHARACTER

Like most more traditional theater artists, Chaikin believes that the actor must try to have the broadest possible life experience, so that roles will not get misshapen by the performer's constricted understanding. He suggested that Open Theater members make a point of having contact with blind, deaf, and seriously ill people, that they go to night courts, Buddhist services, draft boards, ghettoes, Bowery flophouses, prisons. A theater artist, Chaikin says, must actively work at becoming open, at shedding "prepared responses" that cut off genuine receptivity. Rather than "screening out much of what bombards us and focusing on a negotiable position, [the actor] must in some sense be in contact with his own sense of astonishment."

But, unlike most more traditional teachers, Chaikin feels that the influence between an actor's on- and offstage lives goes in both directions. Not only do life experience and personality affect stage characterizations, but something of the persona remains after the show:

When we as actors are performing, we are also present as persons and the performance is a testimony of ourselves. So each role, each work, each performance changes us as persons . . . In former times, acting simply meant putting on a disguise. But now it's clear that the wearing of the disguise changes the person. As he takes off the disguise, his face is changed from having worn it. The stage performance informs the life performance and in turn is informed by it.

Partly because he feels that an actor's work and life relate in this way, it is "a kind of actor's morality" for Chaikin to perform only material with which one feels engaged: "You shouldn't do what you're not connected with. You don't have to be able to explain the connection or be 'politically correct' or anything, but there has to be something that you have a connection to." Chaikin once described the Open Theater's aim as "to give form and expression to what one *does* care about." He has little patience or respect for "people who would do whatever role is flattering or pays a lot." Even if their performances are polished, he says, "Usually when people are doing that they don't explore and they don't probe very deeply." The shallowness of the work begins to infect the offstage life, starting a vicious circle in which both get circumscribed.

Presence and empathy. Since the basic value of theater for Chaikin is the recognition of shared aliveness, he wants the spectators always to feel the presence of the actors as well as the characters. In contrast to Method advocates, who anathematize the performer's showing through the role, Chaikin wants the audience to have a heightened awareness of the actors. To a large extent, he believes, the ability to create this response is simply a gift that certain performers have. It is "a quality that makes you feel as though you're standing right next to the actor, no matter where you are sitting in the theater . . . , a kind of deep libidinal surrender which the performer reserves for his anonymous audience."

All actors can heighten their aura of presence, though, by directing their attention outward, rather than focusing only inside the world of the play. Chaikin insists that performers be totally alert at all times to the actual moments and the actual space in which they are working. He told the Open Theater members to cultivate a "consciousness of not only what's going on inside you but what is going on around you and in the room and area that you are in":

The basic starting point for the actor is that his body is sensitive to the immediate landscape where he is performing. The full attention of the mind and body should be awake in that very space and in that very time (not an idea of time) and with the very people who are also in that time and space.

Only when the actor is attuned to the entire play and the audience–actor situation of the particular performance is the theater work truly alive.

This presence is related to the Alienation Effect. While Brecht proposed to distance the audience from the action mainly for didactic reasons, his theory was based on an aesthetic recognition that theater involves two simultaneous realities: the fictive world of the play, and the actual situation where the performance is taking place. Spectators must not be tricked into looking *through* the actors, the physical setting, and the actual time, without seeing them, to enter the realm of the drama. Rather, the performers, the playing space, and the actual time must be acknowledged along with the theatrical world they conjure.

This sort of double reality, precisely, underlies Chaikin's presence. A single human form becomes at once a breathing, mortal person and a timeless theatrical personage, a single space both a playing area and a theatrical environment, and a single time both linear, progressing time and the abstract time of the play. The audience always sees both the actor and the character. Speaking of the *Verfremdungseffekt*, Chaikin has explained how a performer creates this duality:

Moment to moment, the play is between actor and audience . . . The audience is the actor's partner as he plays the role of the character for the other characters. Yet the actor should not – and does not have to – wink, woo, or pander to the audience: there is a tacit understanding. The actor, as his character, is sincere in relation to the other actors but performing in relation to the audience.

Such a performer functions "like a double agent who has infiltrated the two worlds."

While Chaikin's engagement with presence is not directly political, he shares Brecht's interest in the didactic potential of Alienation. "Acting at a distance," he says, "has the power of spotlighting the forces at work"; it can move the audience beyond thoughtless emotion to a more objective consideration of the events portrayed.

At the same time, Chaikin wants his theater to transmit direct feelings, unimpeded by intellect. "The V-effect," he explains, "was to *observe* and *look* in the middle of all that push-button emotion of Germany during that period. It really came out of that particular sentimentality." Our situation now is different. The tendency toward ready-made emotions is at least counterbalanced by a terrible decimation of feelings, a lack of permission to enter strong emotional territory. Theater today, according to Chaikin, must address and provide an antidote to that coldness as well.

So, unlike Brecht, Chaikin feels that actors not only must remain aware of their real selves and actual surroundings, but *also* must empathize completely with their characters: They must "reflect the condition directly" rather than "respond to it, mediate it." He told the Open Theater, "The most important thing in acting is to understand – to be able to empathize, to subjectively see." The goal should be "understanding a character, not judging."

Chaikin accepts the incompatibility of his requirements that the actor be visible and disappear, be distanced from the character as well as empathetic. "I think that they're two different and disparate values," he explains, and to some extent the material will determine which value should predominate. Finally, though, he thinks it is possible, however paradoxical, to be present as an actor and yet inside the character at the same time.

Entering the character. Virtually all of the major teachers in New York in the early sixties based their training on Method principles, that is, the belief that a performer's basic entrance into a character comes from effectively remembering or imagining emotions that parallel what the character should be experiencing. For Chaikin, this approach is not without value: "Every actor draws on his own life; very often such associations enrich performances." The Open Theater members were urged to have – and most did have – a strong grounding in the Method.

But actors must, then, move beyond this training. A performer who relies too much on emotional recall and projection risks molding every character to the contours and limits of that actor's own psyche rather than stretching to fit the character. As this becomes a habit, the ability to empathize will decline:

As the actor develops techniques of emotional memory, by consciously approaching or paralleling the characters' experience through his own, he weakens his powers of empathy . . . ; the ability to transfer oneself to the experience of another becomes underdeveloped. The character of the emotion and the emotion of the character slowly get evened out; even though the mannerisms of the character may be very different, the sphere of feeling stays the same.

Shaping the character's emotions to correspond to those of the actor is a particularly critical problem in contemporary theater, where many characters are not even people. Certainly an actor's repertoire of emotions could not include the feelings of cartoons, phantasms, or personifications of spiritual conditions.

Emotion memory, in any case, incorporates distortions. It relies on impulses that have already been edited:

Feeling is experienced differently at the moment from the way it seems when remembered. A simplifying interpretation of the feeling, classified through some current psychotherapeutic approach, is often invisibly attached to it. Today we are overripe with psychological interpretations of feeling and information about feelings; these often intercept the raw and undecoded feeling itself.

Moreover, the very act of calling up extreme emotions, especially painful ones, is likely to contradict the character's impulses:

The "Method" actor, in his effort to inhabit the character, tries to involve himself with the character's inner dilemma. But the character, if he were a live person, would be doing the opposite – that is, trying to relieve himself of his unhappiness, and to respond to the circumstances around him.

"To make a fight," Chaikin noted, "you have to play against it." Often, the actor's effort to generate emotions not only violates the character's intentions but shows through the performance: "An actor who is pumping at his remorse asks the audience to see the remorse, but not the pumping"; the audience sees both.

The Method also can seduce performers into excessive self-involvement on stage. "I really can't stand the actor who is pumping up feelings and saying, 'It only matters how I feel, and if I'm full enough it's groovy.' I'm just repelled by that after a certain point." The actor totally absorbed in a personal experience is "completely locked out of any ensemble experience," "leaves no room for the spectator," and, ultimately, has little real connection with the substance of the play:

Traditionally the actor summons his sadness, anger, or enthusiasm and pumps at it to sustain an involvement with himself which passes for concern with his material. The eyes of this actor are always secretly looking into his own head. He's like a singer being moved by his own voice.

Chaikin's final objection to the Method is that it does not work. It rarely succeeds in presenting the character – as opposed to the actor. He quipped once, "If John and Jim both were actors who relied on emotional memory, and John played the character of Jim on stage, Jim would give up that approach."

Chaikin believes that the actor's real entrance into a role comes more often from a somatic than a psychological impulse. He has explored ways to work with the shapes and rhythms of actions and feelings.

Chaikin works with Winter Project actress Tina Shepard, trying to use the body to locate extreme conditions, New York, 1980. Photograph by Ricki Rosen.

While a person's emotional memory contains only the experience of
one individual, in a filtered version, Chaikin feels that "all of one's
past – historical and evolutionary – is contained in the body." And
somatic impulses are direct, uninterpreted. Thus, although we are,
most of us, out of touch with our physicality ("In America many
people live in their bodies like in abandoned houses, haunted with
memories of when they were occupied"), the actor must become
resensitized. A performer need not actually recreate the physical or

emotional condition of the character; Chaikin would no more recommend that someone get stoned and exhausted to play in *The Connection* than a Method acting teacher would. But the actor must recreate the *form* that physically embodies and so communicates the character's way of being.

Chaikin is particularly concerned with rhythms. All speech, all human action, he says, has a rhythm that is tied, ultimately, to breathing. To enter a role at a particular moment, the actor must incorporate its pulse. Otherwise, the state will not be communicated to fellow performers or the audience. Any shift in the character's feelings must also be embodied in a change of rhythm. He has talked, for example, about "a kind of upbeat" that may precede launching into a new intention. And the theater event as a whole has a rhythm, however complex and shifting, which the actors must realize together.

This approach to internal conditions through their forms is valuable not only for the original entrance into a character moment, but also for its recreation in performance after performance: "The internal is charted territory; the access to it is through its shapes and rhythms. Although the inside needs to be replenished each time, there is another kind of attention that must be tuned to the outside."

Still, Chaikin does not consider the somatic route a unique, one-way road. He cautioned a student in 1978: "Don't let anyone tell you to go from the inside out – or the outside in. It's a circle."

THE COMMUNITIES OF THEATER

Ensemble. Chaikin once said, "The single most important concern [of the Open Theater] is the continuity of an ensemble of actors and the collaboration of talented writers, director, etc." He continues to feel that an ongoing company is "the only way."

Although he cares very much that the work atmosphere be congenial, Chaikin's goal in ensemble collaboration has always been to make theater, not to develop a Utopian community or perform group therapy. He was out of step in this respect with much of the collective theater of the late sixties and even, at times, with people in the Open Theater who wanted the company to become less of what Chaikin termed a "task group" and more of a support group or commune. In 1969 he told the *Terminal* actors, "If all we stay with are our hangups and we define ourselves completely in relation to them and we get all excited in our work when we find an expressive release for them, we haven't gotten very far."

Chaikin became interested in ensemble work because he felt that actors could not really be "present" unless they became more sensitive to one another. He told an interviewer in 1968: "I had been acting in many different plays and at the Living Theater, which was the only [repertory] theater in New York at the time . . . I never felt an ensemble sense on the stage, that people were in the same place . . . So I started making exercises to meet." He wanted actors not simply to mesh interpretations and intentions on stage but to become receptive to one another's rhythms and to the developing energies of the piece as a whole. Long-term collaboration, he felt, would facilitate this sort of sensitivity.

An ongoing ensemble also would be able to develop a common working vocabulary. While Chaikin sees some use in continually wrestling with diverse theater assumptions, he thinks it much better to start with shared values and a shared language and then try to expand the possibilities for expression.

There is the danger, of course, that a company working together year after year will begin to fall into familiar patterns, becoming predictable and stuck at a certain stage of growth. Wary of this, Chaikin never plans workshops more than one season at a time. But he feels that if the individual people are gifted and the mix is a dynamic one, the benefits of long-term collaboration greatly outweigh the drawbacks.

Audiences. Chaikin is much more ambivalent about the other part of the theater community: the audience. Neither the Open Theater nor the Winter Project was ever primarily a performing group, and during each workshop's first few years, Chaikin tried to keep public showings to a minimum. One observer described the early Open Theater as "exclusionist," a company of "monastics," its director "worried about contamination" and "reluctant to take the troupe out into the world." Chaikin has always wanted the embryonic stages of explorations to be spared the pressure to please. "You don't learn while you're performing. Performing only makes use of what you already know. You need a laboratory, a workshop, a floundering around in order to develop." Although both the Winter Project and the Open Theater gave public productions beginning in their second seasons, Chaikin considered these valuable only as a chance "to see where we were in problem solving; how far we had gotten, and what was left for us to do."

The nature of Chaikin's misgivings has changed over the years. When the Open Theater was rehearsing for its earliest performances in 1963 and 1964, Chaikin tried to prepare the company for rejection. He gave notes like "Going from the private to public is going from the known accepted to the implied unaccepting," "People will be walking out," and "Be prepared to be attacked – not armed – but know that full approval is not forthcoming." After the first few seasons, though, he realized that the greatest threat from the audience was the lure of its approval. He told the Open Theater on one occasion, "Even though we must sometimes be supported and encouraged, praise is beside the point. Even self-praise. It sets up a criterion other than the organic one."

Actors, he said, must overcome the "temptation to play for the audience[,] to please them, to engage them, to beguile them in such a way that the inquiry is shallower." Often, he feels, one can be misled by following the most conspicuous spectator reactions, especially laughter:

There are often a few guffawers in an audience who are out to show everyone that they're having a good time. Their laughs don't necessarily reflect the mood of the audience. The actor who is drawn in by the laughs and plays to get more will lose the intent and meaning of the work. The actor must find a balance: he must be aware of what the audience is receiving and at the same time be faithful to the precise requirements of the play and his role.

Chaikin dislikes the changes that often occur within his ensembles as they begin to prepare for public performances. Resentments and jealousies develop as the relative democracy of the workshop ends and Chaikin begins to impose final decisions about cuts and role assignments. The *Serpent* company, he says, declined from a "Utopian community" to one fractured with tension:

When we got into the roles – that Tina would play Eve, that Ray was going to do Cain – there was a terrible feeling of betrayal . . . They would all tell me in one form or another – repeatedly, I mean, in whatever form they would tell me – how they thought Tina was rotten, and that Paul Zimet couldn't talk as an actor, that yes, it was true that he could move a little bit, but he couldn't talk. This part of it had a lot to do with the dynamics of the group experience, which I didn't foresee, or I think I maybe somewhere did and didn't want to.

Other strains come simply from moving out of a safe, closed arena into the public eye. Chaikin told the actors in 1968, "Performing is sharing . . . It is giving birth, and the pain and trauma of birth is part of the move from private to public."

Chaikin's political involvement and his view of theater as something shared by actors and spectators always pull against his exclusionist tendencies. Since the later years of the Open Theater, he has increasingly considered questions about the audience for whom his work is to be played. And while he still insists that research must be protected from the pressures of public scrutiny, he is anxious to show work that he feels is ready.

Chaikin does not expect his theater to appeal to a mass audience. This suits him, in a way, since he also prefers to perform in intimate houses. Larger theaters require "telegraphing to the balconies" in a way that ruptures the experience. Complex and delicate work, he says, cannot be done "in Madison Square Garden."

In fact, he is not concerned about being universally accessible:

There will be a certain part of the audience that won't understand. If one goes by the criterion that the more people who understand it the better, then one can only reduce the language that you speak in theater to the language, for example, of a television series, which does take the most reduced language to speak to people.

The message in Chaikin's work is often in the overtone, and "if you're going to take that chance of doing overtones, you must also know that a lot of people won't tune in, because a lot of people are going to tune in strictly to the pitch itself."

But, in contrast to what he sees as self-indulgence in much Method-dominated theater, he is not satisfied as soon as an image has meaning for the performer or the company. He recalls his frustration, for example, with one actor who, although very inventive, was not concerned enough with being understood:

I would say I didn't get what he was doing, and he would say, "But it has meaning for me." And I would say, "But not for me, and I'm playing the audience now." There was this thing he did of going through the play monitoring his own connection, his own responses. And he would say, "If I'm not connected to it, the audience can't be." I agree with that, but the opposite doesn't follow, that if you are connected in some way, that [connection] will transmit to the audience.

Theater is about meeting an audience: "It's very important to us, to be clear while speaking of deep and subtle things, and the more one tries to speak of deep and subtle things, the more the responsibility to be clear is."

Since he recognizes the spectators as present, living people, Chaikin is interested in who they are. For artistic as well as political reasons, he has made a point of performing for nonhabitual theatergoers, in prisons, hospitals, schools. And he has paid attention to the makeup of his general audiences as well. While some of the Open Theater's New York following, he says, were avant-garde chic, a kind of "culture-vulture type that devours the current cultural commodity," most, including many artists, seemed to come out of real interest in the work. Having a sense of community with the spectators is important to Chaikin. He would not do *The Dybbuk* at Papp's first choice, Lincoln Center, not only because he hated the hangar-like coldness of the Beaumont Theater, but also because he did not like the character of its audiences. When he found out that his New York *Endgame* run was largely sold out to subscribers from the Manhattan Theatre Club's staid, wealthy neighborhood, he was dismayed and concerned that people he thought likelier to care about the play might not be able to get tickets.

Chaikin's interest in audiences is tied to what he calls "levels of address." He realized while acting off-off-Broadway that his performance shifted somehow according to his feelings about who was in the house:

One night when I was about to go on stage, I was told Gwen Verdon was in the audience. Ours is a small theater, and I knew that somehow her being there, watching, would alter what I was doing, perhaps very slightly, but it would have an effect. Now suppose there were 200 Gwen Verdons in the audience. Perhaps we could endeavor to provide this sort of specialized communication.

Real-life interactions involve not only what actually is said or done but also the complex colorations imposed by each party's assumptions about the other. These "different levels that one addresses another one on" range "from the most familiar, habitual relationship to something very cosmic." And, Chaikin reasoned, "the same thing is true with the actor and the audience and with the piece and the audience": These dynamics too are variable and depend on the assumptions each has about the other.

Chaikin believes that the actor always fixes upon a certain level of address. "The audience . . . is in fact always endowed with a quality unless one ignores them completely, which will always end in a total lack of communication." Every performer has some notion, makes some decision, about who the audience is. Most often, this choice is made unconsciously and uncreatively. But performers can and should control how they approach the spectators. Chaikin has come to feel, in fact, that one can *create* certain dynamics in the audience by addressing it in a given way: "In attributing a particular quality to the audience, one invites the participation of that quality." This may even be a key to "presence": Perhaps the actors' heightened sense of live spectators sharing the space, time, and event generates or invites the audience's heightened sense of aliveness.

Whoever the spectators are, it is crucial to Chaikin that they stay alert to the presence of the event. He does not want to draw the audience so far into the stage experience that they lose their awareness of its immediacy and aliveness:

Much of the new theater that I see . . . is much more like the movies than like theater. It takes you into a kind of dream . . . and you become very passive . . . It makes me feel bad because it's exactly what to me is not precious in the theater. To me what's precious is that one is there.

Most of the tacks Chaikin saw or tried for directly engaging the audience's presence finally seemed misguided to him. During the late fifties and early sixties he was intrigued with Happenings and environmental theater as ways of redefining the actor–spectator roles. But he could never see himself limiting his expression to the abilities of untrained, even unrehearsed, performers; and merely reallocating the performing and viewing areas to intermingle everyone seemed an uninteresting "arbitrary experiment." Chaikin thought for a time that actors might address and even touch members of the audience, but he eventually rejected this approach as not only ineffective but assaultive:

You can be touched and disqualify it, annul it. After the initial response, whether it's pleasure (which I don't think was usually the case) or you're repelled by it, then you can work it out to annul it. In any case, you feel a little violated.

The audience must be actively included in the theater, but in more subtle ways. Chaikin urged the Open Theater performers, for example, to consider themselves part of a community encompassing the spectators as well as their fellow actors: "When not in a scene and watching from [the] side, [you] are the same as audience . . . Don't consider [the] audience in [the] limited role of critic or friend – someone who will praise or blame – but as yourself doing something else at that moment." To underscore this connection, he prefers, wherever possible, to let the audience see the actors move from being people like themselves into inhabiting the characters.

THE POLITICS AND ECONOMICS OF THEATER

For Chaikin, the political issues facing a theater group include not only the content of its work but the context in which it performs. In the Open Theater, especially, finding an alternative economic structure was a priority. The company kept admission charges low and voluntary whenever possible, so that no one would be kept out for lack of money. They performed in prisons and did benefits for political causes and theater groups that could not get funding on their own.

More recently, with grants tighter, New York living expenses higher, and company members older, Chaikin has had to temper his idealism and concede that audiences should pay so that artists can be paid. But he still feels that the political and economic aspects of a production cannot be ignored if the project is to have integrity.

Chaikin is repelled by the workings of commercial theater, by the idea and the process of making theater into a business. He finds, first of all, that the casting structure there tends to reduce actors and characters to types, "reinforc[ing] the rigid and convenient stereotyping of ourselves, actor and audience alike." More basically, though, he feels that real exploration is crippled by the commercial theater's immediate need to please critics and audiences, that "It is necessary to close off the impulse to 'make it' in order to open oneself":

I think that it's almost impossible to grow [under the pressure to please]. There are examples of people with a certain kind of stamina and a certain sort of competitive esprit that can tolerate a kind of competitive arena. But I personally didn't think I could, and other people can't. But it can be almost a sport. I've never been involved in sports, or interested in them.

In the early years, Chaikin accepted that Open Theater members might support themselves in the commercial theater, though he "wanted very much that nobody should come there as a stepping-stone toward the Broadway world." But when *America Hurrah* became a hit, he became disillusioned:

There was nothing left of the exploratory thing or the attempt to strengthen the work or even to confirm what we had done through occasional rehearsal or review, which was to me really important. So I was very disgusted. I couldn't get anybody to rehearse at all. The women wanted to go to the beauty parlor because they were being photographed so much, and the men wanted – something else, I don't know what . . .

And, in fact, from that group one guy is a big commercial actor, another guy has a television show of his own, and they're all over doing all kinds of things including commercials. And, in fact, it was what they did want.

This experience convinced him that very few people can function in that big-time, mainstream world without becoming corrupted by it. When one becomes "invested in certain values . . . there's a given boundary to one's willingness to explore"; becoming involved with "a status thing . . . bring[s] about a kind of equilibrium; it sort of distracts you from an abyss."

He found that acclaim itself became "a kind of responsibility" that consumed time and energy: "For us there was no impetus left to do anything else, to do any research: There was not the time or the space. We were being processed as a 'success.' " Chaikin became committed after *Viet Rock* and *America Hurrah* "to never doing anything off-Broadway or on Broadway again."* This is not, however, an abstinence that he finds especially onerous: "It's so precious, those moments that one is working in a really creative way, that there isn't any bribe that seems equal to it."

Remaining in noncommercial theater has not prevented Chaikin from receiving a great deal of critical notice, and for a long time he was uneasy with his growing fame. Having gone through wanting to "make it" as a Broadway star, he had rejected those values with the militancy of a convert. Gradually, he has become more comfortable with "being a little bit public." No longer "doing it like a monk," he even can admit that he enjoys aspects of success. He appreciates that it helps him get opportunities to do what he wants to in theater. And he was very moved at receiving the first "Lifetime Achievement" Obie award, though he could not bring himself to come to the ceremony to accept the honor. He remarked once that "being well-known" has the advantage "that I get to meet really interesting people who ordinarily wouldn't pay any attention to me."

Chaikin has always thought of critics, partly at least, as the enemy. He objects not only to their role in the grading system of commercial theater, but also to their shaping of audience expectations: "The critic digests the experience and hands it to the spectator to confirm his own conclusion. The spectator, conditioned to be told what to see, sees what he is told, or corrects the critic, but in any case sees in relation to the response of the critic." The Open Theater's experience bore out Chaikin's misgivings. After *The Serpent* had been reviewed, for example, the actors felt that "the whole quality of the audience changed . . . because the audience was looking forward to

*Chaikin has directed at the New York Shakespeare Festival Public Theater, which functions under an Actors Equity Off-Broadway contract, but it is a nonprofit organization.

certain things that they had read about." Once the reviews of *Tongues* and *Savage/Love* came out, Chaikin found that spectators were terribly "respectful" and therefore less free. (In fact, Chaikin decided that the funnier of the two pieces, *Savage/Love*, should be shown first, to help counteract this new tightness in the audience.) Zimet recalls that the critics' responses sometimes even directly affected actors' performances; for example, after reading in a piece about *Nightwalk* that he played a bird, he felt his previously nonspecific character "become birdlike."

While Chaikin always has given a limited number of interviews for feature articles or books, he says he has tried to operate as though reviewers didn't exist. He once described the Open Theater's policy:

We don't invite critics. We don't keep them out if they come; they can come in, but they're not invited. We've done everything possible to avoid an opening night, so that the first time we perform anything we do it as furtively as possible, so that if the critic does come there's no eventfulness in that critic coming.

Chaikin does read everything that comes his way about his own work, and he can be visibly pleased or rattled by what is written. He finds the whole system upsetting and counter-creative.

Despite his feelings about the role of reviewers in the grading process, Chaikin tries to draw on critics' talents in the creative process. In the early years of the Open Theater, Gordon Rogoff and Richard Gilman attended workshops and participated as in-house advisors. Chaikin continues to use certain critics as visiting dramaturges, inviting them (along with other people) to observe work in unfinished, pre-performance states; he then considers their responses in shaping the final piece.

Lately, he even has had some positive comments about reviewers. In 1974 he told an interviewer that he respected the views of certain critics who had taken the trouble to observe his work over several years. And he says now that an intelligent, sensitive reviewer can and should help to shape the direction of theater.

Chaikin described himself once as "neurotically suspicious of money, afraid it'll ruin us." In a notebook kept during the Open Theater's first season, he included "no money" among four precepts that made their work possible. He insisted that the company keep production costs low so that the group would not become more vulnerable than necessary to the financial consequences of reviews. He was dubious for a long time even about accepting foundation and government grants.

"The danger," he said at an Open Theater meeting, "is that we will try to behave in the approved way in order to get more money."

Chaikin felt also that the Open Theater should mantain autonomy in management as much as possible, dealing with outside producers only when necessary (on tour, for example). He said once that he considered producers in the same category as landlords: pariahs to be avoided as much as possible.

Since disbanding the Open Theater, he has had to rely more than before on producers. But he has restricted his dealings to a few noncommercial organizations, and has been careful to make only temporary affiliations:

One of the things that's been my survival mechanism since I've been doing productions has been to bop around from institution to institution instead of staying in any one. So I do something at LaMama, and I do something at the Manhattan Theatre Club, and I do something at Joseph Papp's. Because otherwise the institution starts to inform the company in some way, and the sensibility and the consciousness.*

Even so, a kind of defensiveness often hovers about these projects. Directing *The Dybbuk*, for example, Chaikin deliberately used as few Shakespeare Festival staff people as possible, so that his designers, crew, and so forth would not owe their primary allegiance to the organization. Just before *Re-Arrangements* began workshops at La-Mama, he insisted that a funny, cutting remark he had made about another show there could be quoted, and then later agreed that he had really just been proving to himself that he didn't have to censor what he said about LaMama.

OPENNESS

Finally, a key aspect of Chaikin's theory is his refusal to fix on any aesthetic. He told an interviewer that it would be "intolerable" if the Open Theater were to freeze at a given point in its development, because "its whole character is this thing of changing, of changing, of getting rid-of, like snakeskins." At the start of one new season, he told the company, "After each year of work I think, 'what a bunch of crap that was last year.' My feeling at a given time is 'now

---

*In fact, both Ellen Stewart and Joseph Papp have been supportive of Chaikin in very practical ways over the years. Stewart offered the Open Theater performance space as early as 1965–6 and helped sponsor the Winter Project's *Re-Arrangements, Tourists and Refugees,* and *Trespassing.* Papp provided rehearsal and performance space for the Open Theater in the early years and later for *Electra,* and he produced *A Movie Star Has to Star in Black and White, The Dybbuk, Tongues, Texts,* and *Antigone.*

is the only possibility.' "* It is crucial to him to go along with "what becomes alive as you work" rather than hold onto some initial concept: "Growth means one has to be able to shed, and to give up."

In his Open Theater notebook during the first season, Chaikin wrote that discovery is "to go where you don't know. And you only know some of the ways of going." To explore, one must accept the inevitability of false starts and the possibility of failure; only then can artists "go beyond the safe limits and become adventurers." Looking back as the Open Theater was disbanding, he recalled, "We worked with a lot of permission to fall on our asses . . . Everybody got to do poor work, but in a creative, questioning situation."

Breakthroughs, ironically, are one of the biggest threats to remaining in process, because "when you make a real discovery of some kind, you have to be careful not to become so devoted to it that you get stuck and can't evolve beyond it." It is difficult to move away from work that feels rich and start again to stumble in unknown territory. Still, the immediate prelude to discovery often feels (and looks) like utter confusion, while moving confidently in place can feel (and look) just great:

Just as the actor is about to achieve a stride into the next step, you are visited by obstacles and despair. Just before evolving further, obstacles and despair that makes the actor want to retreat back to that step which precedes the possibility of evolving.

Within one group some people are growing and some people stay in one place, and some seasons bring out the one and some the other. The one who stays in one place has a great power within the group because at all times he is able to identify where he is and where he was. The one who's moving is always somewhat lost because he's not at a place he can clearly define. He's between a place he knows, and moving to where he doesn't know. To move from one known place to another known place is not really to move at all.

*Even during interviews, he was always enthusiastic about discussing current projects, but often merely obliging about recalling the past.

3   The workshop investigations

At a Winter Project workshop one afternoon Chaikin demonstrated an exercise he had designed to locate and express extreme, primitive emotions. Explaining that the actor should prepare by becoming as neutral as possible, he began doing head rolls; his jaw loosened, his shoulders dropped, and he eased into a kind of release. He cautioned about confusing alert neutrality with vacuity or limpness, and let his body go flaccid for a moment to show the difference. Next, he said, the actor should try to find somatic entrances into emotionally extreme conditions, through movement of the spine or the limbs or the head or, especially, through breathing; and as he spoke, Chaikin's body started to change. He explained the importance of keeping in motion, of maintaining a pulse, because discoveries would not come out of stillness or rigidity but only from active receptivity. Meanwhile, a distinct condition began to take shape. His right arm reached upward, his neck contorted, his chest hollowed, his head moved back, and a raw, empty sound emerged from his throat. Without dropping that state, but using a normal voice, he said he noticed that his left arm was not involved, so he needed to explore how to integrate it; as he spoke, his left arm became part of the process. Then, explaining the importance of not clutching onto a condition, but allowing it to transform and even dissolve, he released it.

A few Project members tried the exercise – and then the work took an unexpected turn. An actor said that what had struck him most about Chaikin's demonstration was not the exercise itself but the way Chaikin had simultaneously been totally in the world of the workshop, as he explained the process, and totally within the condition he was exploring. So a new study began. The workshop started to examine the dual dynamic of Chaikin's presentation, applying it in ways that had nothing to do with the original investigation.

This incident reveals a great deal about the nature of Chaikin's workshops. Several of his deepest concerns intersect in it: the search for ways to express things on stage that people cannot generally express in their lives; the use of the body as well as the psyche to locate unfamiliar conditions; a recognition of the actor's presence along with the character's. But the incident also shows something

67

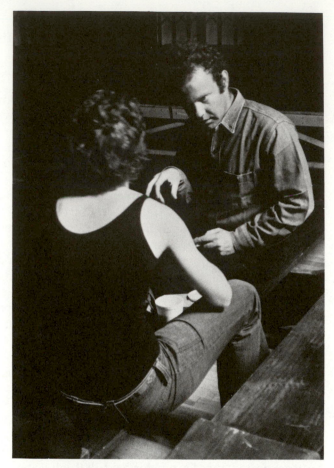

Chaikin (*right*) in an Open Theater workshop with actress Tina Shepard, New York, 1973. Photograph by Inge Morath/Magnum.

about Chaikin's work method: One exercise often spawns other unforeseen lines of work, and the exploration moves in whatever directions emerge and seem promising.

The focus of Chaikin's activities is the workshop. His main contribution to theater, he says, is behind-the-scenes research with actors, musicians, writers, dramaturges, and other directors. This is his "real work."

The structure of these laboratories is elusive. Chaikin navigates by intuition. He may drop an exercise after a few minutes or develop it over several years, but "every one leads to ten others and the work is embodied in our mistakes, discussions, thoughts, and discoveries." An apparent false start may be the catalyst for a whole different line of study, or may reemerge five years later in a new context and take off. And while Chaikin often stays in the background, letting others initiate and lead, beneath the apparent diffusion it is his energy that fires the others, his insights that propel the investigations.

In part, Chaikin's stimulation of his ensembles is intellectual. He reads widely, particularly in philosophy, cultural history, and modern poetry, and often recommends or discusses books that have inspired him. But his real contribution is his talent for translating impulses into stage action. "When questions are alive to a company of actors," he says, "there is in any of them a dangerous point when discussion must stop and the questions must be brought to the stage in terms of improvising actions":

Forming an exercise is one of the most important things a theater person can do. When he can envision a kind of behavior, a kind of ambiance, a kind of interrelating, a kind of environment, a kind of physical life, the kinds of sounds, and then find the proper exercise, the actor is invited to envision as well as to inhabit that realm.

Even when one is working with scripts, exercises can be formed "to enter the material . . . to *locate* the world which the writer has designated."

In the early years of the Open Theater, Chaikin was looking, in part, to develop an alternative system of actor training. "I thought that things did have prescriptions. You did this, and then you got that from it. [I thought] that one could assume that things accumulated in that way."

Unlike much of the American avant-garde in the sixties and seventies, he always stressed disciplined study, including vocal and physical technique work. Amateurism and "freedom" from serious training seemed to him self-defeating rather than liberating. "The theater is to make visible and one must develop the means to make his discoveries visible." The Open Theater invited and hired teachers to work with the actors, and members of Chaikin's workshops taught each other approaches that they had learned elsewhere.

But while the Open Theater did concentrate on physical work in the late sixties, Chaikin never espoused the Grotowski position that unrelenting bodily discipline is a basic tool for gaining access to the actor's purest expression. He felt, moreover, that one must acquire craft cautiously as well as rigorously. Some studies tend to segregate the performer's voice, body, and intention, rather than helping to integrate them. The actor must take care not to become imprinted with the style and mannerisms of a particular discipline, be it dance, yoga, martial arts, or voice studies. Finally, one must beware of mistaking skill for creativity: "When a painter with a brush faces a blank canvas, the technique in no way does the painting."

Chaikin's real research has concentrated in a more elusive area: the imagination. He has tried to make visible and vivid what before could only be imagined. Although the work has followed nothing like an organized agenda, for all its tangents and sprawl, it largely sorts into a few major areas. Chaikin has, first of all, been exploring ways to highlight the liveness of the theater encounter, to accentuate the presence of the performers, audience, and event. And he has continually searched for forms more expressive than those of naturalism and everyday life. Developing new languages to address the particular urgencies of our time – emotional numbness, violence, the inability really to see or hear one another – he has at the same time been preparing speakers of those new languages.

By the end of the Open Theater, Chaikin no longer felt that there could be a general system of stage training. He does not, finally, advocate even his basic interests, let alone specific exercises, as universals. The record of his investigations, he says, must not be taken as a collection of "recipes." Exercises should be developed ad hoc to grapple with specific problems, and then thrown away. Though he still believes one can get clues from other people and, in fact, sees lasting value in some lines that he has developed, he has come to feel that "every work for the theater, every company about to do the same work, even different actors within the same company require different approaches." Each artist must discover an individual kind of expression based on individual sensibility, aesthetic, and culture, or else "simply imitate both the process and the findings of another." Chaikin's advice to artists who wish to follow his example is to let their work constantly redefine its own boundaries, and not to copy his experiments.

Indeed, over the years, Chaikin's own research has aimed less and less toward specific, preset results. "The only exercises which are really interesting," he said in 1975, "are those which are not contained in any already determined achievement that the exercise will bring about." He avoids, even, using descriptive names, since they can prevent accomplishing anything beyond what the label prescribes. When the goal is precisely charted in advance, often "to explain the exercise has all the benefits of it; to do it doesn't add much." Chaikin hopes less that his exercises will have measurable effects than that they will be "a kind of yogurt culture" that will "turn the whole thing."

UNDERSCORING PRESENCE

Chaikin's fundamental interest has always been to heighten the sense that living people are sharing immediate fleeting moments – to emphasize presence. In the early years of the Open Theater, he tackled the problem in rudimentary ways. He had the actors try, for example, to play alternately "in some way in which the person is very present, and that's part of the corporeal, conscious understanding of the actor as well as the audience," and, for contrast, in the manner that "one sees a lot, where nobody's home." He would ask someone to walk first with an "awareness of how his body and head fill, vacate, and move through space" and then to walk "with absolutely no feeling for space." Or several actors working together would alternate between moments of visual or physical contact with each other and moments when they did not acknowledge one another at all. Chaikin's "wattage" exercises, which also date from the early Open Theater, were attempts to explore the degrees between total involvement and total withdrawal. An actor would start to do something in a state of minimal awareness, gradually increase the wattage to full presence, and then recede. The low-energy behavior might be the same activity, even at the same tempo, as the high-wattage actions, or it might be a neutral, absent state from which the animated behavior slowly grew.

Extending this study of presence, the Open Theater improvised scenes in which characters switched "on" and "off." At first these exercises were set in familiar, boring situations that people often tune out: offices, queues, subway platforms. Later, the company explored how modulating degrees of awareness work in more charged settings and interactions. In the Winter Project, Chaikin applied the wattage work to performing recognition scenes:

If you suddenly see somebody as life, as this person, whatever the relationship of the person is to you, if you suddenly see it all, then you probably go back into blindness, and then you may see again, or you go into at least a kind of dimness, or who you see changes, et cetera. A recognition scene does not sustain in one dynamic. It changes. It flows.

A journeyer (Tina Shepard), at left, observes the "sleep world" in a scene from *Nightwalk* contrasting "on" (presence) and "off" (absence), at the Space for Innovative Development, New York, 1973. Photograph by Inge Morath/Magnum.

Acting in an ensemble. Part of the present situation at most performances is the other players, so Chaikin has constantly sought ways to make actors more alert and responsive to one another on stage. Some of his early ensemble exercises were adaptations of Viola Spolin's theater "games": attempts to shift the focus back and forth among continuous scenes; work on passing, receiving, and molding imaginary objects; new variations on mirror exercises (Peter Brook did similar mirror work several years later). Spolin's "parts of the whole" became a series of machine exercises, the actors improvising the interrelated parts of a nonexistent machine. These contraptions were sometimes metamorphosed into social situations, maintaining the same dynamics and even types of sound and movement; or, working in reverse, actors would transform scenes into machines that captured their rhythms and energies. Though many of these exercises, in their original Spolin form or in Chaikin's versions, continue to be used in theater schools, Chaikin himself found them "initially freeing" but ultimately facile; he abandoned them after a few seasons.

An Open Theater "chord" exercise in workshop, New York, 1968. Photograph by Hope Herman Wurmfeld.

In the mid-sixties, the direction of Chaikin's ensemble work was shaped partly by the general cultural infatuation with sensitivity training and communal experience. The early Open Theater, for example, did "trust" exercises, adopting, adapting, and inventing ways to increase mutual trust which, they assumed, would carry over to a playing situation: They fell against and caught one another, led blindfolded partners around the room, touched and explored each other's bodies with their eyes open or closed. This work, which Chaikin found obvious and uninteresting after a season or two, was later carried on by the Living Theater and others, and has remained popular in "alternate" theater training.

The ensemble exercises that Chaikin has continued to use over the years are mostly ones that he invented himself or developed far beyond their sources. Some of these also reflect the sensitivity-training ethos. A number of early exercises attempted to subsume the impulses of individual performers into a single shared response. The "chord," which has come into wide use, was an Open Theater standard through the sixties. One participant, a visitor to the workshop, described:

I stand in a circle with the other actors, my arms around the shoulders of the people next to me, their arms around my waist. I close my eyes, relax, and listen. I hear breathing – from the others, from myself. I listen to it and feel it. It is regular and hypnotic. It turns into a drone, and I drone too. Now it is a humming, and I hum. It rises, and gets louder and then falls back to a soft dissonance in which I can distinguish my own voice, and, if I try, the voices of my two neighbors. I can hear it all around me; I am within it. I match myself to it. I don't want to alter it, but to let it alter me. I no longer know where I am physically. I no longer remember who is at my right and left, although we are holding each other. The communal sound is dying out. But then it starts up again, droning louder, and again I go with it. But it dies back fast. I hear breathing again. I wait, relaxed and listening. Chaikin says "okay" quietly; I open my eyes and see feet in a circle. Looking up and dropping my arms, I see Brenda and Paul next to me; I remember them now.

Each person was to become so receptive to the impulse of the group that everybody was following and no one leading. The Open Theater did "chords" with drones, hums, vowel sounds, and even movement, all the actors adjusting to the ensemble so that their gestures formed a single, organic shape.

In "breathing and talking together," a number of actors would find a common breathing rhythm; then, improvising answers to questions that were posed, they would start and stop speaking as a single group, simultaneously. Sometimes several actors would try to achieve a shared pulse animating their entire bodies – either a breath pattern of inhaling and release or a "heartbeat" of tiny explosions.

The most subtle, and interesting, of Chaikin's attempts to unite the ensemble in one dynamic were his "conductor" exercises. Performers were to tune directly into someone else's energy without imitating the form of the other's action. This work stemmed, in part, from earlier experiments: Nola Chilton had used recorded music during improvisations to affect the actor's mood; Viola Spolin had asked performers to adjust an improvisation to various metronome settings. But Chaikin wanted workshop members to take their cue from another person's behavior. One performer initiated a gesture and/or sound with a distinct rhythm and tone; the others then tried to meet it with *different* gestures and/or sounds of their own that had the same pulse and feeling as the original. Sometimes the conductor worked with sounds alone and the others only with movement, or vice versa. The workshop leader might move the focus from one person to another during the action. Or there might be several conductors, with different actors assigned to each. There also might be no particular person designated to lead, each actor picking up the energy being shaped by the group.

More complex exercises involved improvised scenes. Here the actors might follow either a performer within the action or someone outside it doing abstract sounds and movements; in either case, by regulating the mood, that person's behavior determined much of the content of the scene. Sometimes there were multiple conductors, either inside or outside the action, with groups of actors following each. Or, again, there might be no assigned leader, the actors sens-

"Jamming" with movement in a wedding-dance scene from *The Mutation Show* at St. Clement's Church, New York, 1973. Photograph by Mary Ellen Mark/Archive.

ing among themselves, moment to moment, who was dominant and following that person. This, Chaikin says, "starts to be much closer to living circumstances, where someone is starting something and other people are moving out of it, and it changes, but it's not arranged at all." Conductor exercises, in various forms, are among those Chaikin has found of lasting worth, "a sort of staple." He has continued to use them from time to time in his workshops.

Usually, in performance, actors must not meld but coordinate with one another. "Jamming," which Chaikin adapted in the mid-sixties from the jazz jam session, was designed to help performers integrate their work with one another's during the course of a performance. Using all kinds of vocal sounds, including hisses, clicks, huffs, syllables, and words, actors improvised a musical piece; or using various types of movement, they created a group dance.

Jamming was then extended to sentences: While one person said a line straight, another took off from it, making echoes and reverberations; an actor could also jam (or scat) alone, either starting with sounds and words and building to a comprehensible line, or beginning with the whole phrase and then, as in a musical development, improvising with its elements. Now the actors were exploring not only formal patterns but meaning:

One actor comes in and moves in contemplation of a theme, traveling with the rhythms, going through and out of the phrasing, sometimes using just the gesture, sometimes reducing the whole thing to pure sound . . . Then another comes in and together they give way and open up on the theme. During the jamming, if the performers let it, the theme moves into associations, a combination of free and structured form.

Chaikin felt that this exercise should help sensitize actors to the progressive line and texture of any performance piece. He told the Open Theater before a run-through of *Nightwalk*: "Rhythms, jamming [are the] most important thing. Each performance should be a jamming." He has continued to find this work "very valuable to do a little bit," not for some concrete technique it teaches but, rather, "like that yogurt culture again." The point is "not to try to stick it in here and apply it, but just to do it and get it in the room, and then leave it alone."

Addressing the audience. Presence involves the *audience's* sense of shared aliveness and immediacy with the performers, and Chaikin has continually experimented with ways to heighten this actor–audience relationship. In the early years especially, he tried direct interaction. Workshop exercises often included give-and-take between active participants and spectators. On several occasions, Chaikin explored moving this dynamic into actual performance. During work on *The Serpent*, he experimented with a section "where any actor can come out and talk to the audience"; processions through the aisles at the beginning of *The Serpent* and the earlier version of *Terminal* were intended partly to create a link between the cast and spectators. In several instances Chaikin even had performers physically touch people in the house. At the end of *Viet Rock*, the actors mingled with the viewers: "Each chooses an audience member and touches his hand, head, face, hair. Look and touch. Look and touch. A celebration of presence." But he felt that this business became "sentimentalized . . . automatic." After a similar experiment in *The Serpent* – when Eve and Adam ate the apple, the company "exploded into people who touched things and people" and moved out into the audience – he abandoned this course.

The studies that Chaikin has continued to pursue have been more delicate ones involving attitudes and assumptions, and have largely had to do with his notion of "levels of address." He began this line of experiment in the earliest days of the Open Theater with "dedications":

The idea was that we were always addressing ourselves to someone or some element or some force. The idea is to select it. I call up a thing or a person and I *dedicate* what I am going to do . . . You say: for you, to you, in honor of you, I dedicate the next two hours. I may forget you as I am going through it, and I may consciously return to you; it may be nothing more than the gesture saying "I'm doing it. I don't know what my dedication to you will do, but I address you and share this time with you."

Sometimes, the Open Theater publicly dedicated performances to political figures, such as the Indians occupying Wounded Knee, the United Farm Workers, or Angela Davis. Other times, Chaikin asked the company to make private, individual choices; these might be close friends, acquaintances, or even strangers. But the point was, as one actor explained, to select someone who "would call up a particular part of yourself that you want to share with the audience."

Having settled on a given audience, the actor needed to make subtle adjustments in performance in order to make contact. The process, Chaikin explains, involves considering, " 'I've chosen the one to whom I'm dedicating this performance. Now . . . what level of me do I summon in order to summon the other so that we meet?' That level is the performing level." By expecting a certain manner from the audience, he says, "you are calling it up; calling it up, you are making an open place for it to come in." The dedication and the level of address provide "a meeting place for the actor and the spectator."

During the Open Theater's first season Chaikin experimented with different relationships between performers and the audience. In some exercises, actors pretended that the spectators were "trees, creatures, qualities." In others, they tried first to "play to the audience" and then to "pull away from the audience."

In the fall of 1966, the group began more elaborate "expecting" work. From a series of *"Midsummer Night's Dream"* exercises, in which the spectators were, again, thought of as trees, squirrels, and pebbles, the company moved to an audience of people:

The audience is very discerning – impress upon them how charming you are, how sensitive.
The audience is not discerning – impress upon them how stupid they are.
The audience is just like us.
        like saints . . .
Audience has power to decide which of you is most attractive.
Actors attribute audience to be sophisticated and charming . . .
Actors are convinced they are pulsing with life and if the audience (which they are assuming is frail) came up on stage they too would be pulsing with life.
Audience nazis.
Audience prisoners who actors have arrested.
Audience angels in heaven . . .
They are foreigners and do not understand too well.
Audience is parole board and actor prisoner.
They are some from whom you have been severed for a long time – you are now reunited.

In the most rudimentary exercises, a group of actors decided upon an identity for the "spectators" (actually other workshop members) and tried to elicit the appropriate qualities from them by answering questions posed by the workshop leader. Sometimes actors repeated a simple improvisation for a supposedly different set of viewers. They also performed stories and monologues shifting their assumptions about the audience, often in mid-speech.

Chaikin also explored how "expecting" operates in interactions other than the actor–spectator one. Workshop members improvised scenes in which one performer developed a character based on what the other characters expected, picking up evidence from their behavior. For example:

Two actors who are confused endow the third actor with clarity.
Two manly [actors] attribute unmanliness to the third.
The person upon whom this is registered becomes immoral – puritanical – a hero – clairvoyant, etc . . .
Assume the third person is a liar – switch roles imperceptibly – third person incapable of being depended upon in emergency.
Assume third actor is a spy.
He is a mistake (like a cripple).

The attitudes might, again, be changed in midstream. Some of these exercises were connected directly to the presence/absence work: one person would presume and, thus, generate real contact with another, then rupture or dissolve it.

The Winter Project explored for a time how built-in imbalances in the performer–spectator relationship color what the audience receives:

The basic equation was talking and listening . . . Now if the hearer feels he can talk at any point back to the person who is talking, it's one thing. If the hearer feels that he can't, he has to be silent, has to be de-activated during the time the speaker is speaking, it's a different experience. We were just studying different things about the actor and the audience, the role model being the listener and the talker.

The Project did a number of exercises exploring how spectators at a performance process their responses, since they are permitted to make them visible only in very limited ways. One group of improvisations, invariably comic, focused on the feelings the spectator brings to the theater and imposes on the performance. The actors played audience members at a poetry reading or piano recital, each having a secret piece of information, such as "You're the pianist's [or poet's] mother," "You're only interested in the performer's genitals," or "You're only interested in seducing the person sitting next to you." Sometimes it was assumed that the performer could see the spectators, sometimes not. The idea was to discover the responses and make them visible within the tiny area allowed by the formal situation.

An offshoot of this work was a study of how the attempt to *show* interest affects listening. In some exercises a listener tried to demonstrate rapt attention or keep up a series of responses (such as "I know, I know") while someone else monologized. The Project found that trying to express attention generally tended to block hearing. They adapted versions of this improvisation, with the "I know" refrain, for performance in *Re-Arrangements* and *Tourists and Refugees*.

Presentational performing. Chaikin has experimented with several quasi-theatrical forms that acknowledge the reporter along with the report. Storytelling, singing, and interviews all involve someone addressing others here and now but testifying about something that may be from another time or even another mode. And "the dynamic thing," Chaikin says, is that, as in theater, "those two things are going on at once."

In his work with storytelling, mostly between the mid-sixties and late seventies, Chaikin stressed that the actors had to maintain a double relationship: with the story material and with the present audience. They might shift their emphasis from one to the other, but they always had to keep this dual connection.

Two born-again Christians (Ronnie Gilbert and Paul Zimet) sing the religious ecstasy of going "home" to Jesus in *Tourists and Refugees* at La-Mama, New York, 1980. Photograph by Sylvia Plachy.

The performers were not, though, restricted to any particular vocabulary. As they began to enter the experience they were narrating, they could expand beyond traditional verbal means:

The story can go into parts of the body and can then extend. It keeps moving. It can move from the past description to the present telling or both at once. And what it moves to in terms of the body or sounds or voice or song or silence or face is brought about by the actor. And I keep trying to open the actor to the other possible ways that those two things can be going on.

A way of exploring presence in the theater, storytelling was also a major source of material for Open Theater and Winter Project performance pieces.

Singing, like storytelling, involves frankly performing for an audience in the present while inhabiting another mode or giving testimony to something that happened before. Chaikin has included singing in his workshops from the earliest Open Theater sessions right through the Winter Project. He introduced his companies to a wide vocal repertory: American jazz, Balinese chant, grand and lyric opera, Brazilian samba, Egyptian popular music. And the actors experimented trying to sing "in a direct way, without guile," using selections from different languages and styles, performing individually and in groups, doing rounds and other multipart forms.

This work not only gave the actors experience performing in a boldly "present" way, but also provided a good opportunity to grapple with nonnaturalistic style. Actors' notes show that Chaikin felt the insights they gained would carry over to spoken performances:

Singing – don't be embarrassed by it being a special mode – it's rehearsed, formal, that's part of it. Also true of poems and prepared text . . .

Beware the mode of pretending it's natural.

He had the Open Theater and Winter Project listen to examples of very formal speech, such as Siobann McKenna reading *Finnegan's Wake* and Judith Anderson playing Medea, and try to perform stylized poems and chants, applying their work with vocal music.

Chaikin's singing exercises had dozens of variations over the years. The Open Theater sometimes used a conductor to regulate the dynamics and intensity of a song performed by other actors. They also experimented with singing as someone else, either a well-known figure or another member of the company. A different extension of the work in the late sixties was "body songs": Each actor kept a piece of music in mind and performed a difficult Grotowski exercise cycle in relation to it. The idea, one actor later explained, was to do the cycle so that "you're not working with getting the headstand right and the this right and the that right; you're just working on moving from one position of the body to another to another to another through the song." Chaikin also had the actors try to "sing" a selection using their bodies rather than voices, expressing the rhythms, dynamics, flow, and feelings through movement; one workshop member might perform a piece vocally while others sang it with their bodies. The Winter Project studied musical traditions of various cultures, trying to discover their different sensibilities in this way.

Toward the end of the Open Theater, Chaikin began doing "interview" experiments. A person being questioned would try to make present a past or current emotional state, while staying within the

A pair of anonymous, impish interviewers question a strait-laced doctor (Paul Zimet) about his sexual fantasies in *Re-Arrangements* at LaMama, New York, 1979. Photograph by Nathaniel Tileston.

interview format. Sometimes, in the Winter Project, Chaikin would heighten this duality by having the actor's voice remain totally in the reality of the workshop while the body inhabited the condition being described: This variation came, in part, out of Chaikin's demonstration of locating extreme conditions somatically. But usually the interview testimonies, like the stories, were allowed to employ a full theatrical vocabulary of words, sounds, and gestures.

Question-and-answer exchanges became a way of exploring inner states. A character in mourning, in physical pain, in love, in retreat from feelings, in a world of the dead, in a place of extreme physical desires, might be asked, "What thoughts are a comfort to you?" "Do you think you're more sensitive than most people?" "What do you think the next moment will be like?" Interviews also became a way of developing material for performance works. Beginning with *Terminal*, each of Chaikin's pieces has had characters and conditions discovered partly through interviewing, and in *Re-Arrangements* and *Tourists and Refugees,* the structure was retained in performance.

FINDING NEW THEATER LANGUAGES

Chaikin's work with interviews, singing, and storytelling has been not only a way of exploring presence and constructing performance material, but also part of his basic search for stage forms more expressive than naturalism's copies of everyday behavior. He wants his theater to show "the precious buried parts of ourselves where we are bewildered and alive beyond business matters, in irreducible radiance," to make "something theatrical out of something abstract." His attempt has led him to look for new languages and new methods.

Working somatically. Chaikin's Winter Project exercise of locating powerful feelings through movement and breathing has a long genealogy in his work. Since the early days of the Open Theater, he has been looking for ways to use the body as a primary route into characters and conditions. He believes that by circumventing the verbal and psychological levels, actors can tap directly into feelings that do not have reductive labels and interpretations attached.

One of his first attempts at working somatically, and perhaps the most widely adopted of Chaikin's Open Theater exercises, was sound-and-movement transfers. In contrast to Method techniques, which rely on an actor's emotional engagement with a condition to generate its physical form, sound and movement was an attempt to work from the outside in. One actor would begin a simple, repeatable gesture using both body and voice, not selecting in advance what the action should express, but playing with it until it touched on a clear condition; that actor then approached a second, who tried to copy the forms exactly, thereby being led to their emotional content; the second then altered them and transferred a new sound and movement to a third actor, and so forth. Using kinetic impulses to locate inner states, actors were able to discover emotions that had not been in their experience before.

Originally, this exercise was done with the actors in two lines, a person from one transferring the gesture and sound to someone in the other. But dozens of variations developed. It was done in pairs, with partners trying to achieve a shared statement and splitting to regroup if they could not. Sometimes each actor was given a physical limitation or handicap to circumnavigate. Or, by prearrange-

Chaikin helps Will Patton and Tina Shepard to work physically on a refugee condition in a Winter Project workshop, New York, 1980. Photograph by Ricki Rosen.

The same refugee-condition image in performance in *Tourists and Refugees* at LaMama, New York, 1980. Photograph by Sylvia Plachy.

ment, a specific quality, such as suspicion or love, or a theme, such as war or "you can't catch me," would color the whole exercise. It also was done using changing degrees of presence, the actors switching "on" and "off" while they worked.

Applying this work to storytelling, the Open Theater used sound-and-movement exchanges to enact a simple scenario decided in advance. Or, extending the basic transfer exercise to a verbal level, someone would take over a story in the middle, picking up its dynamics as precisely as possible from the first actor, then either maintaining or altering them before passing the story on to a third narrator. The Open Theater even did transfer exercises with scenes: A two-character scene would be picked up in progress by a second set of actors, who would attempt to match exactly the tone and energy already established.

Chaikin also had actors simply "try on" different bodies to discover the emotions to which those physical states corresponded. The Open Theater experimented with various walks (for example, funereal, foot dragging, chain-gang struggling, rushing to buy flowers for a date) to connect actors with characters through their bodies rather than through words or emotions. He had the actors move as if they were flying or floating, as if the air were changing density or temperature around them. Sometimes, they worked purely technically, shifting weight forward or back, keeping limbs spread or close, thrusting the head, chest, or pelvis out. They also imagined body parts and functions interchanged, moving, for example, as if a hand were one's head. In a related exercise, based on Nola Chilton's physical adjustment work, they let physical images of inanimate objects (such as weapons) inform their movement in order to discover emotional states. Sometimes actors would adjust their behavior to reflect a color that was named.

They also explored how the face – which, Chaikin says, is "a trained liar" – could be used to communicate rather than conceal. Lee Worley developed an exercise in which performers created "life masks" by feeding emotionally charged phrases to their faces, usually to a slow count of five. This work was extended, then, to silent "conversation." Parts of the body and, in some cases, vocal or other body sounds (such as slapping, stomping, or snapping) might be added to the means of expression. At times actors would look for the sound of either their own or another performer's mask. In other body- and face-communication exercises, small groups improvised scenes in which they had to "talk" with each other, sometimes in fairly specific ways, without using language.

Expressing hidden faces. One of Chaikin's priorities has been to express parts of experience that are usually obscured in life. The early Open Theater, for example, wanted to show the horror latent in American media and advertising myths. Chaikin said at the time:

What kind of country is it that is populated by "perfect people" talking about cigarettes, toilet papers, spaghetti sauce, detergents, and the thousands of other products we consume? And "Who are these consumers?" A night watching TV convinces us that they are "perfect people" – and if these are the images of our aspirations, God help us.

In one series of exercises, workshop members played TV and magazine stereotypes speaking in clichés and commercial slogans. Often these skits were set in the most "unperfect" situations – a sewer-main explosion, a shipwreck, a visit to Dachau. They explored how people coped without losing their masks, without really seeing. "Perfect people" improvisations and, later, mini-plays written by van Itallie were included on several early performance programs. Often an imperfect (that is, normal) guest at a perfect party was drowned in the swimming pool or otherwise killed while the more correctly behaved company sipped their dry martinis.

For Chaikin, the sometimes facile satire in this work had a deadly serious basis: It was, he said, about closedness versus vulnerability, absence versus presence. He wrote in an early notebook that the perfect people study was really about "the stages of the killing, destroying, obliterating – it's about murder." Although he moved on from the perfect people after a few seasons, their descendants appeared in performance pieces much later: simpering dinner guests mouthing semicomprehensible inanities in *Nightwalk;* corporate wives gossiping and discussing native cuisines of the countries they exploit in *Tourists and Refugees.* Chaikin's later work also included other kinds of public "outsides" that pointed to unsavory beneath-the-surface realities. *Tourists and Refugees* characters that slid between personas as Wall Street businessmen and thug "enforcers" for multinational corporations were, in a way, mutant descendants of the perfect people.

Chaikin wants theater to look behind personal as well as social and political facades, at what individual people experience but do not generally show. "This challenge of the unspeakable in a natural situation may be that when a character is drinking water he is wondering if there is a God. When we locate the inside of a situation in its abstract and elusive texture we then try to make this thing visible." Chaikin wrote in a notebook:

"Perfect" dinner guests (*left to right*: JoAnn Schmidman, Ralph Lee, Ellen Maddow, Raymond Barry, Shami Chaikin, Tom Lillard) are observed by the two journeyers (Tina Shepard and Paul Zimet) in *Nightwalk* at the Space for Innovative Development, New York, 1973. Photograph by Inge Morath/Magnum.

We're alone with ourselves even when we are outside with each other. Our attention alternates.

The outside living is the relating, the behavior, as opposed to the images, sounds and words occasionally inside. The outside is the behavioral functions which react to outside stimuli as opposed to the private which reacts to memory, the digestion of the present experience (while it is going on) and the primitive, mysterious level of perceiving.

The question is: can we see them? these levels – can we play them? And finally can we make them touch?

Some of the Open Theater's early work in this area grew out of its social satire. Actors would establish a perfect or, at least, proper situation and then act out the forbidden impulses in it. They might, for example, physically attack someone or start groping sexually, all the while maintaining a socially correct conversation. In a cocktail party "unnoticed action" improvisation that van Itallie devised, the actors let their bodies respond to the blaring of Wagner's *Liebestod* while they kept their voices, as much as possible, at the party. This exercise was then expanded to explore the general problem of expressing one quality vocally and an opposing quality somatically: A particularly successful example was an actress singing "Whistle a Happy Tune" while writhing on the floor in agony; according to an

"Perfect" tourists (Paul Zimet and Atsumi Sakato) encounter a pair of multinational-corporate wives (Tina Shepard and Ronnie Gilbert) in *Tourists and Refugees,* in rehearsal, New York, 1980. Photograph by Ricki Rosen.

observer in the workshop, she used a "jerky rhythm . . . as the motor for both physical agony and vocal lightheartedness."

Another early Open Theater exercise, called "insides," provided a different structure to reveal the passions and longings that people hide. Actors would begin a naturalistic scene in which the external action really formed a veneer covering very different impulses. Then, rather than constructing realistic signposts or symptoms to show a character's private feelings – the way, for example, Chekhov's plays do – the actors would enter these "insides" and enact them fully. They could draw now on nonnaturalistic sound and movement as well as dialogue from the scene; sometimes the means of expression would be restricted, for example, just to the voice or the body.

In the basic exercise, one or more characters alternated between the "outside" and "inside" modes, picking up the external action each time as though there had been no break; the others in the scene either froze or continued their activities without acknowledging the aberration. Sometimes everyone simultaneously switched into the private self, then returned to the social, visible world; or, if one character's inner story involved other people, they would play the appropriate roles, then all return together to the outside. In another variation, two sets of actors played the external and hidden sides of a single situation, either sequentially or simultaneously, using different playing areas, with the inside actors improvising from the outside actors' scene. This work, related to "conductors," sometimes took the form of a dream exercise in which a "sleeping" character's movements and sounds provided the clues for other actors to create the character's dream.

"Locked action" and "machine" improvisations were also used to express the invisible. For locked actions, an actor would try to sense a character's psychic rut or trap and give it concrete form by becoming stuck in a repeating gesture of movement or speech. Variations of locked actions were used in several performance pieces, including *The Serpent* and *The Mutation Show*. Machine exercises explored how people become automatons: A character would perform a task more and more by rote until, finally, the action was totally mechanical. The Open Theater did series of office improvisations in which people became the machines they had been using.

The early Open Theater also explored hidden connections and impulses through its "transformation" work, a development of one of Spolin's "games" along with early expressionist dream–play technique. Mid-scene, actors might change their characters' age, sex, species, or relationship to others; the time of day, year, or history; the location; the physical scale; and so forth. Liberated from the restriction of naturalistic consistency, they could show hidden associations, fantasies, and passions. A tyrannical foreman and a group of recalcitrant workers could suddenly become an animal handler and tiger cubs or a hammer and nails; someone starving for affection could become a derelict, a puppy, or a thirsty shrub. The freedom to turn reality inside out also provided a way to reflect a fragmented and absurd universe. Transformation exercises were useful, too, in training actors to stay alert to the present performance, since each person needed constantly to adjust to the others' shifts.

Sometimes the changes were restricted to certain elements, such as age or location. Taking the work in a different direction, van Itallie devised an improvisation between one person with "a fear . . . of soaring emotionally or intellectually, of going or being high in any fashion" and another who had "made a conscious decision to scale all available heights"; these traits were to stay constant, while the age, size, sex, beauty, and sense of inner life of both characters could alter. Other experiments used transformations of dynamics (tone, volume, rhythm, tempo, pitch) and theatrical styles.

Developed as an acting exercise and improvisational technique, transformations became a favored device in early Open Theater performance pieces. They were at the center not only of many group-created works, but also of plays written by company playwrights, particularly Megan Terry and Jean-Claude van Itallie.

To explore the complex nature of feelings, Chaikin also in the mid-sixties developed a series of exercises that used different spatial areas to represent simultaneous though apparently incompatible impulses:

I had simply thought, especially in my strong opposition to the kind of actor training that I was getting at that stage, that feelings were not so discrete. You didn't just feel angry or not angry, but rather they were very mixed up. And that we were in contradictory conditions at one time.

And why not take this into a geographical or a spatial frame rather than say that they're internal: Have each part of the geography represent a state which the ensemble would agree was part of their experience?

He designated concentric circles on the floor as different states of being; often, the outermost embodied indifference (or real life!), a middle ring dread or wasteland devastation, and the inner circle perfect harmony (or illusion). Actors could move freely across boundaries and pull others from adjacent spheres into their own – though sometimes it was agreed that no one could enter the illusion circle except by invitation, which meant that a rescuer had to venture into the circle of horror. The exercise was sometimes done as the "inside" of a naturalistic scene, with one actor serving as a catalyst to switch into the "circles." An improvisation of a boat trip, for example, dissolved into concentric areas embodying the pleasures of the flowing water and foam, the fear of drowning, and the indifferent, "absent" interactions on the deck. Curiously, the mode that the actors had most difficulty and least interest in playing in these exercises was perfect harmony. Again and again, Chaikin has tried to find stage expressions for bliss, and has found it elusive.

Chaikin came to use the circles format as a general tool. For example, the areas might define theatrical styles; as actors moved from one spot to another, they switched a continuing story from, say, soap-opera manner, to light comedy, to Brechtian *Lehrstücke*. He also used spatial arrangements to explore role playing in human interaction. The actors' respective roles in a prearranged situation were determined by their places on the floor plan; as they changed places, they exchanged parts.

Expressing the essence. Inspired by Büchner's *Woyzeck*, the first play in which he acted after the Open Theater, Chaikin has long been interested in using discontinuous action to explore a story or situation. Early in the Open Theater, he developed "stop/start" and "instant scenes" exercises. In the simplest version, actors just moved around the workspace until one of them began an improvisation, which the others immediately entered, played out, and dropped; then someone began another, and the process was repeated. Instant scenes were also done with prearranged scenarios: When Chaikin called their names, performers would come into the playing area and enact a key portion of the story until other people were called on to replace them, and so forth. Sometimes one cast played all the way through but, still, did only the major events, omitting connective material. The goal in either case was to assume a role instantly and capture the core of each fragment in a short time.

Instant scenes were an early movement in one of Chaikin's most consistent directions: finding a way to show a concentrated essence of a story or condition. The early Open Theater's "sound summaries" were attempts to capture a character or situation in a few seconds. The actors tried, for example, to make the sounds of old ladies grousing, a hospital emergency room, admiring parents, New Year's Eve on the radio, a public library. The goal was to find a synopsis of the noise rather than a parody or a gibberish impression of it.

An important inspiration came from the Chinese theater. During Chaikin's summer in London with Peter Brook, a Chinese director (a political refugee working as a waiter) spent an afternoon demonstrating Chinese theater for the group – and the session was a revelation for Chaikin. This director began with a simple story line, which Chaikin recalled years later: There is a couple in China; the man goes off to work in the morning and the woman says goodbye to him; then she goes to her trunk and takes out various things, including a mirror, and she looks at herself in the mirror; death comes in to punish the woman for her vanity; finally, the husband returns to find her dead and sails to the island of the dead and brings her home. The director reduced the story to a few isolated moments. These images were alive rather than frozen, but they moved very little, almost not at all.

The presentation thrilled Chaikin. Eight years later, he recalled:

What I loved about it was the spareness, was the way in which a single image would resonate with ten thoughts and other images, rather than playing out the other nine . . . It was the way the image was done so very, very succinctly. I loved that! I loved the way in which it was distilled.

He was particularly excited by the clarity of the work – that "You didn't have to work to figure it out . . . It didn't feel esoteric. It seemed very direct." In fact, his contact with this approach was pivotal: "It introduced something really very new, which was to try to find the essential thing and see if it's possible to play, and then leave the rest out, and let the rest be sort of assumed."

The following season, Chaikin reproduced the demonstration for his workshop as precisely as he could. Then during work on *Terminal*, he had the Open Theater apply the Chinese technique to the story of Agamemnon's return. The company refined the plot down to a few moments, the actors moving within the scene from one key image to the next. This sequence was not intended for performance but rather, again, was to be like a culture that would spread through their work.

In fact, although Chaikin did not apply the technique directly in performance for several years (the Open Theater tried it on a Sleeping Beauty scenario, but abandoned the project quickly), it colored nearly everything he did. Extreme spareness, always his inclination, more and more became a conscious goal. He worked at paring away, omitting some elements of a situation or character in order to put others into relief. "I was for the details," he says, "but the chosen details, the very, very chosen details."

Highly distilled "phrases" and "emblems" became, first of all, a general workshop tool. Before this study, Chaikin says, "we didn't have any knowledge of how to repeat improvisation . . . It could just die the second time so that the actors couldn't even get near it." But by putting each section of an improvisation into a phrase and returning to the phrases, the actors could remember the core of each scene and recreate it. They used the same principle to repeat stories. After telling a story, the actor would try to find an emblem that captured it. Sometimes, when one workshop member repeated a story, others would join in with the emblem and use it to enter the experience.

The economy of the Chinese theater also seemed to Chaikin a clue for crafting performance works. When the action is refined down, the audience becomes more actively engaged:

If an emblematic part of an action is played out, with the actor living *in* the action, there is a resonance beyond what there would be if the entire action

A distilled image capturing a domestic moment (with Paul Zimet and Tina Shepard) in *Re-Arrangements* at LaMama, New York, 1979. Photograph by Nathaniel Tileston.

were played out. The spectator completes the action from the part of it which is being performed. The emblem becomes a meeting point for the actor and the spectator.

Nearly all of the Open Theater's pieces included compressed bits of action that implied much larger conditions and stories. In *Nightwalk*, the simple image of one traveler quietly tucking her head under her companion's arm suggested a long, caring relationship. The Winter Project performance works all included segments of domestic scenarios refined into tiny nuggets, much like those of the Chinese demonstration. For example, in *Tourists and Refugees* two characters sat at a table drinking coffee, seeming abstracted and uneasy; then they moved to the next moment, looking away from each other, strained with anguish, barely able to swallow.

Another major input into Chaikin's work at distilling forms came from closer to home, from a very early Open Theater exercise. During its second season, the workshop developed an improvisation in

Another domestic moment from *Re-Arrangements* (this time with Will Patton and Joyce Aaron; Ronnie Gilbert and Paul Zimet, *behind*). LaMama, New York, 1979. Photograph by Nathaniel Tileston.

which Rip van Winkle woke up after twenty years of sleep to situations that were completely new to him; other actors would make up a "world" and Rip would try to enter it – not merely imitate what he saw, but explore it with some surprise and attempt to relate to it. Among the worlds created were one of mechanical communications, one of narcissism (where people talked without listening), a bargain basement, and an Arthur Murray dance studio. In creating or joining these situations, the point was not to parody, but to enter a way of being.

This work extended far beyond the original improvisation. Leaving the Rip scenario behind, one or more actors would simply establish a condition through sound, movement, and rhythm, and then others, if they felt in tune with it, would join in. They would try not to copy or transform the original, but to participate in it. Sometimes the worlds embodied different cultures, such as the life-styles of Asian peasants, middle-American whites, urban blacks. But the richest work involved states of being more difficult to characterize. There were worlds, Chaikin recalls, that the company "couldn't put a name to": "All we could say was, it was a condition of experience."

He began seeking emblems for these abstract worlds, trying to distill them into "modes." This ongoing study really is the culmina-

The "men's world" (Raymond Barry and Tom Lillard) from *Nightwalk* at the Space for Innovative Development, New York, 1973. Photograph by Inge Morath/Magnum.

tion of two intertwining lines of Chaikin's research: the Chinese theater economy and the Rip Van Winkle worlds. A mode is a succinct expression of a way of being, an inner world expressed in essential form. All of Chaikin's workshops since the early seventies have used modes as a basic tool of exploration as well as a central element of performance vocabulary.

Playing music. Chaikin has explored both how music works in the theater and how theater can enter the less literal, less literary realms that music addresses. A part of this study, from the early Open Theater through the Winter Project, has been simply examining nonlinguistic dimensions of sound. At one extreme, Chaikin tried looking at noise as a concrete entity inhabiting the space along with actors, scenery, and props. An Open Theater exercise around the time of Grotowski's 1967 visit, and probably reflecting his influence, attempted, for example, to "make sound do things. Cut through walls, push over broom, open window, move imaginery block, roll out like thin ribbon, surround light bulb, capture it and bring it back, going through a pipe, a narrow tunnel." Another somewhat later experiment involved passing the "shape of [a] sound across [the] room to another person who passes it back."

Chaikin's more ongoing study has been of the expressive qualities of sounds, including and beyond those traditionally considered music. In the mid- and late sixties, the Open Theater explored the emotive powers of speech noises, trying to convey the core of a poem through its aural elements, ignoring the meaning of individual words. The Open Theater and the Winter Project did experiments to communicate the message of a song entirely through its music. They examined how changes in register, timbre, volume, and rhythm affect what is transmitted to the audience.

The Winter Project studied how a text changes effect when it is sung or accompanied, and the differences for the audience between *a capella* and accompanied singing. One actress worked for several weeks on a cycle of poems that a Project composer had arranged. She recited and sang them alone as well as against the piano setting, and the workshop tried to pinpoint ways in which the music underscored or blocked the emotion of the words. They tried to discover which kinds of treatments supported and which kinds distracted from the meaning of the texts. The group even explored how the relative placement and lighting of actors and instrumentalists altered the overall effect.

Most important, though, music has provided Chaikin with a general model and tool for drawing theater into more subtle and abstract types of address. One of Chaikin's ongoing interests in the Winter Project was "thought music," something that he never quite defined but that had to do with the fleeting, often contrapuntal interplay of feelings and ideas. Sometimes instrumental sounds were used in the workshops to help actors locate and express unnamable conditions. In one series of Winter Project exercises, a musician offered a noise – made, during one session, with penny whistles, a saxophone, and seeds in a mailing tube – and actors used it to find an emotional state; sometimes the actor tried to match the sound vocally, other times just to respond to it. Performers also worked in reverse, the actor intoning a noise, and composers then trying to meet or complement it. These sound pairings were used in *Tourists and Refugees* during refugee "testimonies."

Chaikin has even explored how speech can harness the expanded sound possibilities of various instruments. In one Winter Project session, an actor tried to speak through a French horn, keeping his words comprehensible while taking on the horn's resonance. And several chants in *Trespassing* were wailed into the sound chamber and board of a piano, creating an eerie, howling echo.

Musicians have been central members of Chaikin's workshops, especially since the mid-seventies. Because he has been no more satisfied to limit himself to an inherited repertory of instruments than to stay with a received vocabulary of theater forms, Chaikin has always chosen collaborators who used not only traditional Western and non-Western instruments but a variety of found and invented objects. Their experiments fed both workshop explorations and the developing performance pieces, and were often incorporated in the final works. In *The Mutation Show* a rubber ball was dropped on a drum for a particular effect; *Re-Arrangements* featured music made on brass bowls, a spinning bicycle wheel played with a wooden mallet, and a mobile of forks, as well as a clarinet and double bass; the *Tongues* accompaniment included chains and broiler-tray gongs.

Music also has provided models for alternative approaches to play construction. The Open Theater tried adapting specific classical forms, exploring, for example, how "the three or four movements that go into a symphony or a sonata would inform another way of making a structure." Although Chaikin came to feel that this sort of literal transposing was not very useful, he continued to experiment, applying musical principles to the shaping of plays. Indeed, none of his theater works has had a narrative plot. (*Nightwalk*, tracing a kind of journey by two travelers, came closest to following a traditional story line.) His works have been built, rather, from the interplay of motifs. These subjects are visual, aural, kinetic, thematic, or, usually, a combination of several types. And the most important connections among them are as much rhythmic and dynamic as situational or informational.

The immersion of the workshops in music has colored performances in subtle ways as well. For example, rehearsing *Tourists and Refugees No. 2* for the Caracas Festival in 1981, Chaikin urged the actors to "move it a little toward the music of the thing." In part, he was concerned with adapting the work to a largely non-English-speaking audience. But, beyond this, he wanted to emphasize dimensions other than the literal: "In terms of movement as well as language," he said, "we can move toward the music of the characters."

Rediscovering the old languages: words and texts. Part of Chaikin's interest in verbal communication has been to explore its debasement. But while the early Open Theater satirized or shunned social speech that seemed degenerated, in his later work Chaikin has tried to confront it. One continuing interest has been how certain kinds of expressions have been distorted and hollowed out by popular culture. But rather than mock them, as in the "perfect people," or avoid them completely by using nonverbal language, the Winter Project tried to investigate what has become of these phrases, how they can be used, and what can be used in their stead:

At one period, we did a catalogue of the stock ways to say "I love you." And I really think we practically covered it. One thing that became very clear was that no one could say those words anymore without immediately feeling a little estranged from them . . . But those expressions, even if they are contaminated, are the only way we have to refer to certain things that we can't live without. That study has been a very important part of the Winter Project.

Still, Chaikin's main engagement with language has been exploring what it *can* do, trying to tap its powers. As early as the fall of 1968, he began intensive work on "how we put the message that we want to convey into a word and then into a phrase in order to communicate." He felt that the Open Theater's weakest area was the verbal, and he wanted to study different aspects of speech: "breathing rhythm – voice independent of words and voice applied to words." In a letter to the company in June 1971, he outlined some of the issues he still wanted to explore:

words as code – as hieroglyphs, decipherable through context, syntax, and silence.
What is the voice of a particular language? What voice do you use to speak to your mother, your lover, yourself?
Examples: 1. What is the voice speaking from the words of the New Testament?
2. What is the sound of Walt Whitman's "Leaves of Grass?" . . .
These are examples of particular worlds of thought where the words are picked and can't be substituted without losing.
The thought and intention are expressed in word and rhythm.
Each poet has a different language even though they may use the same words.

He wanted to discover how to use the word as "the intimate entrance into that which it represents." Language in theater needed to become integrated into the total expression, rather than information tacked on. "The thing starts," Chaikin told the Open Theater, "before the speaking or singing; the singing and speaking are the singing or speaking part of it."

Some of Chaikin's work on language and voice grew from his fascination with the sign speech of the deaf. Before the Open Theater, he had studied lipreading and learned to sign. This involvement with soundless verbal communication, together with his passion for music, led him to reexamine the concrete elements of language, the interrelationship between the actual sounds and the meaning of a word. Open Theater exercises explored the oral and aural differences between, for example, voiced and unvoiced consonants, open and closed vowels. Chaikin invented an exercise (which the company called "My House Is Burning," because he first demonstrated it with that line) in which actors worked to make each individual sound in a sentence express the full intention. Jamming for a moment on each consonant and vowel, they tried to find the connections between the music of the words and their meaning. In a related exercise, actors tried to reduce a spoken line to the *sound* of its intention, usually dropping the actual words while keeping some of the syllables and rhythms; at times, other workshop members would seek the sound of a first speaker's meaning. These exercises were applied to storytelling and scene improvisations. All of this work, Chaikin said, was "a balancing between very specific technical disciplines and mysterious areas having to do with breathing rhythms and space." He wanted to study the word simultaneously as a chunk of sound, a nugget of information, and an expression of feeling or intention.

Although he has become known more for his improvisational and play-creating work, Chaikin has always been interested in translating the words of writers into living performances, that is, in staging scripts. One reason he started the Open Theater, in fact, was to explore ways of performing in nonnaturalistic *plays*. The company's earliest programs included works by Brecht, Beckett, and Eliot as well as Open Theater playwrights van Itallie, Megan Terry, and Sharon Thie.

During the first few years, the Open Theater was not much concerned with more traditional material. Asked in 1964 if the actors could play Shakespeare, the Greeks, or Chekhov, Chaikin replied that although some of them could, it had "little to do with our workshop": "Our work is more helpful in understanding the abstract theater of Beckett, Genet, and Ionesco, and the social theater of Brecht or Joan Littlewood."

As Chaikin's interest in language grew so did his focus on texts. In 1969 he performed in the Open Theater's production of *Endgame*. And in his own workshop, he spent more time on poetry and scripted plays, dealing especially with Chekhov, Shakespeare, and the Greeks. During the last few seasons of the Open Theater, Chaikin had regular, separate meetings devoted to scene work, and this study continued uninterrupted even after the company had officially disbanded. Since the end of the Open Theater, Chaikin has devoted a good deal of research and most of his teaching (in the Working Theater, at various universities, and in private classes) to traditional and modern classical texts, and has directed and acted in plays by Chekhov, Beckett, Büchner, and Sophocles.

THEMATIC INVESTIGATIONS

In all Chaikin's research, content and form have been inseparable. He has learned about life conditions and connections by discovering the stage forms to transmit them, and has been led to new theatrical vocabularies by the nature of the particular life questions that he was tackling. Exercises from the inside/outside improvisations to Chinese-inspired distillations have involved simultaneously exploring a situation and finding ways to express it.

Often, though, since the earliest days of the Open Theater, Chaikin has focused very specifically on a theme. For example, during the 1966–7 season, the company did a study of excommunication rites, prompted by Chaikin's fascination with the Spinoza excommunication: "I thought it was a kind of structural recreation of certain things that are done on social levels, on political levels, on religious levels, and that there was in the form of the excommunication ritual something to examine. I was just so struck by it." Working largely with documentary materials, the group enacted a number of ceremonies, among them the excommunications of Spinoza, a Catholic heretic, and a Buddhist monk. They also invented excommunication services of their own. Chaikin was looking "to find the essential forms that would connect so to the heart of the phenomenon that they would really capture and express it." The group's study of excommunication was not specifically intended to be performed, but the subject came into their work again when they were preparing *Terminal* and *The Mutation Show*.

A theme Chaikin has returned to again and again is mourning. While other cultures have prescribed forms for working through bereavement, ours really has none:

The only persons who are permitted to mourn now are persons who involuntarily, at a funeral, when the grief is too great, say, "I want to jump into the grave with this person" or something like that. There's no permission, there's no openness, there's no possibility for it otherwise. I feel mourning is healing.

The "dance on the graves of the dead" in *Terminal*, New York, 1971.
Photograph by Max Waldman. © Max Waldman, Archives 1984.

Chaikin explored this problem while working on *The Serpent;* the
workshop (briefly) considered making the piece a ceremony by
women whose men were dead or off at war. For *Terminal*, they
created rites to address the "graves beneath this house," the "bones
beneath this floor," trying to make a channel between the living and
the dead. *The Dybbuk* ensemble explored the question again. They
invented rituals to perform at the burial site of a bridal couple
murdered in a pogrom, deciding finally to have townspeople silently
pray and lay single stones at the tomb; and they experimented with
different forms for Leye's private moments at the graves of her
mother and her love. The Winter Project did improvisations of
mourning ceremonies, and members discussed what kinds of memorial observances they would want for themselves. Chaikin tackled the issue again in *Antigone*, which included a dirge for both the
dead brothers and the young woman about to die. And *Trespassing*
was about finding ways to meet the experience of death.

Chaikin's mourning studies have even crossed over into real-life
ceremonies. When Winter Project member Charles Stanley died in
1978, the company drew on workshop improvisations and discussions to make a service for him. Daniel Seltzer's sudden death days
after he returned from the Paris production of *Endgame* set Chaikin

The attendant (Tina Shepard, *below*) to a dying woman (Gloria Foster) becomes a kind of advocate and alter ego for her in *Trespassing* at La-Mama, New York, 1982. Photograph by Sylvia Plachy.

about this work again with terrific personal urgency. He organized a wake, then helped put together two more formal memorials, in New York and in Princeton, of music, readings, and personal testimonies. Still, he feels he has made little headway in finding expressions for mourning, and the problem continues to haunt and inspire him.

At the opposite end of the spectrum, Chaikin has repeatedly tried to find ways to express exultation. It is a part of the human emotional makeup he says, but contemporary culture has given it no space. "How come only the religious can exult? I believe it's a passion that's there for the a-religious." From the early "circles" work, through the post–apple-eating ecstasy of *The Serpent*, and, again, in the Winter Project's studies, Chaikin has tried to find ways to understand and embody this territory of feeling.

Indeed, beginning with his 1967 Open Theater workshop, Chaikin's emphasis generally has been less on developing a repertory of theatrical forms than on using the stage to investigate and express specific themes. This shift in stress is what marks Chaikin's extension from acting study into serious play making.

Early collaborative play making:
The Serpent

Twice while he was at the Living Theater, Chaikin tried his hand at playwriting, drafting his scripts in a spiral notebook. *The Barrel*, a short three-character piece, showed a woman who had become crazed and whose life had diminished during the ten years her fiancé was in prison; as her narrative moved into the past, a character to whom she was speaking assumed different roles in the story, which was contoured with sharp rhythmic shifts and "full stops." In *The Policeman Didn't Get There in Time*, the focus moved back and forth among party guests and their hosts, all interacting with one another and additional unseen guests; their encounters, sometimes defined as much by rhythmic patterns as by action, ranged from light chatter to revelations of tensions, terrors, and passions that were wholly unacceptable in the social situation.

Although both of these plays pointed toward areas that Chaikin continued to explore in the early Open Theater, he was not satisfied with them. Several Living Theater members worked on his first script for a while, but he "so didn't like it after about six rehearsals, despite the fact that they were working on it very well," that they dropped it. Chaikin was intensely engaged with his second play for a month, but then decided that it also "was no good." His return to play making was gradual and circuitous, via the theater laboratory.

In the earliest weeks of the Open Theater, friends occasionally sat in on workshops. Their enthusiasm led Chaikin to arrange a few demonstration performances in the group's loft, open without charge to anyone who happened to hear about them. In 1963–64, the Open Theater's first full season, the company presented a couple of more formal programs, and starting the next year, they performed fairly regularly.

Even the earliest showings were not just observed work sessions. Chaikin felt that actors could not take the risks of real exploration with outsiders watching and that, in any case, most audiences would be bored by an actual investigation in progress. So the material to be shown was planned and rehearsed in advance.

Some selections were little more than structured demonstrations of exercises. The opening number often was a prearranged warm-up, consisting of, for example, "sound-and-movement" exchanges moving into a "chord." But, mostly, little plays were created to showcase the work.

The Open Theater's "insides" exploration was presented in a piece called *Variation on a Clifford Odets Theme*. Van Itallie devised what he described as "a realistic scene of the boring variety, such as might have been written by Clifford Odets." The characters were a couple and their daughter: The wife was "bitter, romantic (i.e., envisions a better world for the family, a world where they are rich and well-mannered, perfect perhaps)"; her husband was "self-indulgent, affectionate, proud, stupid"; and their child was "precocious" and restless. Van Itallie wrote aptly banal dialogue for the outsides and set certain "rules of the game" for the insides: "The characters were to remain the same, the basic intent of the scene was to remain the same; the setting was allowed to change, the 'language' in which the characters expressed themselves could change as long as no actual verbal dialogue was used that hadn't already been spoken." Although the insides were discovered through improvisation, by the time of performances, their basic shape had been pretty well set by Chaikin and the actors. In fact – contrary to the myth that grew up about the work – apart from group warm-ups and a few open exercises, the Open Theater rarely improvised in performance.

Another piece that van Itallie built around a Chaikin exercise was *Picnic in Spring*. Using the "circles" work, it explored the "instant image of a dream [about] . . . the end of love, including remembering, yearning, and the knowing it is impossible." The actors began in a frozen tableau of a picnic, which slowly moved into a relatively naturalistic "scene of lyrical happiness, sun, and harmony." Then, suddenly, during a game of catch, the (mimed) ball began to take longer and longer to travel through the air, and the scene moved into slow motion, with the illusion that the forest was growing larger. Van Itallie's scenario noted: "Trees that were only a few feet from each other are now miles away. The forest becomes so big that everyone is lost." When the woods had grown enormous, the actors switched from tossing a ball to throwing spoken lines provided by van Itallie ("Where are you?" "I am alone." "Never.") across the infinite distance. Then they moved into concentric circles of illusion, lament, indifference, and terror, continuing to use only the words of van Itallie's dialogue, but saying them according to the modes of the circles. This section, Chaikin told the actors, was "to express what was necessarily unexpressed in the ball game: the great remorse over the death of a living love and the sum of human sorrows." The piece ended with this dream.

The Open Theater also performed a Rip van Winkle improvisation, which began with a comic domestic scene, changed into a dream "conductor," and then, after Rip awoke, moved into "worlds." And they showed several versions of "perfect people" parties, as well as sketches that incorporated transformations, instant scenes, machine exercises, and conductors.

A few pieces did not come from specific exercises. *Contest* was a short, comic-grotesque play that the Open Theater performed in its first season and then, on occasion, for more than five years.* The actors began by walking around aimlessly, looking either up at the sky or down at the ground. Then a policeman emerged in the group and herded all but one person into a line; that person, put on a soapbox, began to laugh, and the others tried, in turn, to make the laughter stop. "What they want," van Itallie noted, "is to be on the pedestal, to laugh at the others and at the audience[;] and to be on the pedestal is to enjoy the wanting of the others." Each contestant who failed was pushed down and had to crawl to the end of the line, but a successful contestant would win the laugher's position on the soapbox. While they were on line, the contestants had to be "perfect" – perfect school teacher, secretary, hippie, bank president, and so forth – to please the policeman, who could arbitrarily penalize anyone he decided was misbehaving. He also could make up and change rules, such as timing, at will. *Contest* was very funny, partly because laughter is infectious, partly because the contestants' antics tended toward the bizarre, and partly because its basic metaphor somehow touched home. Chaikin told the actors at one point:

This scene is about brainwashing and the giving over of the human to being a contestant in a world which prescribes the rules which go counter to the human, but are nevertheless irresistible to everyone . . . Whatever else goes on on stage, don't notice it. You can't see it. Just play the contest and be hideous.

THE SERPENT

In October 1967, when Chaikin began his workshop on the Bible, his collaborative play creating moved into a new phase. The earlier per-

*Fascinated by the contest form, Chaikin considered using images of organized competition in several later performance works as well. Finally, in *The Other*, he created a "suffering contest" between Palestinians and Jews, complete with a blackboard and scorekeeper.

formance pieces had largely been showcases for Open Theater explorations. Now, as one actress put it, Chaikin's group "wasn't really a workshop" anymore but was "geared toward production of a new piece." This changed emphasis characterized the last six years of the Open Theater, Chaikin's *Fable* ensemble, and his San Francisco collaborations with Sam Shepard. In the first two seasons of the Winter Project, Chaikin again had a company devoted to research, with no pressure to develop something showable by the end; but because of stipulations in its grants, the Project's subsequent seasons were oriented toward creating pieces for presentation.

The Open Theater's earlier ensemble works had only partly prepared Chaikin for the scale and complexity of the new undertaking:

I had done small things before, manageable pieces. But this went through so many steps, and I had no idea how the next step would follow or what the nature of that period would be. There was no way to know what we were doing when we were doing it. I really didn't know what we were doing most of the time. So there was a lot of just general inspiration that we were working from.

The first issue was selecting an ensemble – which meant not only, as in past seasons, finding a good work group but also, ultimately, choosing a cast. Chaikin initially invited about fifteen actors from Lee Worley's beginners' workshop of the previous season and a handful of veterans from his own group. During the first month, a few new people were admitted, including some Open Theater actors returning from the London *America Hurrah*. Then, as the nature of the process became clearer, several were weeded out. By the first performances of *The Serpent*, there was a company of eighteen.*

The work began with terrific intensity. The actors were excited not only by the investigation itself but by their sense of being an elect group, specially chosen for the project. Chaikin, in turn, was energized by their fervor and commitment: Each member had agreed to attend all four, four-hour sessions each week, and to accept no employment requiring more than two weeks' absence during the year.

Chaikin wanted to explore connections over "vertical time," links with mythic roots, rather than horizontal, linear history. He hoped

---

*The acting company consisted of Joyce Aaron, James Barbosa, Raymond Barry, Jenn Ben-Yakov, Shami Chaikin (Chaikin's sister), Brenda Dixon, Ron Faber, Cynthia Harris, Philip Harris, Jayne Haynes, Ralph Lee, Dorothy Lyman, Peter Maloney, Ellen Schindler, Tina Shepard, Barbara Vann, Lee Worley, and Paul Zimet.

to discover forms that would express both the deepest, most private areas of experience and the external, public experience that communities share. He said of the investigation: "The inner and the outer – there's the impossible study."

His original intention was to project the life of Jesus between adolescence and crucifixion – to look at the rebel and innovator, and to imagine how his religious and social values might have been shaped. The subject especially appealed to Chaikin because it had mythic dimension, yet it incorporated a sense of cultural alienation. Moreover, the paucity of hard historical facts afforded a great deal of creative freedom.

To get perspective on the Jesus story, the company started working through the Bible from the beginning. To their surprise, they found themselves deeply connected to the Genesis myths. "It became clear," Chaikin later said, "that although we had rejected these stories as being true in any way, they still claimed us." Within a week the Open Theater had decided to drop the original idea and to make a piece from the opening chapters of the Bible.

The company was fascinated, first of all, by the emphasis in Genesis on discovery. Everything was a first. That, Chaikin says, was "the key thing" for him in *The Serpent:* "Dramatically, that gave us a lot of impetus – to look into the first murder, the first 'begatting,' the first breaking of the rule not to eat the apple of the tree."

But the pull of the biblical myths went deeper. For Chaikin, the story of Eden was a poetic insight into a feeling of loss that is part of the human condition. "The story of the fall," he wrote in a notebook, "is the event to explain why we live in 'a state of regret.'" Years before, he had made a note about "a veil of shame through which everything is done and felt"; exploring Adam and Eve's transgression provided an opportunity to "completely reunderstand the whole territory of shame, in the light of our retelling of the story." The company also began, in one actor's words, "to sense a connection between the Biblical myths we were exploring and the images of American violence which obsessed us."

Still, the workshop's attitude toward the stories remained ambivalent and skeptical. Certainly they never considered them literal truths. More important, while *The Serpent* followed the narrative of Genesis, it became, at least partly, in Chaikin's words, "a repudiation of its assumptions."

The company read and discussed not only parts of the Bible but also works by Joseph Campbell, Robert Graves, Karl Jung, Dietrich Bonhoeffer, and Albert Einstein. Chaikin read aloud in workshop from Louis Ginzberg's *Legends of the Jews,* a book based largely on Talmudic stories. And group members searched through illustrated volumes and library print files for visual representations of Adam, Eve, and the Garden.

A number of scholars were invited to respond to the developing work. Joseph Campbell visited in January and looked at improvisations of Eden. He then talked about myths as poems that "are either insights into the structure of the universe or functions of the psyche," and about ritual as "the process by which you are engaged into the myth, made to partake in it." He discussed concepts of Utopia and creation in various religions – Zoroastrian, Hindu, American Indian, and others. He introduced the notion of earthly paradise as a place of unity, "timeless, deathless, passionless (desireless), egoless"; after the bite of the apple, opposites emerged, good and evil, man and woman, suffering and joy, I and thou. Campbell also explained how the Hebrews, a nomadic society, rejected (cursed) the earthbound snake, a symbol of the fertility of the soil and an object of worship for vegetation-centered cultures, in favor of the bird or cherub symbol, the free spirit released from the earth.

Susan Sontag, a close friend of Chaikin's, visited the group twice, shortly after Campbell. She reiterated the view that one should not demand internal logic of the biblical stories but should rather see them as explanations for and justifications of particular social situations. She said that material from different periods had been woven together into Genesis, so that, for example, adjacent lines might have been written more than two thousand years apart and might incorporate very different sensibilities. She felt that the group's central problem was finding a verbal language comparable to the somatic forms they were developing. Paul Goodman also observed the work and spoke with the Open Theater about concepts of Eden.

Most of the research, though, was internal delving. Chaikin noted, "The collaboration required that each person address himself to the major questions: what are my own early pictures of 'first man,' 'first woman,' 'first discovery of sex,' God and the serpent, the Garden of Eden, the First Murder, Cain and Abel?" These were questions that people normally stopped asking after childhood merely "because they were unanswerable."

Ultimately, all of the study and discussion was subsumed into action – in Chaikin's words, "projecting ourselves into images and questions" suggested by the inquiry. This work began with an attempt to find an image for Eden. Chaikin felt that "everyone has some sense of a Utopia we're not living in," so the group began by asking, "Where am I in relation to that mythical place I imagine I might have lived in? What could bring me closer – a better job, a revolution, an assassination, a new wife?"

Chaikin decided that the workshop should confront paradise stereotypes head on, rather than try to navigate around them. "To understand the cliché," he noted, "is to understand the boundary" that must be transcended. The actor who censors a banal image "may always stay behind it," but in playing it out, often "a little bit of you touches at certain main arteries that this idea provokes." The company worked through what Chaikin called "the false Garden pictures: the illustrated biblical ones, the modern Hollywood ones, those from *House and Garden* – all the commercials (riding and Marlboros)"; they discussed assorted "isms" – Marxism, anarchism, Americanism – as attempts to get back to the garden. Trying then to move beyond clichés, they considered such possibilities as images from the Osiris myth; a round space with animals moving in a circle; and a harmonious "center from which people flake out," and which would dissolve after the Fall, creating a universe of irreparably separate individuals.

The best images of Eden came through the "worlds" exercise. Chaikin describes:

The stage is totally empty. The action is to appreciate its emptiness . . . , then to project on it the image of your garden. One actor will get up and do his garden and if another actor is sensitive to it, he will join him so that they make a little world. A third actor may or may not join – depending on whether this garden does or does not signal anybody, give them something they can identify with and understand. Then it's over and someone else tries it. Soon somebody will start a world with its own logic, its own rules, and its own sense of things. Then we have the garden. Ah, but it's so delicate, the process.

The company's large, windowless loft, which was painted black, was somehow bizarrely appropriate for exploring the creation of the world in the great, dark, primordial void.

In one early session, an actor began to drift about the floor as though floating. The stage manager noted: "There is no sound, only very fluid movement; and somehow very charming. The group joins him, and soon everyone is floating and very gently exploring each other. Almost like children in a dream." For a while this seemed to be a key. What finally took hold, though, was not a gentle, genial Utopia, but a world that preceded judgments or values.

An actress recalls:

The notion . . . wasn't that the Garden of Eden was . . . so pleasant and nice and warm and cozy – it was that there was no mind to judge that. There is an image . . . in Christian mythology . . . of the lion lying down with the lamb. Joe Campbell . . . spoke of that image . . . and he said in the East they have the same image . . . but the difference is that in the West they are both sort of smiling and they're in this kind of bliss together and in the East the lion is eating the lamb and they're in ecstasy – both – that there isn't a mind to say, "this hurts so it's bad. This feels good so it's good" . . . So we took that as how it was in the Garden of Eden.

Looking for possible inhabitants for the Garden, the actors quickly moved beyond real animals to nonexistent ones. Some were based on mythical, monstrous beasts described in Ginzberg's book. But most were developed from the actors' imaginations, using Open Theater techniques. In some improvisations, the performers tried to find outward shapes for particular internal aspects of themselves, such as "the gentle part." Other times they worked physically: they explored various kinds of motion, tried relocating the body's "center" in a new area, such as a leg, and used different body parts, such as the hands or backside, for a creature's head if it needed one. The company also improvised the inanimate elements of the Garden – stones, a tree, a rippling stream of water.

Originally populated by most of the company, Eden was eventually pared down to half a dozen animals. Among them were a quasi-frog; an unidentifiable, gentle, cooing creature; and a strange beast with its head on the ground, its back arched, and its rear sticking up. Only one animal, based on the Talmud's "king of the birds," stood upright. This heron-like "Ziz," with its dignity and beauty, reappeared in several post-Eden segments of *The Serpent* as an after-image recalling the lost state of grace.

In early improvisations, two Garden creatures became Adam and Eve, but this was later changed to emphasize the first people's first awareness of life. Two actors simply entered from offstage and lay down in the middle of the Garden, Eve on top of Adam; suddenly, Eve awoke with a scream of amazement.

Having humans in the improvisations brought up a question that the workshop had been postponing: What kinds of words would the piece use? Chaikin asked each actor to write scenes for Adam and Eve, Eve and the serpent, and God and Adam. But the company could not supply what was needed, and by early November, Megan Terry was sitting in and writing material for the project. Patricia Cooper and Jean-Claude van Itallie began to collaborate on it as well, and for several weeks, all three playwrights observed and contributed. By the end of January, halfway through the workshop season, it had been decided that van Itallie would be "the chief overseer of the scripts." Roberta Sklar, who had meanwhile joined the company as an assistant director, also concentrated on the piece's dramaturgy, working mainly with questions of language and structure.

The first verbal scene that the workshop attempted was the discovery of language itself. They did improvisations in which Adam unsuccessfully tried to communicate with the animals through sound; when he awoke later with Eve on top of him, the two humans began to mimic each other's cries; then, discovering the concept of naming, they took specific sounds, "Ahhh" and "Eeee," for themselves, and leapt about labeling the animals. Both Cooper and van Itallie wrote up scenes on this theme, but the whole idea was finally dropped as overliteral and uninteresting.

Two crucial images that the company needed for Eden were the snake and the tree of life. In early exercises, four women wove themselves into a strange, beautiful tree. Their long hair hung over their faces, swaying slightly as they moved, and their arms extended palms upward, holding apples. This image was eventually replaced, though, by a more striking one: a combined serpent and tree.

The Open Theater saw the tempter as an alternative to obedience, a force that invited people to transcend imposed limits. Chaikin even jotted in a notebook at one point, "The serpent is the good god." But they also saw the snake as having unleashed enormous confusion and suffering. For weeks they tried to find forms that would suggest their complex sense of it.

One day in the workshop actor Roy London arranged several actors, including himself, into a single creature with five flicking tongues and ten undulating arms and hands. Immediately, the workshop recognized its serpent. They played with the figure for weeks, varying the number of actors before finally settling on a five-part version. They tried different configurations and types of movement, perching one actor on another's shoulders, intertwining limbs, having snake hands come through the several groins (Chaikin's suggestion), and so forth. They also explored different sounds for this beast: In one experiment, for example, a serpent-actor read a snake speech from Ginzberg's *Legends of the Jews* while the four other actors "jammed" along.

Then someone tried putting apples into the creature's hands. And it became a bizarre, stunning amalgam of serpent and tree: Its arms now were tree limbs as well as creature limbs, its sinuous movement

The serpent forms in the garden in workshop, New York, 1967. Photograph by Hope Herman Wurmfeld.

the swaying of the tree in the wind as well as the animal's writhing.
Chaikin recalls the image as "very beautiful" and exciting: "They
were charged and it was very erotic and electric, with all the hands
and tongues going all the time and the sound of the thing."

In early improvisations the serpent formed itself from other
Garden beasts. Later, Chaikin decided to have the five actors tumble
and slide in so that the audience could see them assume character.
The final effect, according to a reviewer, was "first the primordial
ooze, then crawling creatures. Slithering snakes become a tree of
Serpents."

The company viewed Eve's seduction as partly sexual, so they

The temptation of Eve by the tree-serpent (*left to right:* Peter Maloney, Raymond Barry, James Barbosa, Ralph Lee [*partly hidden*], Ron Faber [*below*] in workshop, New York, 1967. Photograph by Hope Herman Wurmfeld.

comprised the tempter entirely of men, and made its dealings with Eve very erotic. But they saw the seduction as intellectual also. They were intrigued by a note in Ginzberg that God would not talk with the snake, because "the evil are good debaters." "The Serpent," Chaikin wrote, "has a very appealing tongue." So they concentrated on finding its "salesmanship." In some exercises, the creature debated with the other actors, trying to convince them that total anarchy was the only way to live. Or the different components of the snake were individualized, one mouth arguing like a Jesuit, one like a pedantic professor, one like a skeptic, one like a pimp, one like a mother blackmailing her children by withholding affection. The serpent worked with different Eves, trying to entice each in turn with its combination of argument and allure.

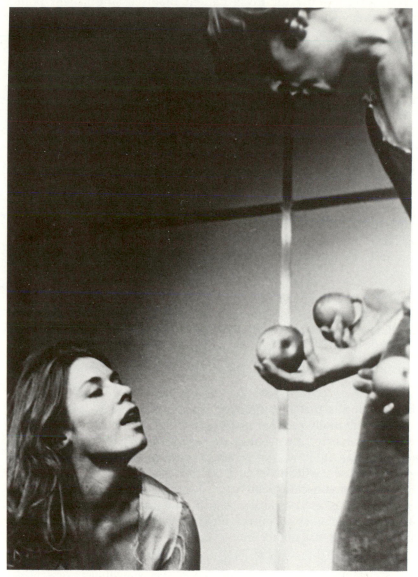

The temptation of Eve (Tina Shepard) in workshop, New York, 1967.
Photograph by Hope Herman Wurmfeld.

Meanwhile, the playwrights wrote temptation scenes. Cooper's snake moved from preverbal hissing into a sibilant "Listen, listen," which grew into its speech. It used a combination of effective argument and intellectual mumbo-jumbo, its different mouths occasionally making a show for Eve's benefit of discussing salient points among themselves. Terry wrote five pages of dialogue, which the group worked on several times, with the beast's various mouths alternating lines. The scene that was finally used, though, was one by van Itallie, in which the tempter tried to debunk God's warnings and authority, to frighten Eve into believing that a new, younger species would come to rule over her if she did not eat, and, most important, to convince her to transcend the boundaries imposed on her, and do what *she* wished to do. By the time his Eve said: "What if what I want to do is listen to God and not to you?" the serpent had won the argument. Chaikin explains, "He really doesn't care whether she eats the apple or not"; the point is that "she's doing what she wants to do."

Different actresses improvised biting the apple and then following whatever impulses came to them. Each Eve copied what the preceding had done, then created her own version. The responses ranged from cries of joy, to asthmatic gasps, to great howls of agony. Tina Shepard's version was a kind of nonjudgmental, thrilled amazement:

We were improvising and I guess most people were doing a bite and then suddenly seeing that it was wrong. And I went up to do it . . . and instead of going into kind of, "Oh, God, what have I done?" it came over me that in a sense it was like going on a trip where it's not that everything was either wonderful or terrible, but that it was absolutely charged with energy. And there was this shaking and excitement that went on – neither joy nor terror, just . . . excitement.

Shepard thinks that her discovery of this moment was what made Chaikin eventually cast her as Eve.

In performance, after biting the apple, Eve gave it to Adam to taste, and he, too, was astonished. Gradually, the entire Garden became infused with awareness and presence. The company then extended this consciousness beyond the playing area. They tried to see themselves as the audience did and, in one exercise, to view particular spectators as mirror images of themselves. For Chaikin, this awakening was about seeing for the first time:

It would be seeing the curtain of the stage, seeing somebody in the audience, seeing one another, seeing one's hand, seeing anything. We wanted a real recognition. We wanted a moment where one would simply take off from a boundary of seeing within limits and see in this way.
One would see with the body and see with the eyes – one would *see*.

In the later performances, after Adam's second bite, the entire company formed a serpent, intertwining limbs, flicking tongues, and squirming sensuously. Then they separated from each other and, continuing the same kind of energy, moved into the audience, handing out apples and, at times, touching the spectators. A critic reported, "When one actress darts into the stalls and, climbing on the knee of a man in front of me, begins kissing him fervently, it doesn't seem terribly strange in the context."

This orgy of discovery was the only part of *The Serpent*, except for the very end, that was improvised in performance. Chaikin noted at the time:

Once the actors are in the house playing out the exploration of this ecstasy, there is the other reality of people – players and audience – and here is where the delicate and mysterious encounter takes place. That encounter is not "made," but permitted. It is not performed at that moment, but let be.

In retrospect, though, he is less enthusiastic. Notwithstanding the company's genuine interest in exploring heightened actor–spectator contact, he says, the scene was done as a kind of mini-Happening mostly because the group never found forms he liked well enough to keep. Moreover, he feels, "It failed 90 percent of the time": "Occasionally it was unbelievable, but most of the time it was trivial."

In any case, after the ecstasy came the apprehension of consequences. In one early exercise, an Adam began to gag on the apple; in another, climbing all over the tree with Eve, he suddenly realized what they had done and tried to reattach the fruit to a branch. The company also explored the pair's new shame at their nakedness; one couple, for example, tried to preserve modesty by covering each other's eyes. Chaikin felt that the workshop should investigate the shame in *actual* nakedness, so they held two sessions in the nude. These experiments turned out to be of little direct value, though, because, to their surprise, the company members did not feel self-conscious or ashamed. In any case, they knew that nudity on stage would have a shock value that would distract from the more subtle points they wanted to express in *The Serpent* – and might get the actors arrested. They were not interested in turning their play into that particular sort of *épater-les-bourgeois* or protest work.*

---

*The Open Theater's discussions and explorations of nudity took place in Oct. and Nov. 1967. Within a year, the clothes line in theater, already stretched by Brook's 1964 *Marat/Sade*, had been crossed by the Performance Group's *Dionysus in 69*, the Living Theater's *Paradise Now*, and, on Broadway even, *Hair*. *Terminal*, the Open Theater's next major piece, did have nudity; a dying man was stripped of his own clothing to be dressed in institutional garb. Although there was not much question of arrests at that point, in performances outside New York it did cause some distracting scandal.

In performance, the initial rapture gradually changed to a recognition of separateness, individuality, and aloneness. The earlier sense of oneness with the audience gave way to a focus on differences. The actors picked out particular traits – gray hair, glasses, a red tie, baldness – and, in early performances at least, mentioned aloud these features which set people apart from one another.

Then came the curses of God. Chaikin recalls:

> That was one of the big problems: God. How to manifest God. I mean, he had to be there. You can't do the Garden of Eden story and leave him out. And so for weeks and weeks and months, one of the questions was, "How can we do it?" And people would come in with things: Somebody came in with a black robe and arranged a special light on herself and spoke with a funny voice through the robe, and it seemed interesting for about two days. I remember eliminating hundreds of things.

Chaikin asked everyone to bring in an image for God. One person projected a slide of Michelangelo's *David* onto two workshop members; another showed a watercolor she had painted depicting God overlooking the Garden. Several actors improvised living pictures: a Nero-like deity reclining on a couch and toying with the universe he was creating; a character resting quietly, then suddenly noticing that there was a void, and so gracefully and thoughtfully fashioning a world with his hands; a creator who watched with terrible anger as a tiny speck on the tiny universe in his palm bowed to temptation. The company also tried showing God as a figure made up of several actors whirling together in a circle; in some improvisations this image was created by the same actors who had formed the serpent.

It was, finally, in exploring the voice of God that the company found a visual image as well. They had worked at first on expressing sheer force in sound. They improvised percussive ways of talking, and tried "to demolish someone with sound only." At the opposite extreme, they worked with the notion of God's voice as silence or breath, trying to adapt an open-mouthed breathing sound to speech and then to use it in a "chord"; this chord might be comprised of the entire company, including the Garden animals, or only the components of a circular, multi-actor God. In a related experiment, several actors sustained a deep note while others in the company built sounds on top of that. Still another idea was that God's voice might appear through its effect on Adam, Eve, and the animals, who would quiver and make a "quaking sound" in response to it.

Eventually, a solution came from the scriptural notion that God cursed his creatures through their own tongues, and from Susan

Sontag's suggestion that God might be within the performers, as in a Dionysian ritual. An actor noted:

Phil Harris . . . took the floor and attempted to use his own voice as the voice of god, coming against his will from his own throat. At first the voice of God which he used was much louder and more angry than his own "Adam" voice. We agreed after discussion that a more meaningful contrast will be achieved by having God's voice really calm and quiet while Adam's body is contorted with fear. This dichotomy ("the arms say yes, the legs say no" – Grotowski) is of course very difficult to do. Roy London had a good idea which he demonstrated: Whenever God was speaking through Adam, he walked over and grabbed Phil under the arms from behind and shook him violently, then walked away.

The group expanded this image, sometimes having London pick up Adam, Eve, and the animals one by one, and later having the various animals lift each other as well as Adam and Eve. Chaikin told the actors that God's voice, coming through the Garden inhabitants, "should be without tension": In fact, he said, "if you don't know the meaning of what you are saying, it is better." Moreover, the one lifting the speakers should not be seen as God, but simply as "a person lifting them."

Containing God's existence within earthly characters, this image supported the company's premise that "man made God in his own image and held up this God to determine his own (man's) limits." It also suggested that God was less vital somehow than the serpent, which was, after all, an independent (and, ultimately, the title) character.

In the final version of *The Serpent*, as God entered Eden, the actor who had been playing the heron lifted Adam for God's words, dropped him for Adam's reply, lifted him again for God's response, and so forth. Then the same was done with Eve. As God began his curses, various animals lifted one another and God's voice came through them. Gradually, God's anger built until, by the end, lines fragmented, phrases came through several actors at once, and individual meanings became lost in a general, horrible din. The clamor was augmented by the low, bellowing groan of a "lion's roar," an instrument comprised of a rawhide strip pulled up through a small hole in a resonating drum or bucket.*

The company felt that God's scourges should go beyond the few stated in Genesis. They discussed what it meant to be accursed –

---

*Richard Peaslee, who introduced the "lion's roar" to the ensemble, and Stanley Walden worked closely with the Open Theater, developing what they called *The Serpent*'s "bruitage."

what the "irreversibles" (Chaikin's word) were in the human condition. Van Itallie shaped a text out of ideas from that discussion, amplified with material from the Bible and Ginzberg. It included:

> Now shall come a separation
> Between the dreams inside your head
> And those things which you believe
> To be outside your head
> And the two shall war within you.
> . . . .
> And your children shall live in fear of me.
> And your children shall live in fear of you.
> And your children shall live in fear of each other.
>
> Accursed, you shall glimpse Eden
> All the days of your life.
> And you shall not come again.
> And if you should come
> You would not know it.

The workshop explored how the effects of God's wrath could be made visible. Influenced, no doubt, by the Chinese theater distillation technique, which Chaikin had demonstrated during the first weeks of the Bible project, the actors refined their results into a succinct emblem for each curse. One Eve, for example, dropped over from the waist, the top of her body hanging, legs bent, arms extended; an Adam hunched his back, squeezing his hands together, his weight heavily on one leg. Chaikin decided, then, that each person or animal, when cursed, should become imprisoned in the image of that state, "in a locked action, one phrase of action which is their synthesis":

Because they were mythic figures, they would remain in primarily one, not necessarily *only* one, but primarily one position, one moment, one activity . . . Things stay in memory where they're rerun in a different way from how they actually happen. Certain things have emphasis and predominate within all the steps that make up the action.

Chaikin considered tying these locked-action emblems to spatial areas, in the manner of his old circles work. The idea was that everyone in the terrain of Adam's curse, for example, would become locked into Adam's phrase, and that this would highlight humankind's inheritance of his guilt. Chaikin even thought of using cages to emphasize the locking, possibly enclosing the audience in visible or invisible prisons, since the spectators too were heirs to the Fall. These prisons were not finally used, but the locked actions remained in the final performance piece; Adam pointed accusingly at Eve, she pointed at the ser-

The curses of God take over the garden, and Adam (Philip Harris) is already in a "locked action," in workshop (with Chaikin, blurred, crossing in the background), New York, 1967. Photograph by Hope Herman Wurmfeld.

pent, and the other creatures locked into various attitudes. Only the heron was left uncursed, a vestige of lost innocence.

According to Genesis, God damned the serpent to crawl eternally on its belly and eat the dust of the ground. The Open Theater had its creature break apart into five actors writhing along the ground, rolling sideways by doing pushups and falling over backward. Chaikin wanted "to make it like snakes, almost like cutting up a live worm and both halves or three parts of it are still alive." This image of a body torn apart and even at war with itself became a metaphor in the piece for accursedness. An early script contained the following note accompanying a reprise of the curses:

Each other actor on the stage engages in a battle against his own body. The theme which is being interpreted physically here will be stated verbally later: If a bulldog ant is cut in two, a battle starts between the head and the tail. The head bites the tail. The tail stings the head. They fight (until both halves are dead).

The "Battle of the Bodies against Themselves" scene was cut in later versions of *The Serpent*, but a verbal statement of the theme was kept in.

The workshop continued its exploration of Genesis with the tale of Cain and Abel. They considered various interpretations, including a Talmudic note that Cain was born of Eve and the serpent, and a version in which Cain blamed God for not saying which action was sinful until after it had been committed. The company discussed the myth as a prototype of the violence in modern society. For Chaikin, though, the real fascination of this murder was that it was the first: "The trigger that kept my connection to the Cain and Abel story was the thing that we found in a Talmudic criticism, which was that he was killing his brother but didn't know it would cause his death." Cain understood "that killing Abel would be to give physical expression of his anger, of his contempt to that other body. But he didn't know that would mean he'd never live again after he finished that."

After various exercises and improvisations, the dramatic entrance into the story came from a legend in Ginzberg: Cain did not know how to kill, did not know which parts of the body were the life centers, so he attacked every part of Abel, until Abel begged to be hit on the head with a stone to end his misery. In sketches based on this, Cain pounded his brother with both arms, or dropped a rock on him, or broke his limbs, or covered Abel's mouth and nose. The final version involved a scoring of these actions accompanied by several actors' strained, rhythmic gasping – the breathing of Abel until his death.

The workshop developed several variations and extensions of the Cain–Abel scene. Richard Peaslee worked with the company on sounds to accompany the murder. The actors also explored the sus-

Abel (Ralph Lee) and Cain (Raymond Barry) in workshop, New York, 1967. Photograph by Hope Herman Wurmfeld.

pense in the story, stopping the action in the middle and then tracing backward to find the point where the outcome became inevitable. They also considered juxtaposing other actions with the killing: biblical scenes of cruelty (including a stoning, a mother eating her children, a woman being killed with a nail through her head); and episodes with clowns and acrobats, to show how divertissements are used to camouflage the horror of violence. They tried using multiple pairs of brothers. One set of actors would begin and then pass the action to a second pair, who might in turn pass it to a third. Or, alternately, three sets of brothers would work through the story simultaneously in adjacent spaces: An action begun by one pair would be completed by another; or the three groups would act through the story at different speeds, or with one group slightly in advance of another; or the pairs would switch partners in the middle of the murder. Finally, though, Chaikin cut all this elaboration:

When I did that three Cain and Abel thing, I'm sure I had an idea, but finally it was just "Boy, that'll really be something! And then when this one is at this point of the act, this one will be at a slightly different point of the

Cain and Abel in workshop, New York, 1967.
Photograph by Hope Herman Wurmfeld.

act, and maybe they'll join up; and we'll have the other actor do something; meanwhile that one will do this; and then we'll see something about the *act* in relation to the steps of the act." But in fact what you saw was a kind of choreography. It didn't have to do with the main part of it, which was: you hate and you want to kill, and you don't know what that's about, and you don't know how to do it.

The Cain–Abel variations were one instance of a recurring problem in the *Serpent* work: Chaikin recalls, "I was very filled and very energetic. And I also had a sense of a kind of virtuosity that I hadn't put together yet . . . And some of what I was doing was just variations on variations. And some of it came out of something very organic. I just wasn't discriminating very much." In fact, one of the most important lessons from Chaikin's experience in creating a number of pieces is that he now feels better able "to tell what we should promote, and what we should just try."

In any case, the Cain–Abel segment was pared down to its simple, linear form. Then, after the murder, Cain became imprisoned in a locked action. Frightened by Abel's failure to move, he first tried to make him behave as before: He put (mimed) grass into the lifeless hand, and tried to make Abel feed his sheep(played by two actors). When this did not work, he laid Abel down on the backs of the animals and stood behind him, swaying from one foot to the other and waiting for Abel to be alive again. For Chaikin, Cain's locked action did not embody guilt so much as agony at having discovered death:

Its source was an idea of a speech not in the play: "How can I live at all, knowing I am going to die? How can I attach myself to anything precious if I know it's going to perish?" The gesture was a wavering and a noncommitting. The source was never clear, but I hope that the feeling was.

After this scene, in early performances of *The Serpent*, came a section called "Blind Man's Hell": All but three of the actors groped around as if blind, while the remaining three lay on the floor and reached upward, grabbing at the "blind," moving people. Later, this interlude was cut, and the actors who had not been part of the Cain and Abel scene entered the playing space and joined in Cain's locked action, sharing his curse.

A narrator of some kind clearly was needed to link the segments and establish a tone. Van Itallie wrote speeches to accompany the seduction and Cain–Abel scenes, but for a long time it was not clear who should say these lines or what relationship this person, or people, would have to the events being enacted. The company discussed a variety of solutions, including the possibility that the serpent might narrate, taking on different identities during the play. Then van Itallie had the idea that four women would chant the narration in the rhythmic *davenning* style of Jewish prayer, and that they would intermingle statements of their own with the biblical material. At first, the company saw these women as in mourning, separated from their men, who were gone and scattered, perhaps off at war, perhaps all dead.

That scenario was dropped, but the female chorus remained in *The Serpent* as descendants of Eve, vessels containing her experience, and inheritors of God's curses. In early performances, during Eve's debate with the serpent, someone in the chorus echoed her lines and cried out in amazement after Eve bit the apple. During the ecstatic "seeing trip," their facial expressions mirrored Eve's sense of astonishment and discovery, and in some workshop improvisations, Eve actually joined the line of women.

These narrators also came to perform another traditional choral function, expressing the company's point of view about the Genesis stories. A note that Chaikin brought to the company from Dietrich Bonhoeffer's *Creation and Fall* formed the kernel of a central, recurring motif:

> Man no longer lives in the beginning – he has lost the beginning. Now he finds he is in the middle, knowing neither the end nor the beginning, and yet knowing that he is in the middle, coming from the beginning and going toward the end.

The loss of past and future anchor points, coupled with a narrowing of possibilities, seemed to Chaikin a major anguish of modern life. Another choral theme was the image of lemmings running, one by one, then in groups, and finally en masse, "For tens / And hundreds of miles / Until, / Exhausted, / They reach the cliff / And throw themselves / Into the sea."

Chaikin thought that the narrators might have a very intimate, immediate role in the piece if they spoke partly about their real lives. So van Itallie developed a series of "statements" from autobiographical material that the actresses provided:

Jean-Claude asked us to come to his house, which we did, and he asked us questions about ourselves, and we talked about ourselves and our lives. I thought he was fabulous to come up with the speeches that he had the four women do. My own, for instance, were the things I said to him, but he put them in a brilliant way. I could never have done it, but they were from me. They're wonderful.

The chorus now conveyed a deeply personal sense of loss, mourning, purposelessness, and suppressed rage – a spectrum of agonies:

> I hugged my child
> And sent him off to school
> With his lunch in a paper bag.
> And I wished he would never come home.
> . . . .
> My home was Cleveland.
> Then I came to New York

The chorus of women (*left to right:* Cynthia Harris, Shami Chaikin, Lee Worley, Joyce Aaron) in workshop, New York, 1967. Photograph by Hope Herman Wurmfeld.

And I didn't have to account to anybody.
I smoked: pot, hashish, opium.
I slept with a man.
I slept with a woman.
I slept with a man and a woman at the same time.
But I'm a gentle person, and I collapsed.
I pretend I'm enjoying it when I'm not.
It gives him pleasure.
I'm not really there.

In early showings, the women's testimonies also touched on the lives of other company members. They mentioned, for example, that the actor playing Adam had been drafted into the army. Such statements were later dropped.

In performance, the chorus addressed the spectators directly and, in most cases, delivered their first speech from the auditorium before moving into the playing space and seating themselves just outside the Garden. They emphasized the rhythms of their speeches and sometimes accompanied them with a low drone. For the passages of biblical narrative especially, they tried to evoke a sense of ritual. Often, they *davenned* as they spoke, rocking back and forth

The "begatting" in performance at Washington Square Methodist
Church, New York, 1970. Photograph by Karl Bissinger.

with their eyes closed. Their keening was described by one critic as
"wordless, almost soundless wailing . . . among the most terrifying
sounds I have heard in the theatre."

The chorus became part of *The Serpent*'s final biblical segment,
which the Open Theater called the "Begatting." After showing the
Fall and the first murder, they wanted to wind forward to approach
contemporary times. They used the genealogical chapters of Genesis
(5, 10, and 11) and the first Gospel as their texts. (They also tried,
briefly, to incorporate a newspaper obituary column.) And they
sought images for the initial discovery of sex, and then the succes-
sion of many, many generations. Predictably, the first part of the
scene became comic. Chaikin recalls: "People were kind of looking
to see what to do with the other body – how the body resembled
theirs, or where it fit, or what to do. And that's what they were
exploring, with feet in mouths and pulling on ears and things." By
the time of performance, the text that accompanied this group tangle
had been reduced to a drone, chanted by a chorus woman pacing
back and forth upstage, and punctuated with finger bells.

The company worked improvisationally to find images for the
birth, growth, and death of generations. An actor noted, following a
workshop:

After each couple "made it" so to speak, and progressed to *birth*, Shami gave birth to Nancy, Barbara Vann gave birth to twin boys, and Paul gave birth to Tina. It was agony, the "mothers" with legs spread wide, the "babies" descending, coming out, some feet first, some head first, entering screaming into the world . . . The scene was startling since a dozen births were occurring simultaneously and the awful pain of childbirth, woman's curse since the fall, was graphically and aurally portrayed.

After their births, the children were taught to walk and talk . . . As they learned how to walk and hold things they got older and kept getting older and older until at the end, they were walked over to the platform by their mothers, who remained mothers, not aging. And were deposited on the platform next to the other old people, all of whom were left alone, sitting there in their old age like the old people on the upper west side, who sit there on their benches on the island as traffic roars by on either side up and down Broadway. This fantastic transformation took only 15 minutes, but was so powerful in its humanness and "reality" that my eyes were filled with tears in the face of such agony, joy, and sadness condensed into such a small space and short time.

A version of this improvisation was used in performance. As the initial sexual explorations progressed, a man and a woman very slowly approached each other from opposite ends of the stage. When they touched, all of the gropings culminated in a single, giant orgasm. Shrieks of ecstasy transformed into screams of mothers in labor and babies being born, and the growth-to-old-age scenario began. The scene ended with a line of old people facing the audience.

Fearing that the "Begatting" might not pass the Italian censors, Chaikin and the company tried to find alternative ways to do the scene before their European tour. But since each metaphor that they tried seemed more obscene than the explicit copulation, they decided to take their chances with the censors, who, it turned out, did not interfere.

The Open Theater never meant to create an Old Testament mystery play. From the first week of work, they looked for ways to show the strong connections they felt between the biblical themes and modern concerns. One suggestion was to transform the Genesis stories into a modern myth or fairy tale. Peter Pan, Sleeping Beauty, Hansel and Gretel, and Snow White were all considered, but the tale that most held the company's interest was Cinderella. They saw the story as a means to investigate modern delusions of paradise (Chaikin jotted in a notebook at one point. "The pursuit of happiness – Cinderella marries prince and they're miserable"), and they spent weeks doing improvisations based on it. Workshop notes on the

The "first birth" in workshop, New York, 1967 (Philip Harris and Dorothy Lyman). Photograph by Phill Niblock.

fairy tale exploration were extremely enthusiastic, but Chaikin and others now recall it as less than exciting. In any case, none of it was used in *The Serpent*.

The company also thought that an image of human sacrifice might suggest misguided attempts of the fallen to regain paradise. They worked with various children's games to choose a victim. Finally, though, Chaikin abandoned the sacrifice section too: "It was not interesting; it was just an illustration of an idea."

Another notion was to interpolate modern domestic scenes, pictures of life after the Garden. Workshop improvisations included a family dinner; a young couple in love, but getting on each other's nerves; a strong man teaching a weaker man to hammer; nomads constructing a shelter on a cold night; a totally humorless community concerned only with work. Van Itallie wrote a little play in which political protesters, all women, were first heckled by male counter-demonstrators, then dragged into a van by the male police. None of these modern analogues was given much work, though, and none was used in the piece.

The story that did take root as a modern embodiment of the Genesis myth was the assassination of John Kennedy. As early as 1964, Chaikin had noted his interest in staging the Kennedy murder. And, in fact, Jacques Levy's workshop during the 1966–7 season had developed a sequence based on the Zapruder film of the shooting: Four actors, playing occupants of the Kennedy car (they were actually kneeling on the floor) posed in the individual frames of the film; each picture was assigned a number, and someone outside the scene ran the film backward and forward and selected random single frames by calling out the appropriate number. Meanwhile, the watching crowd declared:

> I was not involved.
> I am a small person.
> I hold no opinions.
> I stay alive . . .

Van Itallie, who had participated in Levy's workshop, and had written the crowd's speech, suggested now that this work be incorporated into the *The Serpent*.

Chaikin was not enthusiastic. "It was primarily involved with doing a scene on stage like a movie – where it starts, and then it's as though one were sitting in one of those annoying screening rooms where people go back and trace something and go on and then go back again to trace something." Still, the material had an immediacy and dimension that he wanted for *The Serpent*, and he decided to see if it could be adapted. Stanley Walden broke the poem up and scored it in a staccato rhythm. At first, the audience heard only incomprehensible fragments; gradually, the words became clear.

The crowd at rear waves to the occupants of the Kennedy car as the assassin, at right, takes aim; James Barbosa, at the rear center, has not yet assumed character as Robert Kennedy. In performance at Washington Square Methodist Church, New York, 1970. Photograph by Karl Bissinger.

Meanwhile, the killer, a lone figure standing apart, silently enacted the agony of being shot himself, then joined the crowd's speech, saying the words very distinctly. For Chaikin, the scene gained impact from the counterpoint of the visual images with the scored speech.

The sequence, finally, not only expressed the violence and isolation of Eve and Adam's twentieth-century children, but also echoed the biblical feeling of the loss of order and innocence. Moreover, it seemed to have the necessary weight. Van Itallie told an interviewer: "I think the Kennedy assassination is in our head – at least my head – almost mythologically. I mean it's an image that the Zapruder film made indelible, as strong as anything from the Bible."

As the Open Theater was working on *The Serpent*, Martin Luther King was killed in Memphis, and the group incorporated his murder into the Kennedy scene: A figure became detached from the crowd, began a speech like King's "I Have a Dream," and was shot; then he too moved backward and forward through his action, repeating the fatal moment again and again. While the company was touring Europe with *The Serpent*, they learned of Robert Kennedy's murder, and included that in the piece as well: A man stepped forward, tossing back his hair and offering his hand with a big campaign smile, and was shot; this too was repeated over and over as a "phrase" while the crowd's words became clear.

Another modern section, a surgery/autopsy scene, was developed in the last weeks before performances. The idea was that during surgery certain areas of the brain might be stimulated to produce vivid memories, of the race as well as of the individual. Initially, the workshop thought that the patient's recollections might include one of Eve's sentences, a chorus statement, or God's curses. Ultimately, the memories that were evoked were the rest of *The Serpent,* and the doctor scene provided a kind of dramatic prologue. It also tied the assassination more directly to the rest of the play, since probing the patient's brain suggested Kennedy's autopsy. The segment was changed at some point from an operation to an autopsy, to strengthen this link. Although Chaikin recalls that the doctor episode "wasn't played with the same fullness as most of the rest of *The Serpent,*" it was nonetheless "very important" and "very organic to the play." And for van Itallie, who wrote the scene, it had a special personal import, because he developed it largely from his experience with his mother's brain tumor.

In performance, an actress was placed on a table formed by kneeling actors. The surgeon announced an autopsy, explained his procedure, and pointed out how the brain of a live patient contained memories that could be aroused by the surgeon's knife. Meanwhile, there were occasional sounds of gunshots in the background. In early showings, partway through the scene, actors not directly involved moved behind the doctor to form a large brain, which pulsated slightly as electrical connections were made through the actors' fingertips. This image then reappeared at the very end of the play, composed of the entire company, including the chorus women. Finally, though, this brain image seemed more a display of Open Theater technique than an integral part of the play, and it was not used in the later performances.

Although thematic connections among the various biblical and non-biblical segments were clear from the start, finding a structure to relate them formally turned out to be one of the more delicate and complex aspects of the project. Putting any developing work into a shape, Chaikin has found, circumscribes as well as clarifies the investigation. The trick, at each point, is to balance the need for definition with the need for openness.

The Serpent workshop began addressing this problem early. Chaikin asked each actor to bring in a suggested scenario for the whole piece, and the company discussed narrative and musical models that might serve. As the work progressed, Sklar turned her attention to questions of dramatic construction. And van Itallie became central to the process, trying periodically, he says, "to put together all the impulses anyone had come up with so far and put them into a kind of frame, a form, which I hoped, but was never quite convinced was organic":

Every month or so, I would suggest a total structure, which would be accepted for a couple of weeks, and then Joe would break it down again, which was a big blow to my ego each time; but I could see why he did it. And that process continued.

The workshop considered a wide range of overall forms for the piece: a funeral mourning a common catastrophe; a ritual performed by a group of prisoners or political exiles; an LSD trip; a procession of medieval players or magicians; a confession; a Black Mass; a retreat from the plague; a trial with a paper-mache inquisitor asking questions and making accusations in various "establishment" voices; a ceremony introduced and explained by a herald, who addressed the audience directly; a presentation of the lives of the actors.

In fact, though, *The Serpent* was not assembled until the Open Theater was literally on its way to Europe to begin touring. Van Itallie recalls:

We had escaped doing a premiere in New York, because *America Hurrah* had drawn a lot of attention, and therefore people would have come a lot, and there was fear of the tension that would come from that sort of opening. So we thought we would go away and do it nowhere, which is to say, in Europe. So we were on the boat, and suddenly we began getting telegrams and so on and realized that it was going to be a major European opening. And suddenly the crisis was on.

So I sat down with Joe and Roberta Sklar, and I wrote down the names of all the scenes that we had on three by five cards, and we went through them and we decided rather quickly which pieces to keep and which pieces to throw out. And then I said, "Okay, give me an hour or two." And I sat down with the three by five cards and I put them in a particular order, and I said, "Okay, this is the piece."

This final arranging was so much an eleventh-hour undertaking that minutes before curtain time some actors were not sure what material was in and what had been cut. But, although some changes were made in the following weeks and months, the piece remained essentially the way it was put together on the boat.

Chaikin had felt all along that the Genesis stories should follow rather than precede any modern material, so that the action would be a tracing back to mythic roots rather than a chronological history. The body of *The Serpent*, therefore, started with the doctor segment, which was followed by the Kennedy–King assassination, which led to the Garden. The chorus began the Genesis section, coming up from the audience, and then remained on stage through the unfolding, in order, of the biblical scenes.

But the piece needed a beginning and an end. Chaikin was particularly concerned about how *The Serpent* would start, how the spectators would be led into its unfamiliar theatrical world: "We needed the piece introduced . . . Because we had never done anything like *The Serpent* before, and we had never seen anything like that before. And we didn't know what the response of the audience was to be."

After experimenting with a number of openings – a series of solemn conch horn notes, a prologue by a herald – the company decided to use a procession. They tried several, including a file of people with their hands over their eyes and a New Orleans-style funeral cortege with periodic bursts of joy. What worked best, though, was a musical band composed of actors making sounds with their bodies and with primitive instruments. In early performances, the company started by doing warm-ups all over the stage and auditorium, and moved from that into the procession; later, they began by sitting quietly around the theater, and then slowly built up a musical texture. An actress explains:

Each actor as he or she was ready would go and sit at any place in the auditorium . . . People would come in, step all over you . . . and wonder why this person was sitting there without shoes, on the floor; . . . then the piece would begin with just sounds – each of us had an instrument and one person would start with . . . the sound of claves – two sticks that you hit together and they make a very nice resonating sound – and then there would be an answer of another sound from another part of the room . . . At first it would be . . . just occasional sounds – and then one of the actors started a rhythm, and the others would join in relation to that rhythm in counterpoints. And there was also a particular voice sound which we used which was sort of like a calling across distances, not with words but with just a sound that was sort of projected out . . . It was like . . . when the first bird wakes and makes the sound and then as others wake they join . . . And then there was a procession of the men, mostly . . . They paraded around the room picking up people as they went along.

During this opening, Chaikin says, the entire theater would become "full of a certain kind of music."

Periodically during the parade, the marchers stopped and for a moment embodied a motif from the play: the locked action of Adam,

Eve, or Cain; the aspirated breathing of the serpent; the trilled sound of the heron; the moment of recognizing the audience. Then the procession resumed, moving eventually to the stage area, where the play itself began.

The very end of *The Serpent*, following "Begatting" and "Old People," was changed completely after the Open Theater began performing. In early showings, the company re-formed a brain; the chorus, from inside it, gave a long speech containing emblematic lines from the rest of the play. Then the brain became a giant serpent/tree with eighteen heads and thirty-six arm/branches. The group considered inviting the audience to go to this "tree of life." Instead, they had the organism break up into its component actors and move out into the auditorium. What happened now was to depend on the inspiration of the moment. The only structure was a rhythm – a heartbeat separated by three counts (huh-huh, two, three, four) – derived from the hissing of the serpent.

Sometimes this "invitation for the audience to do something" was successful: One actress spoke of a performance that "ended with a kind of parade, a chain of people dancing all around the auditorium . . . really a celebration"; someone else recalled occasions when "the silence was full, mysterious, a kind of tense stepping back and saying what now." But the same actor noted, "Often the audience would do nothing. A few might smile, someone might heckle, but most looked bewildered, defensive. When we stopped the rhythm there would be a long pause, finally someone would start to applaud . . . only to be shushed by others in the audience. More silence. Then the audience would decide it really was over, applaud, and leave." And once, he noted, when the company encountered an audience "all primed to do something," the actors "didn't know what to do with them."

The open ending was eventually dropped. Following "Old People," each of the actors was "overtaken by a slow kind of dying, not so much a physical one as a kind of 'emptying out,' a living death." Then, as ghosts, they began to sing "Moonlight Bay," an old, sentimental popular song. Continuing their singing as themselves, they left the theater through the audience. It was an odd finale, ambiguous, apparently, even to the company. Chaikin told one reviewer: "The intention is a moment of celebration. The stillness of Cain's waiting, the fact of death – you can really get dragged down by that and die from it. Or you can just go another way." But he has also said that the group's use of "a kind of present-day Utopian melody" was "actually to be an irony . . . It was to cut through."

Although many of *The Serpent*'s innovations have now become wide-spread, especially in experimental theater, its presentational, ritual, collage form was a real break from the familiar stage vocabulary and syntax of 1968. The action did not follow one story, and the performers were not portraying individual characters as much as giving expression to some shared conditions and experiences. Everyone except the chorus women assumed more than one role, and there was only one actual dialogue in the piece, the one between Eve and the serpent.

The play also was intentionally theatrical in the sense of being very frankly the work of performers on a stage. Chaikin avoided stage tricks (such as amplification for the voice of God) and the distraction of elaborate material trappings; there was no scenery at all, and the only props were apples and primitive musical instruments. He emphasized the presence of the live actors, too, by letting the audience see them move into and out of character:

> I had this thought that all the actors would be visible all the time, and that we would demarcate the stage area from the offstage area, but the audience would see the off-stage area as well as the stage area. And there would just be some formal sitting, something that would not be too attention getting, so that we could focus on the action, but the audience would see how everything took place.

The Open Theater toured Europe with *The Serpent* and a program of earlier short pieces from May through July 1968, performing in Italy, Germany, Switzerland, and Denmark. It was a difficult, painful experience. Although the work went well and was received enthusiastically, the pressure of constantly living, traveling, and performing together caused much greater tension than the group had foreseen. Problems were complicated by lack of money and often inadequate hotel and travel accommodations. The pace was exhausting, and there was a growing, sometimes explosive, bitterness between some actors and van Itallie about control of and credit for *The Serpent*. Chaikin wrote to a friend that there was "constant trouble within the company," with various people "pissed off all the time" or "incredibly stubborn about matters which seem so eccentric," or "unhappy most of the time," or "always completely stoned." This was, in fact, the most trying period that the Open Theater ever would undergo. Even subsequent tours were not as tense. One company member explained, "We've learned more and more with each tour how to deal with ourselves, with each other and the work . . . Also some people who had been on the first European tour just didn't keep on working. Those that did went on because they knew that something about it was important to them even given the terrible times."

When the Open Theater reconvened in New York in the fall of 1968, they considered dropping *The Serpent* completely. They gave one performance in early December, with which both Chaikin and van Itallie were dissatisfied. The following week, Chaikin told the company that he felt, regretfully, unable to rework *The Serpent* for U.S. performances:

I would really like to share it with an audience. It is the most important thing I have ever worked on but the periphery relating to it have been very painful and difficult . . .

It's up to me to fix those things that are wrong. I don't think I can. I cannot fix it up without going into it, opening it up . . . It is an unmanageable amount of work. It can't be smashed together; on the other hand, it can't be opened up and go[ne] into . . . in a workshop situation again . . . Therefore, between all the work problems and the fact that four people are missing . . . it is very hard to restart it.

Finally, though, he and the actors decided to take it apart and look at it "as though it were a script by somebody we didn't know":

We started from scratch, from the procession which begins the piece, and then examined and re-examined and re-examined our attitudes to the audience and to the material. Only when we finally began to examine our process of examining were we able to alter our approach to a more creative one, and only at the point where we fully gave up and let the production collapse were we able to begin to build. We slowly did exercises in and around the material and began to reconstruct the work. This time we reconstructed it in a much more formal way because it was much clearer what the intentions were to be.

The Serpent's official American premiere was at Harvard University in January 1969. The company performed the work that winter and spring in their loft (for free), at the Public Theater, and on a short New York State college tour. There was some talk of taking *The Serpent* off-Broadway, a move that van Itallie favored, but Chaikin was adamantly against a commercial run. The piece remained in the Open Theater's repertory through the spring of 1970. It finally was dropped, partly because Chaikin felt it was becoming dated and partly because it really could not be reworked for the pruned-down company.

In retrospect, Chaikin is not wholly satisfied with *The Serpent*. He feels that elements in it were very powerful, but "the whole thing was unreliable: . . . Sometimes it was really terrific, but sometimes it was ghastly." Foreign performances were especially problematical since the company faced audiences that not only were unfamiliar with *The Serpent*'s theatrical forms but could not understand the piece's large verbal sections. "It was one thing doing it at Harvard and another thing doing it in Sicily!"

The critics, on the other hand, were nearly unanimous in their praise. Kevin Kelly, covering the Harvard opening, called *The Serpent* "a lovely and significant piece of work." Walter Kerr, in his first *New York Times* review of the piece, wrote, "Of all the work now being done in this vein, the Open Theater's seems to be plainly the best . . . If you are at all interested in the theater's latest attempt to remake itself, this is the company to watch." The following year, he recalled, "Months after seeing [*The Serpent*] I find myself continually reverting to its bold ambiguities . . . *The Serpent* starts the mind off on tangents that keep extending themselves." And in Kerr's farewell article at his retirement fifteen years later, *The Serpent* was one of three examples he mentioned of unexpected treasures he had found as a reviewer. Kerr's *Times* colleague, Mel Gussow, wrote of the show, "It is amazing that the evening is so short . . . because it is filled with so much imagination, theatricality, and perception." Catherine Hughes gave *The Serpent* only slightly qualified praise in *Plays and Players:* "Although there are moments when invention wanes and any number where the scenes seem overly protracted, *The Serpent* has greater sustained impact, more arresting images, than any other recent example of experimental theater I can recall." And the *Village Voice* presented the Open Theater with an Obie award for *The Serpent*, "for outstanding achievement in the off-Broadway theater."

5 The growth of ensemble playwriting

Chaikin did not turn the Bible workshop's experience into a formula for creating new plays. In fact, his method since *The Serpent* has been different for each piece, with variations generated by the themes, the participants, and the work conditions. Still, in the course of creating a dozen plays with an ensemble, he has evolved some general patterns.

The thematic center has always been provided at the outset by Chaikin. He has chosen his ensembles in part according to his sense of who would be fired by the subject he wished to explore. With the provisional territory of an investigation marked off, the group has begun to "live with it, not only by talking about it but by improvising on it, by doing things on it." They must, Chaikin says, become "obsessed" with and "possess[ed]" by it; then, before long, "you find either that the theme no longer has interest, that it only had a short interest for that time and it's finished, or else that it has a kind of enduring interest." The company has had to remain open enough to allow the focus to shift, as the *Bible* project's did, and even to drop a subject that is not working out: Chaikin did abandon his first post-*Serpent* attempt at ensemble creation after several months of work.

During the early stages, each exploration has drawn on a variety of resources, including readings, discussions, and outside speakers. Usually, playwrights have contributed texts, although the writer rarely has been the central force in the piece, but rather someone invited, in Sklar's words, "to hang around and maybe put out material the way other people put out material in other forms." The core of the investigation, though, even at the beginning, has always been in Chaikin's suggestions and performers' improvisations. Roles have been fluid: Actors might bring in texts; writers, ideas for stage images; musicians, notions about possible characters or directions in which to expand the subject.

On one level, the investigations have been wide open at this point. Tina Shepard, who has worked on most of Chaikin's ensemble pieces, explains:

Chaikin (with actress JoAnn Schmidman) in an Open Theater workshop, 1973. Photograph by Mary Ellen Mark/Archive.

In the beginning you have a lot of time and you use that time to spread out from the opening idea, from sort of the first kernel of the idea and to find all of the ideas that are related to that sort of central place, and all of the different directions that you can take off in from there and all of the different images that have to do with it, with each person in the company.

In fact, she says, "We don't necessarily commit ourselves to work on things that relate to the piece; it's just bringing up, at this point, anything that maybe somebody else will connect with, or everybody else."

Naturally, each developing work has reflected the lives and feelings of the people creating it – sometimes very directly. For example, strains between some of the men and women in the company during the creation of *The Mutation Show* edged that investigation toward a concern with dominance relationships, and probably underlay several specific images, including a wedding ceremony. The imminent end of the Open Theater inclined the *Nightwalk* workshop improvisations toward expressions of lostness and quest; one performer's added sense of abandonment and rage after her mother's death, aggravated by her feeling of being left out in the workshop, injected a particular sting – and, in fact, showed up as a temper tantrum in the finished piece.

Still, all the way through the process, Chaikin has always been seeding, priming, selecting, directing, and shaping *his* play. The work has never been a chance potpourri of company members' most accessible emotions. Sklar explains:

I don't believe it was ever about the randomness of someone having been angry on a given day. There's always someone angry; there's always someone suffering; there's always someone full of joy that they're hiding because the sufferers dominate. And it's the nature of the given work that a director goes over to someone and whispers, "Would you go over there and spill the beans?" – whichever one of those dynamics the director is choosing to tap . . . There is always a number of dynamics available, and the sculptor is making certain kinds of choices.

Gradually, for each play, the emphasis has shifted from generating new material to pulling the work into a coherent piece. From the performers' point of view, this has largely been a question of editing:

As you approach the deadline, you sense that you have less time and that you . . . can't do just anything anymore. You have to start . . . weeding out, start cutting away and selecting the images that have most resonance; or condensing things. So it's a process of first exploding out and then drawing back in again toward the center.

In fact, most of this shaping has been done outside the workshops. Chaikin has met with his dramaturge or assistant director and, sometimes, with a writer or actor. They have discussed general directions, as well as specific cuts and juxtapositions, and have devised provisional structures that have been tried, then altered or scrapped. Usually, this kind of crafting has continued well after the start of public performances.

As a general outline of a creative method has evolved, so has a pattern of difficulties. Chaikin's work groups have been as prone as any to personal tensions – a more serious problem here than in some other types of joint effort, since his process draws so directly on participants' feelings. An Open Theater actor once described it as having "all the friction and sometimes the bitterness of a close family." People in that company and the Winter Project have sometimes described certain colleagues as show-offs or prima donnas, have talked about being annoyed by associates who were too pushy or immature. Often, relations between new and veteran members have been strained owing to insecurities on both sides. One of the fledglings in the *Serpent* workshop – just "graduated" from Lee Worley's beginners' group – later recalled that "the new members . . . felt inhibited by the older members who they thought looked down on their work," while "the old members . . . felt they were being pushed out, that their experience was not appreciated." A performer joining the Winter Project after several years away from Chaikin's workshops expressed worry that someone else might have usurped a formerly secure position of closeness to Chaikin. Chaikin has been aware of and disturbed by these pecking orders, but, in fact, his obviously greater ease in dealing with long-term colleagues has often exacerbated the problem.

Some tensions have come very specifically from the nature of ensemble playwriting. People have found themselves in the awkward position of creating – not merely interpreting – a work over which they did not really have artistic autonomy. Actors, for example, have sometimes had to generate material for a play whose tone and thrust was not clear to them. One performer noted, a few weeks into the workshop on *Nightwalk:*

It's a fog, a huge fog that I'm squinting into trying to find some familiar form to join in with. Joe seems to have the clearest picture because he can say yes this, not that . . . But I don't feel I'm creating a thing in which I'm consciously going about to say what I want to say. I feel like a blind person trying to learn a dance. It's hard for me to come up with ideas. It's too big for me to grasp. I can chew on my little corner but I can't see the whole thing.*

Often Chaikin has pursued a direction that has seemed fruitless, but in which he sensed a seed of something; and while workshop members may have had no idea what he saw there, it has been up to them to realize the potential in the image. The actors have had to remain open and creative during periods when the work has felt dry. The person just quoted wrote at a difficult point during the building of *Nightwalk*, "I don't feel us as a group saying to each other, 'Oh, this is great,' and having things popping out of us right and left. It feels like some people are waiting around for someone to tell them what to do."

The pressure to produce good ideas has been all the greater because roles in the final pieces have depended on what performers came up with in the workshops. In contrast to the traditional re-

---

*Two weeks later, the same person noted, "The fog began to clear a little," and two weeks after that, "The work seems to be on a solid footing now. We only have to proceed in a logical way – forward and it will come together."

The Open Theater *Nightwalk* workshop, New York, 1973. Photograph by Inge Morath/Magnum.

hearsal situation, where such issues would be settled before the first meeting, in these ensemble creations, what and how much each performer would do on stage remained painful questions through most of the work process. Chaikin recalls the bitterness in the *Serpent* company when, preparing for performances, he began to weed out various sections and to assign roles to specific people:

Everybody played every part for a while. One day Shami would do Eve; another day Cynthia would do Eve; or Joyce would do Eve. And then the point came to take an Eve, and when I did that, it was mayhem. Several women in the company were irate, just furious, because there was this absolute democratic thing that we had been doing up until that point. There was terrific unhappiness . . . It was very banal, one of the things people don't talk about.

He cautioned the actors that some decisions could not be "fair" because they were "not based on democratic principles" but on artistic needs. Still, feelings of discontent and even betrayal persisted in the Open Theater right through *Nightwalk*. And when he was preparing *Re-Arrangements*, Chaikin actually retained a scene that he felt was not working well, rather than face the distress that cutting it would cause.

Another problem for the actors has been the lack of any element – such as a script – from which they have *ever* had critical distance. They sometimes have felt desperately unsure about the quality of the work. Because structure generally has been the last part to develop, the pieces have often felt incoherent just days before performances were to begin. And the actors have been triply vulnerable, on the line not only as performers but also as playwrights and, because the work has been so personal, as people. Predictably, the terror was strongest and most disruptive with *The Serpent:* On the day of the Rome premiere, one performer exploded that the piece was "shit" and "a hoax," then took Chaikin's response that she should not perform if she felt that way as a request to leave, and collapsed in tears. Insecurities lessened with succeeding shows, but they did not disappear.

Playwrights have suffered similar problems from the need to be creative within someone else's framework. Each has handled the collaborative process differently: Some have participated actively in the group or observed sessions; others have just communicated with Chaikin about scenes or speeches that might be useful, in some cases contributing new or preexisting texts before workshops began. But all, one way or another, have faced the problem that van Itallie described as "two primary creators trying to squeeze into the same space," a situation that, he said, was "mighty uncomfortable" at times. Susan Yankowitz, for example, found her involvement on *Terminal* "as much a frustration as a challenge":

If Joe or the actor who was to perform a speech wasn't satisfied with it, the speech had to be rewritten. I could argue or defend my work, but ultimately artistic control was not in my hands . . . I found it difficult to write without having a sense of the whole; and yet the discovery of the whole was the process which occasioned the writing.

Since none of *Nightwalk's* several authors was central to the shaping of the piece, they found themselves working with little sense of the complete play. Sam Shepard, sending in material from London, wrote to Chaikin at one point that he was "vague about the real direction of the piece," and that his "main stumbling block" was "how to find a space for myself for adjusting to a way of collaboration."

The playwrights' problems have been complicated by their tenuous position in the groups. In the early Open Theater especially, actors often resented having free workshop exploration hemmed in by writers. To some extent, Chaikin feels, this tension was inherent in the ensemble's methods:

When you work improvisationally a lot, the actors . . . make great discoveries, and they see each other opening out and opening out and discovering parts of themselves that had no expression before. And then a writer comes in and restricts that expression and says, "Look, say this or do this – don't do anything under the sun" . . . And they say, "you're straitjacketing me, who needs you, it was just going very beautifully before you stepped into it."

Chaikin implored the Open Theater to accept its playwrights more fully in the work process: "Unless the writer, too, has an opportunity to experiment, fuck up, go up dead ends thinking that's the way, indulge in personal hangups before being able to break from [them], and most important to have a real participation and dialogue with everybody else concerning the work – it can't work out."

But the writers' position in the Open Theater remained, in Yankowitz's words, "ambiguous and insecure" – in an awkward middle ground where one was "neither an integral part of the group nor an independent outsider providing a finished script." The playwrights, she says, were "made to feel that they're only allowed to go this far and not that far, and that it's an intrusion if they step out of place." While Chaikin originally intended the Winter Project to have writers as full, active members, in fact none ever became a long-term or central participant.

A source of deep resentment in the collaborations has been the question of credit and rights. During workshops ideas and images have interwoven, overlapped, and inspired one another so that it has been impossible, often, to say who created what. "Someone would bring something in," Chaikin says, "and you'd discard it, but in discarding it it suggests something else, and you say, 'Why don't we try this?' You could not have come to that without the other idea." Group creativity has depended on the lack of authorship egos:

I've always found that when one gets very involved in whose idea it is, there's a pressure in the rehearsal situation and in the innovation itself. I think people are very innovative in a charged atmosphere. People just sort of dream up the most extraordinary things. But if, in fact, there's a diploma attached to certain terrific ideas, then the dreaming itself is reduced. You quote yourself before you've said it, which already destroys the way in which it can be transmitted to other people as anything except: "I have an idea," which precedes the idea and which in a way informs the version of it.

In fact, the workshop atmosphere usually has been generous, and people have not often become involved in claiming ownership of their contributions.

Still, ensemble members often have felt undercredited. This has come partly from misunderstandings about one another's participation. In the early years especially, there were astonishingly different perceptions about what the performers, writers, and directors actually had done. One actor, for example, claimed that "most words in these pieces came from improvisation, and then the writers would go home and polish them." A playwright working with the company said, on the other hand, that it was "yet to be seen whether ensemble creating is not just an illusion needed by the actors for the moment in order to bolster their commitment to the piece." Meanwhile, one of Chaikin's directing associates said, "What goes on between the directors, the kind of decision making, the kind of choice making, the shaping of a work as it's going on, is enormous, and is not really communicated to the actors."

The question of creative contributions has been further complicated by the elusive nature of Chaikin's role. Everyone concerned has recognized Chaikin as the center of the process, the person without whom nothing would happen, and who steers and inspires all aspects of the work. As a result, ensemble members often have credited him with what others had done.

In any case, these unstated assumptions exploded when van Itallie wound up with exclusive rights to *The Serpent*. The published script listed him first as author, and the only recognition, for royalty purposes, of the Open Theater's contribution was that it retained the right to perform the play without paying him. Many of the actors felt angry and betrayed, and several were enraged. After this, the Open Theater was more judicious about credit and finances; the actors who were involved in *Terminal*, for example, are still entitled to some tiny royalties when it is performed. But clarifying legalities has not prevented writers and actors from feeling that their contributions have gone unrecognized. One performer, for example, said:

All of the things I did in *Terminal*, I came in with myself. That's why I always had a resentment of the writers. I would see a text a few years later where it says, such and such a piece by so and so, and the actors aren't even mentioned!

Look at *The Mutation Show* as an example. It did not have a writer. I resented the fact that those writers were listed and given credit on the program. Because they didn't do anything. I'm not going to deny them the credit for being present in the room as we worked for a certain period of time. But as far as any contribution is concerned, yes, I resent any significant mention of that.

Writers, on the other hand, have felt that *their* work has not been duly credited. Yankowitz complained at one point:

My name does not appear on ads, and often, not in reviews. It is irritating and amusing to be the author of an "authorless" piece. I'm trying to find in myself the proper balance between detachment and the need for recognition. I don't want to succumb to the demands of my ego for that transient, slightly contemptible gratification. But then again, why should recognition be denied in the service of some illusion that the Open Theater, without its writers, is a totally self-sufficient artistic unit? For certainly, it is not.

Ultimately, the only way that Chaikin has avoided playwright–ensemble tensions has been by eliminating either the playwright or the ensemble. He has gone the first of these routes more and more often, either accidentally (when writers did not work out) or intentionally; *The Mutation Show* and the Winter Project's pieces were created without the real participation of a playwright. The post–Open Theater pieces he has made with Sam Shepard, on the other hand, have been intimate collaborations, with only the two of them (or, in one case, additional musicians) sharing the functions of performer, director, writer, and composer.

THE MUTATION SHOW: PLAYWRITING WITHOUT A PLAYWRIGHT

In October 1970 Chaikin's restructured, smaller Open Theater ensemble* began work on a new piece, on the theme of change. At first, they thought a focus might be the process of learning, and they looked for images of people actively shaping the direction of their lives. By spring, though, Chaikin was describing the exploration as "dealing with human mutation, with ourselves as mutations, contemplating the human form we haven't taken, on the experience of being torn away from ourselves." A major motif became "multiple selves" – how everyone contains various selves, how people often cannot recognize who they have become because of "the legitimacy of the past," how individuals are "wrenched out of their self-hood."

It was risky, thrilling work. It involved, Chaikin said, "bring[ing] the group to acute anxiety, vertigo, a disequilibrium, a confrontation with a kind of crisis." And it had a special personal importance for him, since he was feeling the need to promote change in his own life and work, to prevent the Open Theater's success from causing its (and his) ossification. He told an interviewer a short time later:

I do think there are times in one's life when you should give up a lot of your life and live with whatever's left . . . that if one holds on – let's say you have

*The company, after a few initial weeks of comings and goings, consisted of Raymond Barry, Shami Chaikin, Tom Lillard, JoAnn Schmidman, Tina Shepard, and Paul Zimet.

a terrific vacuum cleaner or a great car – things tend to possess one, and so do nonmaterial things.

W. E. R. LaFarge was writer in residence from October 1970 until June 1971, and John Stoltenberg, the Open Theater's administrative director, was also its writer during the following season. Both attended workshops and attempted to provide material, but neither found a way to contribute usefully to the work. Chaikin decided, however, not to ask in another playwright. He felt that the ensemble should not "go through" writers this time as it had in the past, and he was wary of bringing someone new into a project that was already well under way. Instead, he and the ensemble would rely on their own resources, with Roberta Sklar, the codirector of the piece, concentrating as before on matters of language and structure.

Chaikin felt, though, that the work was weakened by its lack of a participating writer, and as late as the final preparations for an audience, he considered trying to get a new playwright, though he decided against it. Reworking the piece after several months of performances, the ensemble again talked about bringing in a writer. Again, they concluded that it was simply, and unfortunately, too late.

On one level, the work process was not significantly different for *The Mutation Show* than for Chaikin's earlier plays. Speeches were developed from improvisations, workshop discussions, and provisional texts brought in by actors or directors. Chaikin and Sklar continually edited as they went along.

Still, the relative nonverbalness of the final *Mutation Show* resulted partly from its lack of a playwright: The company had more facility creating nontextual material than dialogue or speeches. And there was no one giving the kind of exclusive, skilled attention to words and dramaturgy that writers previously had given.

Ultimately, in fact, not having a playwright did cause changes both in the process of developing *The Mutation Show* and in the product. The Open Theater's writers, however closely involved in the workshops, had provided an alternative perspective. Their ideas had often been the foil or even the resistance that helped to balance and sharpen Chaikin's own. Sometimes, having a bit more critical detachment, they had been able to see latent structures and directions in half-formed material. Here, as in nearly all of Chaikin's subsequent work, there was no comparably strong second vision playing against Chaikin's. And in this case, the subject was especially hard to control, since it offered no particular story line and, indeed, had as a theme things-that-change-and-cannot-be-pinned-down. Chaikin followed his instincts about what the piece seemed to encompass, but the work did not find its real shape and tone until after months of performances.

One major source of material was storytelling. Company members told stories that they felt somehow related to the theme of change or that, for whatever reason, they wanted to tell the group. The ones that struck a chord were repeated and distilled into "emblems" or "phrases." The ensemble generated additional material through "interviews" of potential characters.

They also, as before, drew on outside speakers and published writings. Joseph Campbell talked with them about ceremonies that mark human change: puberty rites, naming children, and so forth. Company members read *Soledad Brother: The Prison Letters of George Jackson*, Richard Wright's *Black Boy*, and David Cooper's *The Death of the Family*, as well as works by Freud and Laing on learning and the stages of maturity. This was the period, too, of the Open Theater's excommunication study, and some of the research on Catholic and Jewish rituals was brought into the project.

But the core of the investigation, as always, was theatrical, an exploration through stage action. One early exercise involved showing the different facets within a single person. The company members drew up a list of selves that they all contained: the "acceptable self," the "narcissistic self," the "no-bullshit self," the "mask," the "human animal," the specifically "male or female self," the "myself in the world self." Then, as Chaikin called out an item from the list, the actors tried to express that part of their personalities.

This work led to exploring how identities can freeze, how limited personas gain special legitimacy. One factor, the company felt, was naming: Labeling a thing often alters and limits it. (At one point, there was a question in the piece, "If you saw something which had no name, would you recognize it?") But the biggest factor is simply the accumulated effects of living: A person's habits gradually harden into a protective but inhibiting shell. A taxi driver, folding his body into a car seat for eight hours a day, eventually creates the shape of his body; people similarly mold and limit themselves in nonphysical ways.

The actors improvised dozens of "mutants," freaks stuck in a single defining self. Although these characters did not speak, the actors, Chaikin, and Sklar wrote short descriptions of them, which were presented by an announcer. By performance time, there was a gallery of five grotesques. "The bird lady," sporting a silver lamé bikini and a pastel feather in her hair, primped, cooed, and fluttered about. "The man who smiles" was presented as one who "would have no face" without his constant, ear-to-ear grin. "The man who hits himself," clouting himself into a stupor, was someone who "has had the same nightmare for 35 years." "The thinker," with a thinking-cap beret and a self-satisfied glow at the wonder of her thoughts, was one who "thinks she thinks, but she doesn't know what it is that she thinks." (This character came from a story about *showing* how well you do whatever it is that you are doing.) Last came "the petrified man": "He's always under attack. Each day he moves less and talks less."

Chaikin wanted to parallel these stunted personalities with social and political images. His notion for "History on Trial" was that only partial truths get recorded, and our sense of the world is shaped by this distorted, truncated picture. But the idea never found a theatrical, as opposed to intellectual, life, and was dropped. Chaikin also developed a "healer" scene in connection with the mutants: Each freak was cured by dancing with and thereby transferring the affliction to a healer. But, though Chaikin loved the theatricality of that segment, and, in fact, revived it during the preparation of later ensemble pieces, it seemed extraneous to the concerns of this work and was cut.

Chaikin thought that one focus might be "the slaughtered child, or slaughtered beast inside oneself," and during the summer preceding the workshop he asked the actors to read material on wild and isolated children. The company was particularly struck by the case of the wolf-girl Kamala, from J. A. L. Singh and Robert M. Zingg's *Wolf-Children and Feral Man*. They made extensive notes about the child's behavior living among the wolves, the rescue of Kamala and her sister, Amala, by missionaries, and her subsequent development.

Various actors tried playing the animal girl. Some exercises explored her "wolf breathing," trying to distinguish it from "civilized" breathing and use it to tune into a less self-conscious way of experiencing the world. A series of improvisations depicted Kamala at various stages. They began when she was five, living among the wolves; missionaries came to take the children from their cave (constructed of mats), frightened the animals with the sound of castanets, collapsed the cave, and scattered the wolf family. The story resumed four years later, when Kamala was in an orphanage but still persisting in wolf ways, chasing chickens and trying to play like a cub with puppies and children. Finally, Kamala at fifteen was walking on two feet, eating like a human, singing hymns, and collecting eggs from the chickens.

At one point, the group assigned numbers to the scenes and ran the scenario forward, backward, and a-sequentially, performing whatever action corresponded to the number called. This work was dropped, though, because it related more to *The Serpent*'s Kennedy–King segment and the "Agamemnon" exercises that Chaikin was doing at the time than to the mutations investigation.

Some of the Kamala exploration focused on seeing and learning things for the first time:

You don't know what sound is, you don't hear it . . . You know what breathing is. Someone wants you to make a sound – you don't know what that is – find out how to do what he wants.

You're in a low cage, you want to get out. You know you did one thing before that was right – find out how to "tell" that person that you want to get out.

The point was to discover the concept and the skill of communicating through sounds.

The company also read about isolated children, including a little girl named Anna, who lived alone in an attic for more than five years, and a "pig boy" who kept swine and was shut up with them at night. They were most struck, though, with the case of Caspar Hauser, a German child who was kept for years in an attic too low for him to stand up in, whose sole companions were toy horses, and who could speak only one sentence.*

All of the actors tried playing Caspar, seeking in themselves "the part that is alone, unemerged, the vulnerable naive part," and looking at "the mutated, critical part" through those eyes. They attempted to describe things as Caspar would see them: a crowded beach, a dog, a cockroach, a cigarette, a refrigerator. They examined his connection to language, using his one sentence to express various needs and impulses. And they did their "My House Is Burning" exercise – trying to communicate the full meaning of a statement through its sounds – using Caspar's words.

Some improvisations explored Caspar in his attic feeding bread and water to the toy horses. Others showed him discovering the outside world: seeing people and trying to identify them, learning how to walk, hearing a steeple bell, trying to ask questions, learning

---

*The group read Anseln von Feuerbacks's account of Caspar in the Singh and Zingg volume. They did not know Handke's play at the time.

something new and becoming rigid with amazement. The group was particularly intrigued by accounts of Caspar's catatonic reaction to new experiences. They developed an exercise in which the boy, being taught to walk, suddenly looked up and for the first time saw the sky filled with stars; the actors tried to find physical expressions of astonishment so great that it was almost unendurable. Expanding then from the literal story of Caspar Hauser, the ensemble looked for general images of isolation, limitation, and overprotection. Chaikin set up various improvisations with characters inside or emerging from a crate, "Caspars" trapped in, torn from, or breaking out of their terrible, comforting insulation.

Eventually – influenced, again, partly by their Chinese theater model – the company distilled the Kamala and Caspar scenarios into a few key moments. First, the wolf-child was snatched from her pack by hunters. The scene began with an announcement:

> The Animal Girl
> She was raised with animals.
> She ate and drank and slept with an animal pack.
> One day she was torn from her cave, and carried away, and made civilized.

As Kamala, Amala, and the mother wolf sat calmly breathing, the hunters played a brief call on recorders, accompanied from outside the scene by drums and a tambourine. The "wolves" froze, began to pant in fear, then froze again. Now, in panic, the two wolf-children ran in opposite directions. After several unsuccessful lunges at Kamala, her hunter changed his tactics, crouching nearby and copying her breathing. Seduced into trusting this "wolf," Kamala stepped into his noose. As Amala was roped also, the near silence of breathing turned into a cacophony of Amala's howls and percussion instruments. An announcer chanted:

> We will name her.
> We will straighten her bones.
> We will give her words.
> We will caress her.
> . . . .
> We will dress her.
> We will train her.
> We will name her.
> We will name her.
> We will name her.

Like much of the verbal material in *The Mutation Show*, the chant's dozen lines were culled from several pages of material (in this case,

A hunter (Tom Lillard) pretends to be a wolf in order to capture the wolf-girl (Tina Shepard). St. Clement's Church, New York, 1973. Photograph by Mary Ellen Mark/Archive.

the combined product of workshop brainstorming and various company members' provisional texts), including "We will bind her tongue; we will invade her; we will stuff her; we will channel her rivers; we will flatten her mountains; we will celebrate her; we will decorate her." As Chaikin and Sklar honed and formalized the text, they crafted it not only to the developing themes of the work but also to the particular dynamics – somewhere between a rally-cry and a litany – that the announcer had brought to it in improvisations.

The second Kamala scene was the animal-girl being taught to walk. Totally bewildered, she was raised upright, given shoes, and manipulated step by step, with one foot placed out front, then the other. Left on her own after a bit, she hobbled in her shoes to the front of the stage and stood for several moments, breathing like a wolf and looking out at the audience. The chant resumed: "We will name her, / We will caress her, / We will name her." Apart from these two scenes, Kamala appeared in *The Mutation Show* only in brief images, mostly reprises of the capture and the walking lesson.

Kamala is roped. St. Clement's Church, New York, 1973. Photograph by Mary Ellen Mark/Archive:

Caspar's two scenes showed him coming out of a three-foot cube. For the first segment, two actors brought on the crate and one stepped inside. The announcer introduced the action, with a speech largely drafted by the writers and then edited by Chaikin and Sklar:

> The Boy in the Box.
> He lived alone in his box all his days.
> He never saw distance, light, the night sky, or another person.
> One day he was torn from his box and carried to a hill where he
>   was left.

To the sound of a "lion's roar," the actor outside opened the crate and began to yank at arms and legs; finally he upended the bin, and the terror-stricken Caspar tumbled out and huddled on the ground. Caspar was lifted onto his keeper's back, and they undertook a long (mimed) journey over changing, difficult terrain. After first

"The boy in the box" (Paul Zimet) is
thrown out of his safe isolation. Photographer unknown.

clinging desperately, the boy soon began to look around, straining
to see as far to each side as he could, sometimes moving his upper
body out nearly parallel to the ground. Caspar's breathing was the
same as the wolf breathing; and twice he passed out from astonishment. Eventually, he began trying to communicate with his carrier
by breathing sharply – an embryonic attempt at speech, which came
from Kamala improvisations. Finally, the keeper tried to set his load
down, prying loose the grasping arms and legs, and tearing the
again-terrified boy off his back. Caspar was left sitting on the floor,
squeaking and shaking in fright.

  The second Caspar segment grew partly from actor Ray Barry's
interest in the radical Black Panther leader, George Jackson. The
Caspar box seemed to him to express Jackson's experience of solitary
confinement. On one hand it was an excruciating isolation; but, at
the same time, being in that box, in jail, made it possible for Jackson
to develop beyond the influence of his fearful, protective, and au-

Caspar and his keeper (Raymond Barry), both
in wonder, during their journey. St. Clement's
Church, New York, 1973. Photograph by Mary
Ellen Mark/Archive.

thoritarian mother. Barry devised a scene in which he explained
from inside a crate why he would not come out: The only alternative
to his cage was a kind of selling out, and his loss of freedom actually
facilitated a larger independence.

Over several weeks, this segment became totally transformed. Its specifically political facets were dropped, and it became part of the Caspar scenario. The workshop had once discussed what Caspar might do with his bodily excretions, since they were probably the only objects he had apart from his toy horses. Barry started working on this question with his Jackson/box improvisations.

This study became connected, then, to another part of the exploration, an investigation of breaking: Breaking out of things and just breaking things both seemed to be related to the theme of change. The company found a number of images that they liked, including cracking an egg on the stage and bringing a paper-filled circus hoop down on an actor's head. Kamala's attempts to escape the hunter were connected to this work on breaking away. And Barry's Caspar image became tied to it as well: Now, instead of refusing to leave his box, he crashed his way out in a kind of violent birth.

The final version of the scene began with Barry inside the crate, bashing against its sides and top. His clamor was amplified by cymbals, whistles, castanets, a washboard, and a "lion's roar." Meanwhile, several other images occurred around the playing space: the egg- and hoop-breaking gags; the beginnings of Kamala's walking scene. Finally, the box-boy burst out, smeared head to foot with strawberry preserves, which suggested gore, body juices, and excrement. Kneeling, groping blindly outward, he described his experience.

This was the most developed text in the play. It recounted being alone in the box with just body fluids, then being outside for the first time seeing light, people, and nature; the world was "another box the top was blue the bottom was many colors it had many colors moving and turning." Changed by the experience and so no longer the isolated, amazed person he once was, the character concluded, "I don't know if this happened to me or to someone else but I know it happened."

Like the segment it climaxed, the speech came from a number of sources. Parts of it were from improvisations in which Barry explored both Chaikin's notion of seeing for the first time and the idea of Caspar playing with his excretions. Sklar noted:

The fluids and the shit were part of his toys. There were poles on each side with rough stuff around it. They had big bushes at the top. And they were green. I grabbed some. They couldn't get away fast enough. It felt good against my face. Later they put me in a white room with white sheets and white people, but my fluids were dirty.

The line "[I] saw stars moving across the light in front" grew from work on Caspar seeing stars for the first time, and from George

After breaking out from the box, the boy (Raymond Barry) tells his story. St. Clement's Church, New York, 1973. Photograph by Mary Ellen Mark/ Archive.

Jackson's statement that he had not seen the night sky in ten years. Other parts of the speech, including its ending, were developed out of "internal monologue" improvisations that the group had done, not specifically in connection with Caspar.

The work on breaking moved in two directions, one more fruitful than the other. Chaikin hoped to find political images for breaking out, or violent change, and the group worked briefly on bits they called "Burying the Rulers" and "Firing Squad." In the first, a figure that stood for the authorities was torn from its seat of power. In the second, an actress recalls, "We used to stand up in a line and Joe would say 'bang' or hit something, and we would all fall down dead. I wonder why. I don't know why. We did it a couple of times and then we didn't do it again."

The more rewarding exploration, a look at things that turn against people and trip them up, developed into slapstick gags. In addition to the egg and hoop acts, the group worked up pieces not specifically connected to breaking: An actress kept accidentally spilling cups of water; someone mopping up kept getting his feet caught in the bucket (by performance, this routine had been reduced to cleaning up the mess that others were making); a person going out turned to say "See you," and smashed into the door, which opened the wrong way; a group did a little soft-shoe number twice, finishing each time with a grand hand-gesture of presenting some attraction – and twice nothing happened; an actress tried to eat strawberry preserves with a spoon and repeatedly missed her mouth; one person zoomed across the stage on a little wheeled cart, followed by another actor who splatted onto his chest.

Along with the extreme images of Caspar, Kamala, and the mutants, the workshop explored human change on more universal levels. They discussed the moments of insight that mark and help create growth in one's life. Somebody mentioned, for example, the moment in *Black Boy* when Wright realized it was his mother's terror of whites that made her slap him when he suggested fighting back. Taking off from Campbell's talks, they considered the social rites connected with points of change – birth, naming, puberty, marriage, the onset of old age, and death. They decided to work up a section depicting rituals that had shaped their own lives. Initial improvisations of a wedding ceremony took off so well that they did not even look for other images.

Exploring marriage traditions brought the workshop into very personal, volatile territory. It touched on kinds of change that were particularly alive right then for the ensemble. Several members of the group had become keenly involved with the women's movement's reexamination of female–male relationships. And, in fact, interactions between the women and men in the group were under stress: A marriage between two actors was in the process of ending, and there was growing strain in Chaikin and Sklar's collaboration.

In any case, the group developed a wedding ceremony that they saw as parallel, in part, to their Caspar scenes: A woman was passed from one kind of dubious protection to another. The scene began with a brief ceremony in which Tina Shepard, as the befuddled bride, was passed from Paul Zimet, the father, to Tom Lillard, the new husband. They tried, Shepard explains, to zero in on the precise moment of the change: "Paul and I walked down and then Tom came. And then at the point of taking the real step, we stopped and we dropped it and went back. And then Paul and I went down and Tom came again. Then we again froze on the step and started teetering on it." Ellen Maddow's musical accompaniment underscored the crisis. Finally, she blew a kind of siren; "the sound broke it, and the whole thing split apart."

The bridal pair was followed down the aisle by a bizarre assortment of couples. These were mostly images distilled from a gallery of families that the company had developed to parallel the gallery of mutants but that was not finally used in the piece. Now these odd pairs of characters, each with its action reduced to a "phrase," changed the wedding ceremony into kind of a parade. First came "the twitchers," a happy couple with a persistent tick that they did not acknowledge. They were followed by "amphetamine freaks," with huge grins across their faces. Next were the wolf-girl, on all fours, and the hunter, with his hand on her head. After them a totally disoriented bride came twirling down the aisle with her groom trying to steady her, to fix her in place. Then an "out of synch" couple who could not manage to get their walking coordinated contrasted with the contented-looking homosexuals who followed them holding hands. Those two men, in turn, preceded "the screamers," who carped and scolded their way down the path. The next pair was a woman with a bicycle horn between her legs, and a man who kept blowing the horn to her amazement and embarrassment. And the final couple was a kind of mutant "perfect" couple: "the bird lady" and "the man who smiles."

While the last characters were coming down the aisle, Maddow began playing "The Anniversary Waltz" on her accordion; and the procession transformed into an elaborate "Wedding Dance." The actors did a basic waltz step with a few variations and jammed physically on the music and the movement. They also left the dance rhythm periodically to move into and out of brief images from the play and sight gags.

Meanwhile, Maddow announced the dancing partners, a list basically constructed by Chaikin. She began, "The bride is now dancing with the groom" and "the groom is now dancing with the mother of the bride." But before long she was pairing the mother of the bride with the mayor, and the bride with the "secretary of affairs." Soon it became the president waltzing with his assassin, the cow dancing with the butcher, and the judges waltzing with each other. By the end of the wedding, Maddow was announcing: "The trees are now dancing with the wind. / The earth is now dancing with the stars." The actors all moved into images from the show, and the dance ended with a blackout.

In addition to these segments *about* kinds of change, the workshop developed a network of mutations involving the theater event itself: They established conventions, then transformed and redefined them; they took motifs from one section and planted them in other parts, either changed in form or altered by the new contexts.

Most props in the piece had their identities totally reshaped during the course of the play. For example, Barry's Caspar/box segment defined strawberry preserves as gore and excrement; then, for the eating gag, it was transformed (uneasily) back into food. A rope used to capture the wolf-girl reappeared in another section as equipment for masturbating.

The playing space was changed, by the addition of broken eggs and spilled water, from a timeless theatrical milieu, where the likes of Caspar and Kamala took form, to a messy floor, where a group of stalwart performers would have to avoid pools of muck; then, after leaving enough time for an audience to forget the slime on the floor and again accept the space as a theatrical environment, the actors began their housecleaning, mopping up and pushing eggshells under a rug. And once again the space was just a dirty floor.

The most striking of the show's mutations, though, was of the performers themselves. The workshop had decided early on to have a section in which actors presented real autobiographical data, in order to show the different selves they contained in addition to the performing self. At first, each actor was wheeled out in a box, and the person pushing the crate gave information. Then Chaikin decided to do the scene with photographs. He had long been fascinated by the way photographs freeze one image, which comes to define the person. In fact, he had thought the piece might include a series of characters paired with photographs that showed single, extreme aspects of their personalities. For example, Jack the Ripper, a meek-looking, balding man, would be juxtaposed with a portrait of him looking demonic and drooling blood. This idea was never worked out, but photographs came to be used in the biographical segment.

In the final version of "The Human Gallery," each actor held up a poster-size blowup of a former "self." Zimet's grade school picture

The "human gallery" faces the audience. St. Clement's Church, New York, 1973. Photograph by Mary Ellen Mark/Archive.

showed him wearing a white shirt and tie, with his hair neatly combed back and a sparkling innocence in his eyes; Shepard displayed her high school graduation portrait, complete with a wholesome 1950s Peter Pan collar and pageboy. Lillard used a military identification photo taken against height markings, Shami Chaikin an old publicity shot of herself as a nightclub singer, JoAnn Schmidman a nude baby picture, Maddow a snapshot of herself at perhaps age five, and Barry a portrait of himself as a late fifties' "Joe College."

As the six stood with their photographs, Maddow started giving basic physical data:

I am Ellen Maddow. I am 5'5ι tall. I have dark hair and dark eyes . . .
Tom Lillard has a barrel chest, slim hips, and sandy-colored hair.

Then she proceeded to bits of background information:

Ray Barry was employed as a gardener, a cook, a waiter, a busboy, a dishwasher, a longshoreman, a construction worker, an English teacher, a social worker, and a sculptor.
Tina Shepard's uncle John is a federal judge.
Tom Lillard's cousin Fred is a Ku Klux Klansman.
In the sixth grade Paul Zimet won the American Legion Citizenship Award.

Shepard's biography, an extremely detailed catalogue of family relationships, was inspired by a eulogy that she and Zimet had actually heard delivered at his grandmother's funeral:

This is Fanny Zimet
Beloved wife of David
Mother of Melvin and Shirley
Grandmother of John and Paul
Great-grandmother of Mark and Debbie
Sister of Rose and Flossie.

The list seemed to serve as both identification and a statement of credentials. The workshop incorporated the idea into the piece, using it for Shepard because she had a particularly complex family tree. The effect of the entire scene, finally, was to transform the actors from inhabitants of a stage world into human beings with parents and pasts, who had changed a great deal to become the people performing as the Open Theater.

Like *The Serpent* and *Terminal*, the new piece had a full complement of material before it had a structure or overall tone. But working without a playwright or dramaturge, the ensemble had a great deal of difficulty in crystallizing a shape for it.

During the first weeks, they had thought of the piece as a journey or quest. This format remained, even though the theme of change in order to achieve something or arrive somewhere was soon overshadowed by a sense of the inevitability and terror of change. The company marked a "journey path" on the floor with red tape going from up- to downstage center, and many early improvisations were performed as passages down this route.

Another structural model that the company had in mind – an outgrowth, actually, of the "interview" work – was an exhibition gallery. There would be a showing of the various characters, such as the wolf-girl, the "box-boy" Caspar, "the petrified man," "the bird lady," the "families," and the Open Theater actors. Shepard explains:

We were thinking that maybe it would be like a museum, and that there would be an exhibit here, and people could walk all around it and talk to it and ask it questions, and the character would speak or not. Whatever its condition was, it would respond in that way. We would each do the character that we were working on, one at a time, I think. And everybody else would come around and ask questions.

For a while, too, the box image seemed to provide a unifying motif. In addition to the Caspar scenes, the "Human Gallery" was done from boxes; and Schmidman worked on an improvisation of Kamala in a box.

Finally, though, none of these formats alone seemed able to hold the piece together. All three were kept in: "journeys" for Caspar being carried, Kamala's walking lesson, and the wedding parade; "galleries" for the mutants and the "humans" (the actors); and the box for the Caspar segments. In fact, the Open Theater's shaping of the material was minimal: The company simply ordered and interwove it. In contrast with *The Serpent*, which had the autopsy/surgery scene as a frame and within that the chronological order of Genesis, *Mutations*, as the work was called at this point, had a purely abstract, musical structure based on the development and counterpoint of motifs.

To pull together the themes of the piece and draw it to a close, the company worked up a section called "The Mutants Give Testimony." It was intended as a kind of bearing witness, a "declaration of the selves that you have been – different voices of past lives, which is also a metaphor for the levels of the self." The company considered making this like a Quaker meeting, or *Interview* from *America Hurrah*, with individual people emerging from and being reabsorbed into the crowd. They also thought of adapting the form of the curses section in *The Serpent*, with different actors being lifted to speak, then allowed to drop back onto their knees. And they experimented with "judgment" improvisations (a carryover from the end of *Terminal*), having people in a line talk before some kind of magistrate for an allotted time. Finally, for performance, the actors just sat on or stood by stools placed around the playing area and shifted the focus back and forth.

The content for this scene was developed improvisationally, drawing on all the work from the past months. Sometimes Chaikin passed around index cards with suggested "testimonies," sometimes the actors pulled things out themselves.

Much of the material that was finally used consisted of emblems from the play. There were a few nuggets from earlier speeches, such as "I don't know if this happened to me or to someone else." And there were reprises of nonverbal images: "the bird lady," Amala howling, "the thinker," "the man who smiles" (now running in place and trying, unsuccessfully, to break through his smile into speech). Maddow brought in musical motifs and rhythms from earlier sections.

Some of the testimonies came from readings or actors' stories that had not been used elsewhere in the piece. One person's account of a drug-related experience in which he felt alienated from his voice was compressed into two lines that someone else delivered: "I swear to tell the whole truth and nothing but –. This is not my voice." The phrase "What's happening? What's happening?" an emblem from another story, was used several times. An autobiographical tale that an actress had presented was first distilled to "I always had a woods near my house" and then, finally, was incorporated nonverbally into her testimony. Some material was also added that did not come from the *Mutations* investigation but seemed to help draw the play's themes together. One actor, for example, said, "What do you see when you look at me? What do you think I see when I look at you?" – a line from an old Open Theater exercise.

"The Mutants Give Testimony" dissolved into a section that the company called "The Winds." It was a jamming on the testimonies, the entire preceding piece, and whatever other energies happened to be in the room. It both recapitulated the themes of the play and suggested an alternate way of seeing. An actress explained:

> The piece was about people locked in patterns and people not locked in patterns. Our upbringing trains us to lock ourselves in and say, "This is me – and some days when I don't feel like it, then I'm not me." . . . What ["The Winds"] was about was that even though there were characters that were fixed, they'd pass through me, flow in, and I could take on this one and that one, and none of them are me, and they are all me. It was just this thing of different things blowing through.

Characters and conditions from earlier in the piece flashed through different people: An actress momentarily became "the petrified man"; someone else recapitulated the line "I don't know if this happened to me or to someone else"; various people became wolves for an instant.

At the end of the jamming, the actors sat breathing quietly with an awareness of the present space, moment, and audience. One reviewer described this close as "an ear-aching, pin-drop silence which stretched on and on as the audience savored the aftertaste."

Although *Mutations*, performed on a Mideast tour, was very well received, Chaikin was not satisfied with it, and when the Open Theater returned to New York, he decided to reopen and totally rework the piece. Only then did it find its final form. The journeys, galleries, and gags coalesced into a kind of carnival parade, and *Mutations* became the presentational, high-spirited *Mutation Show*.

One important change was the transformation of the narrator from a neutral announcer into a sideshow barker, herself a grotesque frozen into her role. This barker, sliding between speech and an odd guttural chant, presented the various attractions. She introduced the five calcified mutants, who came through a little curtain at the back of the journey path, walked to the front of the stage, and

The barker (Shami Chaikin) presents "the man who smiles" (Tom Lillard). Photograph by Hank Gans and Claude Furones.

retired back; then she announced "the boy in the box," "the animal-girl," and so forth. An apparently minor change, this new character helped to unify the play.

As *Mutations* metamorphosed into *The Mutation Show*, certain elements grew stronger and better integrated. The gags became part of the general carnival mode. The zany wedding procession and gallery of mutants now had a matrix that perfectly suited their tone. And two other parades were added, mostly recapitulating earlier moments in altered form. For example, an actress carried an actor in an odd, comic reprise of Caspar's journey. Kamala twice came down the path on which she had learned to walk, this time wearing gold, spike-heeled shoes (her first try was flawless, the second wobbly).

These processions also presented a few new images. In one, a man tried to move forward, as if reaching for something, and a woman kept pulling him back; then they reversed. There was also a festive musical parade, in which the actors, as themselves, came down the journey path playing assorted instruments.

One other important scene was added during the reworking: a prologue of "Rules for the Audience." The section grew, in part, from an early workshop discussion about rules, how they are handed down by families and social institutions, and how, often, there are rules against seeing the rules. The company drew up lists of unspoken regulations that are observed in various situations, including a theater event. This connected to questions very much in the theatrical air at the time about the role of spectators and actors at

A mutated reprise of Caspar's journey (Shami
Chaikin and Raymond Barry). St. Clement's
Church, New York, 1973. Photograph by Mary
Ellen Mark/Archive.

a performance (issues with which the environmentalists and early
post-modernists, such as Handke, also were grappling). When the
company thought of structuring the piece as a series of galleries, the
question of audience assumptions and behavior became practical as
well as theoretical; for an early open rehearsal, they drew up necessary instructions, telling spectators when to walk around and interview the attractions, when to take seats, and so forth. Since the
gallery-exhibition format was dropped and the first performances of

Mutations were to be for foreign audiences, many of whom might not understand English, the idea of announcing rules for the audience fell away. Then during the reworking, the notion was revived. The show got a new opening that mutated the whole theater event, changing and rechanging its nature.

In performance, when the audience was settled, an actress walked to the front of the playing space, paper in hand, and read a series of regulations. As she began her list, instructing the spectators that they were not permitted to smoke or take pictures, she seemed to be a house manager enforcing fire and union codes. When she continued, "No crinkling paper," her function became hazy, and by the next rule, "No firearms," it was clear that she was part of the show, that what was going on *was* the play. As she continued, then, giving instructions like "Make arrangements for sharing your armrests (or legroom)," "Try to avoid having sexual fantasies about the people in the play," and "Try to think up a comment during the play so you can have an opinion later," she produced an alienation effect. The performance was transformed again – this time from an abstract reality, that is, a play, into a literal, concrete event taking place in the real lives of the spectators and actors.

The Mutation Show's sets and costumes, by Bil Mikulewicz and Gwen Fabricant, respectively, were simple, frankly theatrical, and in keeping with the circus tone. Zimet, for example, sported trousers striped like raccoon tails, with a large, striped gusset in the crotch, striped suspenders, and a vest; Schmidman's costume was a slightly too large silver bikini over dark tights covered with pale fishnet hose; Shami Chaikin wore patchwork trousers made from brightly colored men's ties, topped by a fake shirt, tie, and vest combination held on by two strings around her bare back.

The set consisted of an eight-foot-square curtain upstage on a movable metal frame, strips of tape on the floor going forward from that curtain to outline the journey path, Caspar's cube, the stools for the testimonies, and a few little wheeled carts for the gags. But there were more props than the Open Theater had ever used before: ropes, strawberry preserves, an egg, a hoop, glasses of water, and so forth. This relative extravagance of objects, and the musical instruments, helped keep the show visually lively, despite its simplicity, and supported the carnival mood.

Critical response to the piece was very enthusiastic. The earliest review, of an open rehearsal, predicted that it "will be every bit as powerful as 'Terminal' and 'The Serpent.' " And *Mutations* was awarded first prize in the Belgrade International Theatre Festival (BITEF), where the company had performed during its return from the Mideast tour.

Back in New York, the reworked *Mutation Show* received unqualified praise from Mel Gussow of the *New York Times:*

As it stands, "The Mutation Show" is an important work of art, perhaps the group's finest achievement to date.

By saying that, I do not mean to slight the company's "The Serpent" and "Terminal," two cornerstones of contemporary theater. My special enthusiasm for "The Mutation Show" is provoked by the profundity of its theme and by the fact that the ensemble of actors has gone one step further in searching their own resources and personalities for communicable truth.

Gussow was impressed, too, by the tight refinement of the work. "There is no wasted time or energy," he wrote. "Everything is precise and concise." Arthur Sainer in the *Village Voice* described the piece as "a marvelous work, the freest, most joyful creation that the ensemble has involved itself in since its inception in 1963." And *The Mutation Show* earned the Open Theater its third Obie award, for "The Best Theater Piece" of 1972.

But Chaikin was less thrilled than the critics. While he says, when pressed, that he did finally like *The Mutation Show,* it is the only major Open Theater work that he never describes as his favorite. "It had too few words. And it was too unreliable; that is, the performances were good and not good in too unreliable a way, and so I questioned the structure."

Still, since *The Mutation Show,* Chaikin generally has not had playwrights really participating in his ensemble creations.* He has worked, instead, with a dramaturge, Mira Rafalowiz, and assistant directors. While engaging with him in the kind of continual dialogue for which he had previously relied on playwrights, they seem largely to help clarify (and ratify) his ideas, rather than providing a strong alternate vision. Although Chaikin has never changed his stated desire to work closely and integrally with a writer, in practice the lack of possible enrichment from a playwright's involvement has apparently seemed a fair price for freedom from the kinds of struggles that the Open Theater experienced with writers in its early works.

Electra and *A Fable* are exceptions, but Chaikin considers these pieces the work of playwrights with contributions by the ensemble, rather than collaborative creations.

The major exception to Chaikin's tendency away from real collaboration with a playwright has been his work with Sam Shepard. Chaikin and Shepard met at a dinner party in 1964, shortly after the Open Theater had come into being. Shepard, at that point, had written mostly poetry and was just starting to focus on theater. "We really had a rapport," Chaikin recalls. "After dinner, we walked a long distance together along some highway, and we talked. And I told him to come to a workshop at the Open Theater." Shepard was around the edges of the company, then, for the rest of its existence: "I went to a lot of workshops. Every once in a while, Joe asked me to write something and I would do it. I was always like in and out, contributing to the work just in little particles, in little pieces." In 1966, he wrote *Icarus' Mother*, which was performed by Open Theater actors. Later, he created three monologues for *Terminal*, "Cowboy," "Stone Man," and "Teleported Man." None was finally used; they are published in Shepard's *Hawk Moon*. And he wrote several key speeches and scenes for *Nightwalk*. But, though Chaikin thinks of Shepard as one of the writers who nourished the Open Theater, Shepard always felt uneasy there: "I never knew my place in the Open Theater, you know? I didn't have a place in the Open Theater. I was hanging out with different people, and I would come by. I felt a kinship with Joe. But I didn't know how to function as a writer there at all."

After the Open Theater disbanded, Shepard suggested to Chaikin that they make a play. They decided to proceed without an ensemble, to create something alone together that Chaikin would then perform. They exchanged several letters about the area they wanted to explore, and Shepard suggested the title "Tongues." But when Chaikin arrived in San Francisco in the summer of 1978 to start work on the piece, they had no specific themes and no usable text – "almost nothing," Shepard says, "but a desire to work together."

The actual collaboration period was extremely brief, Chaikin explains, because "Sam has an aversion to New York and he's terrified of flying, and I couldn't stay there [in San Francisco] because I can't stand to be away from New York for too long." But the lack of an ensemble facilitated fast work: Only two people, rather than eight or twenty, were exploring each idea. Moreover, without so many creators' egos to be protected, sections that seemed barren could be abandoned quickly and ruthlessly. After three weeks of intensive conversations, writing, and rehearsals, *Tongues*, a piece for solo voice and percussion was ready for an audience. The following summer, after a dozen more letters back and forth, Chaikin and Shepard spent three weeks developing *Savage/Love*, a play for voice, percussion, and horns.

One might have expected some problems from these "two primary creators trying to squeeze into the same space," especially since the other theater pieces of those creators had been so different. In contrast to Chaikin's distilled collages, Shepard's plays had been flashy, kaleidoscopic trips – chemical, musical, psychological, or literal – through very personal, mid- and western American terrain.

In fact, though, Chaikin and Shepard never found themselves at odds over the basic nature of their work together. Indeed, on some level, their deepest theatrical concerns had long followed parallel tracks. Each had been trying to express inner territory. And each had been exploring the relationships between language and music: how language can produce different voices and modes; how musical elements, including structure, can be adapted to the theater. The collaborations were rooted in this shared ground. Moreover, as they began working up subject matter, both men found that they could easily relate to the other's experiences. There was only one point where an impulse of Shepard's was foreign to Chaikin, (a line in *Savage/Love* about wanting to die before one's lover); but Chaikin wanted to include it in the piece, to try to enter that realm of feeling. And although these joint creations are closer in form and mood to Chaikin's work than to Shepard's, Shepard says that his respect for Chaikin precluded any concern about feeling pressed into someone else's way of seeing:

When you're collaborating with someone who you can learn from, it's very different from collaborating with someone who you're struggling with in some kind of competitive way. Like you're showing each other your chops. Musicians call it chops. If you can play a scale sixteen ways, you've got chops – and there are ways of playing together where you show that off. But when you're working with someone who actually has an experience that penetrates deeply, and you know you can learn from it, the relationship isn't that way. I feel like I'm an apprentice to Joe. I don't feel that in any kind of pejorative way, like a servant, but – I feel like he's my elder. So there's no problem with me in terms of feeling like his ideas are infringing on my vision.

It also helped the collaboration that both Shepard and Chaikin brought experience in several areas of theater. In addition to writing, Shepard had directed, composed music for, and performed in his own plays, and he had recently become a movie actor. And besides contributing to the Open Theater, he had created *Cowboy Mouth* with Patti Smith, so joint playwriting was not new to him.

The functions of playwright, director, and composer melded in the San Francisco work. Shepard says: "The actual material of the thing doesn't break down so easily into who did the words and who did the music; for me, it really was a collaboration in the truest sense. Nobody can really lay claim to any one aspect. The words were both of ours really." Chaikin agrees, though he adds that because Shepard "is a writer the rest of the time, in that sense I feel like he was the custodian of the words." Chaikin credits Shepard with having directed *Savage/Love* and, for the most part, *Tongues*. (Robert Woodruff came in to help direct *Tongues* in San Francisco when Shepard began performing the music, and directed both plays for the subsequent productions.) But Shepard says, "In a way, Joe directed from the inside."

Chaikin and Shepard began work on *Tongues* by trying to explore Chaikin's notion of "thought music." In the early stages, they used a simple story as a provisional springboard and structure. Chaikin recalls:

The first idea, which was thrown away but is in the piece anyway, was "Let's make up this thing about a person who died and had many other lives. And make a fantasy of the lives." So that's where we started from. Although we departed entirely from that idea, it gave a really very nice trampoline for us to play with.

Through conversations, Chaikin and Shepard would focus on a given area, a kind of voice that they wanted to include in the work. Then, Chaikin says,

We would sit there and make something up. I'd sometimes make up a line, he'd follow it; he'd make up a line, I'd follow it. Or sometimes he would write something and read it back to me, and I would say why I didn't want to go in that direction or – you know how I like everything to be distilled, how I can't stand anything that spreads – I'd say why it would be better like that.

The resulting texts often mixed Chaikin's and Shepard's impulses. One section, for example, sprang from Chaikin's account of being with a friend who had come out of brain surgery blind. But Chaikin's description became fused with an image very much from Shepard's America. "In front of you is a window. About chest level. It's night out . . . On the wall are pictures from your past. One is a photograph. You as a boy. You are standing in front of a cactus. You're wearing a red plaid shirt . . . A mosquito races around your ear. The same mosquito you're hearing."

Some voices in the piece came from experiences they had during the collaboration. For example, in the early stages, they worked all over the city, in restaurants, Chaikin's hotel room, the zoo; and deciding when and where to eat became a daily ritual of almost comic mutual politeness. One day, this led to a long discussion about hunger. They generalized, Shepard recalls, "from that particular mundane hunger for food to many aspects of hunger, hunger on different levels. Fat people, for example, want more than just steaks." That evening, Shepard wrote a speech that was used more or less unchanged in the final piece.

It began with a dialogue (both voices performed by Chaikin): "Would you like to go eat? Isn't it time to eat?" – "I don't mind." – "We don't have to. It's up to you." Gradually it switched gears: "I'm famished . . . Nothing I ate could satisfy this hunger I'm having right now." By the end the person was talking about hunger that could subside only briefly and would return even stronger so that "there'll be nothing left but the hunger itself when it comes back. Nothing left but the hunger eating the hunger when it comes back."

Another section was triggered by a phone conversation between Chaikin and his brother. Chaikin imitated for Shepard the business-like persona that his brother had developed, an image that clashed with but finally encroached on the sensitive, socially conscious person who projected it. And, Shepard said, "It's wonderful. Let's put it in." They developed a spoken letter, performed in a flat, dry tone. What communicated was a stifled attempt at caring and contact:

I'm writing you this today from a very great distance. Everything here is fine. I'm hoping everything there is fine with you. I'm hoping you still miss me as much as you once did . . .
Something happened today which you might find amusing. I know I found it amusing at the time. A dog came into the hotel and ran around the lobby . . .

Although they felt, in Shepard's words, "no urgency to tie these facets [of the developing piece] together or force them to tell a 'story,' " *Tongues* did wind up with a kind of double-yolked center. One repeating theme was voices: the total inadequacy and the miraculous expressiveness of sounds, especially words. Chaikin, as a woman giving birth, experiencing a mixture of agony and awe, said, "Nothing they told me was like this. I don't know whose skin

Chaikin and Sam Shepard during a rehearsal break at the Eureka Theater, San Francisco, 1979. Photograph by Ron Blanchette.

this is." A character tried frantically to find a voice he could recognize as his own, running through an orchestra of vocal timbres and pitches in the search: "That was me. Just then. That was it. Me . . . Must've been. Who else? Why should I doubt it?"* And the final segment was about really learning to hear:

> Today the people talked without speaking.
>   Tonight I can hear what they're saying.
> Today the tree bloomed without a word.
>   Tonight I'm learning its language.

Even more central was the theme of death and dying. This focus came partly from the original story idea of the man who had died, partly from Chaikin and Shepard's interest in expressing extreme conditions, and partly from the fact that Chaikin literally was in heart failure: He underwent emergency open heart surgery days after returning to New York.

I was very sick when we were working on *Tongues*, extremely sick, and I didn't know it. And I'd work with Sam and then I'd go back to the hotel room, unless we had never left the hotel room, and I'd lie and look at the ceiling. It was in a geriatric hotel; I wanted to be there because of the feeling

*This voice, of course, had a direct ancestor in the *Mutation Show* testimonies.

that I wouldn't ever be old and I might as well just be around oldness on this occasion when I was out of town anyway.

Tongues circled back again and again to death. The opening was about a man who lived "in the middle of a people"; was honored, was dishonored, was married, became old; and then one night dreamed a voice telling him, "You are entirely dead . . . You are entirely gone from the people" – and "In the next second / He's entirely dead." The theme resurfaced later in a haunting litany:

> Between the space I'm leaving
>   and the space I'm joining
> The dead one tells me now
> Beside the shape I'm leaving
>   and the one I'm becoming
> The departed tells me now.

Another voice talked about the "moment where I vanished," leaving "the whole of my body." There was an address to a dead one somehow present: "Is this me calling you up / or are you appearing? Volunteering yourself?" And one section near the end was about comforting a dying person, trying to guess what might happen at the moment of death.

Like the Open Theater collaborations, *Tongues* had a large, tangled body of material before there was any structure ordering it. Shaping into a performance piece the more than a dozen sections they had developed, Chaikin and Shepard worked musically, around statement, development, and counterpoint. Although only one character or mode was actually repeated in the piece (the person trying to find his voice), themes from the various scenes played off, orbited around, and built onto one another. Chaikin says: "One of the things we share, Sam and me, is our intense involvement with music. We're never looking for the dramatic structure. We're looking for a shape that's musically tenable." In fact, ironically, it is in working most closely with a playwright that Chaikin has created his most musical, least "dramatic" works.

As the words of *Tongues* became set, Shepard and Chaikin decided that there should be instrumental accompaniment. The original conception for the piece had included music, but they had forgotten about it. Chaikin rekindled the idea about a week before he was to start performing, partly, he claims, because he was nervous about being on stage all alone: "I think actors are insecure anyway, but in my case I perform at these irregular intervals, so I'm insecure for those reasons as well. And I have so many opinions about acting, more and more and more. And here I am performing!"

Chaikin and Sam Shepard jamming during a rehearsal of *Tongues* at the Eureka Theater, San Francisco, 1979. Photograph by Ron Blanchette.

He and Shepard each tried to telephone a musician (the two people who later performed *Tongues* and *Savage/Love* in New York). Then Shepard said he would like to do the sounds himself: "I felt it would be terrific if we could both be in it." "So," Chaikin recalls,

since Harry's line was busy and Skip wasn't home, rather than pursue it I said, "Terrific." And I thought four-fifths "Terrific" and one-fifth "What if he does music like he sort of slaps against some guitar and thinks that's it?" And then it just was wonderful! Sam's a very good percussionist. He's not only musical as a writer.

Shepard brought a selection of instruments to the theater, and they started to jam and experiment. They devised a percussion accompaniment on traditional and invented instruments: bongos, cymbals, maracas, an African drum, a tambourine, bells, chains, pipes, brass bowls, kitchenware. The voice addressing the blind one was accompanied by the high, eerie whine of a brass bowl being vibrated by a soft mallet, a sound that suggested the noise of a mosquito. Seeds inside a long, thin drum pittered and rolled as the tube was rotated during the childbirth speech. A section about wanting to change from a job with noisy, dangerous machinery was accented by the smashing of chains against metal pipes. A rhythmic jingling of bells undercut the possible morbidness of the long series of guesses about "when you die." The final section, about learning to hear, was spoken to the low, pastel gong of broiler trays.

Chaikin and Shepard in *Tongues* at the Magic Theater, San Francisco, 1978. Photograph by James Lapine. Print courtesy of *Theater* magazine.

Both men wanted to keep the focus on Chaikin while making the music an integral part of the performance. They had already decided that Chaikin would face front in a chair, motionless except for his head, his lap covered with a blanket. Shepard sat behind him, back to back, on a low platform, his instruments arranged around him. As he played he periodically held his arms and instruments out so that they could be seen over the top or around the sides of Chaikin's chair. For the opening section, about the man born in the middle of a people, an arm reached to the side shaking maracas, punctuating the speech both visually and aurally; the brass bowl and mallet appeared later, held on the other side of the chair; the tube with seeds was held high over Chaikin's head. Shepard invented and scored the various gestures (which, of course, neither he nor Chaikin could see) trying to give the sense that his arms, playing the instruments, were "extensions of Joe's static body." The effect often was a split-second image of a multilimbed Hindu god.

The total stage picture suggested illness and also, somehow, a priest or medium through whom voices came. Chaikin suspects, though, that the show's visual austereness was the result of medical as much as thematic considerations. "I think I furtively got Sam to agree that this would be interesting, even though we didn't want it to be like *Endgame* or something with this guy in a chair. I think I got him to do that because I had no other choice physically." But, Shepard responded when told about Chaikin's comment, "It wasn't hard to agree. We originally had said it would be a voice piece. And that staging put the focus on Joe's voice and face – on that voice and amazing, expressive face."

Before Chaikin had even left San Francisco, he and Shepard were talking about doing another piece. The Winter Project's *Re-Arrangements* became a kind of bridge between the two California works, incorporating several sections of *Tongues,* and moving into an area that neither man had dealt with much in the theater: love. When Chaikin suggested that the second San Francisco collaboration continue exploring this theme, Shepard wrote back: "I've been wondering about a dialogue concerning love for over a year now, so it's almost uncanny that you suggest it . . . I can hardly wait to start on this with you."

Although they had exchanged letters about the upcoming work, and Chaikin had suggested several books for Shepard to read, including Simone de Beauvoir's memoirs about her life with Sartre, they once again started their rehearsal period with no form or text. What they did have, Shepard says, was the experience of having made *Tongues* together:

We had already established certain guidelines in working before. I have the feeling that this collaboration seemed to go much smoother in a way, in terms of being hooked up to each other so that we didn't have to go through a lot of unnecessary dialogue. The last time it was feeling out what would be a method of working together. And we discovered it. But this time was much more fluid.

They also had a theme, even if the one chosen had serious potential problems. Joint creation involves meeting on shared territory, and, superficially, at least, Chaikin and Shepard did not have a lot of shared territory in their dealings with love. Shepard at that time was in a decade-old marriage and lived in an extended nuclear family; Chaikin formed deep and lasting relationships, but not long-term primary ones. Shepard was heterosexual; Chaikin bisexual. But contrary to Chaikin's initial apprehensions, they easily found areas of shared experience. Shepard was not surprised: "We were trying to deal with the interior of it. And it doesn't really matter what your exterior circumstances are in relationship to it, because the interior, I think, is where you find the common ground with anything."

The work process on *Savage/Love* was a new variation of ensemble-less ensemble creation, different from the work on *Tongues*, Chaikin explains, in that "it was a theatrical dialogue rather than conversation." Shepard describes their method:

We would agree on a particle of the subject, sometimes very small things, and Joe would start to work as an actor, improvising things around that particle. Sometimes the language that he used in the improvisation to investigate what the material was became the language of the script. I would take it down and rearrange it and mess with it a little, and then that became the actual text.

Shepard found himself more and more drawn to Chaikin's use of language:

Joe has a poetic sense without using elaborate or fancy words, without being excessive. The language is stripped in a way that's ordinary, but the ordinariness serves as a kind of jolt. There's something undramatic about a line like "The first moment I saw you in the post office" that makes it have a dramatic impact.

Once again, the demarcations between writing and directing broke down. Some sections were mostly Chaikin's words edited by Shepard; some were Shepard's words filtered through Chaikin.

The play came to focus less on the joys and ecstasy of love, though they were included, than on its pain. A recurring theme was the lover's paralyzing, tormenting self-consciousness, wondering what the desired one sees and how to shape a self that will be most lovable. A voice said, "When we're tangled up in sleep / Is it my leg you feel your leg against / Or is it Paul Newman's leg? / . . . / If you could only give me some clue / I could invent the one you'd have me be." Elsewhere, the speaker struck a pose and asked, "When I sit like this / Do you see me brave / . . . / Which presentation of myself / Would make you want to touch / What would make you cross the border?" Another character watched himself in conversation, trying vainly to make his face and body transmit what he wanted them to show.

Several times in *Savage/Love*, Chaikin and Shepard used the figurative image of killing to express both the hatred in love and what happens when passion dies. One speech, by someone who had just "killed" his partner, ended, "I saw you thinking of something else /

Chaikin, in *Savage/Love*, as someone getting
tangled up in his words and the feelings he is
trying to express, at the New York Shakespeare Festival Public Theater, 1979. Photograph by Thomas Victor. © Thomas Victor
1984.

You couldn't see / The thing I'd done to you." Another voice, a
person watching a sleeping lover, said, "For one moment I think of
the killing / . . . / I want to strangle your dreams / Inside me."

The most wrenching section of *Savage/Love*, and one of the funni-
est, was a part Shepard and Chaikin called "The Beggar." They
began by writing a monologue of somebody pleading for a crumb,
moving from "Could you give me just a small part of yourself?"
to, finally, "Could I just walk behind you for a little while?" When
that speech was written, Shepard and Chaikin felt there should also
be a part showing the reverse, so they created a monologue that be-

gan, "Don't think I'm this way with everybody / . . . / In fact, usually it's the other way around," and ended, "I'm wasting my time right now / Just talking to you." Shepard then had the idea to run the two speeches together as segments of one voice. "It seems to be true," he explains, "that one emotion is absolutely connected to its opposite, and the two sides are actually simultaneously happening. You can't show the simultaneousness of it so much, but you can show how they evolve – they don't really evolve, they just flip."

The bleakness of *Savage/Love* was undercut by its (relatively few) affirming voices, and especially by its humor. A lover tried out different terms of endearment; a character declared he had lost fifteen pounds and dyed his hair brown, all for a beloved he had yet to find. "One of the wonderful things about Sam," Chaikin says, "is that he's funny. There has to be a certain proportion of humor in everything he does. It's as clear as that there would have to be pepper on somebody's food or vegetables as part of a casserole. It's very important. Anything without humor at all is very hard to care about."

Because the work period was so brief, some areas that Chaikin and Shepard had meant to explore were not worked out. Chaikin told an interviewer:

On my way to the airport I realized that we had not dealt with the terror of replaceability one can feel with love. Both of us wanted to include it, we both thought it was integral and even central to the whole thing, and it isn't there because we couldn't finish the piece together because we live on different coasts.

They were satisfied enough with what they had been able to do, though, to give *Savage/Love* a final form. Once again, their approach was more musical than dramaturgical; they worked with shapes, rhythms, and thematic interrelationships, but did not try to mold their material into a story.

Instrumental music also became important in the piece. "As we were writing," Shepard says, "we were really trying to think in terms of being economical enough with the words so that it left space where music could really make the environment for it." In program notes for the San Francisco production, he wrote, "Both of these collaborations are an attempt to find an equal expression between music and the actor."

Two musicians, Harry Mann, who had performed in several Shepard works, and Skip LaPlante, who had been in Chaikin's Winter Project, collaborated on *Savage/Love*. Mann played clarinet, saxophone, flute, and various whistles in the piece, often tooting humor into the monologue. When Chaikin, looking placidly at the audience began to wail a few bars of "The thrill is gone," Mann accentuated the irony by precisely matching his pitch, timing, and mood on the sax.

LaPlante, like Shepard in *Tongues*, used mostly homemade instruments constructed from trash – chains, metal strips, kitchenware, fluorescent tubes, wooden planks – as well as a double bass. During the "Beggar" section, he jangled chains in a wicker basket, making a sound vaguely like coins in a tin cup. For an angry, accusing speech – "YOU / who controls me / . . . / YOU / Who leads me to believe we're forever in love" – he used a homemade bull-roarer, a piece of wood whirled on a string to make a noise like a car motor. For a lover's recollection of "days by the water," he created a muted, glubby percussion by tapping the lid of a peanut butter jar partly filled with water.

Often Chaikin, Mann, and LaPlante played as a trio. While Chaikin spoke of being "haunted by your scent / When I'm talking to someone else," LaPlante made a high, hollow sound by bowing metal strips, and Mann created a piercing, quivering dissonance by blowing two penny whistles at once. For the "I've lost fifteen pounds for you" speech, LaPlante tapped a spunky rhythm on a kitchen bowl, while Mann counterpointed with a jazzy, syncopated alto sax.

The physical staging was less austere this time but still very spare. Chaikin performed from a niche about four feet off the ground, six feet high, five feet wide, and two feet deep. He sat, stood, lay down, and squirmed in his little space; once, during "The Beggar," he left it for a few moments to follow behind his loved one. The musicians, with their instruments arranged around them, were further downstage to either side of Chaikin, funneling the focus in to him. The lighting, designed by Beverly Emmons, was full of "specials," in contrast to her design for *Tongues*, which was seemingly stationary but actually subtly modulating white illumination. Here new voices were marked by light changes, sometimes as extreme as a tight spot from directly above or one side, which helped to punctuate the monologue and define its sections.

After the initial performances at the Eureka Theater in San Francisco, Chaikin performed *Tongues* and *Savage/Love* (with Mann and LaPlante) at the Public Theater in New York, then on tour in Paris and Italy, and again on the West Coast. The critical response to the work was enthusiastic, so much so, in fact, that Chaikin found the audiences becoming "too respectful." Mel Gussow wrote about the production twice in the *New York Times*, first in a daily review, then in a Sunday feature; he described it as "not only an exquisite piece of performance theater," but also, "to a great extent, a consolidation, a precis of the work of these two extraordinary theater artists over a span of 15 years." James Leverett wrote in the *Soho News*, "What emerges is the pure presence of an extraordinary actor – mature, classic in its economy, consummate in its power."

Finally, for all its problems, whether his ensemble consists of one other person or twenty, whether there is a contributing playwright or not, ensemble playwriting remains the most thrilling part of theater for Chaikin. The challenge is to locate common ground with other people, areas where deepest impulses mesh, and then find forms to express those discoveries and transmit them to others. This process, which must be partly reinvented for each project, is more exciting for him than directing preexisting scripts. The key difference is going "from the person to the part" rather than "going from the part to the person." "Personally," Chaikin says, "I just like it better."

6   Directing plays: going from the part to the person

Chaikin told an interviewer once: "I feel I've been misunderstood in a way, because, since I like to work on developing new pieces, people assume there must be a sort of disdain on my part about existing theater. It's just the opposite." Our classic theater, he said, is "precious." Chaikin is ardent about the plays of Shakespeare and the Greeks as well as Brecht and Beckett, and he experiments in workshops all the time with a range of speeches and scenes. Still, in the two decades since he founded the Open Theater, he has directed only half a dozen plays with preexisting scripts, including both classics and new works. He says that he must feel a special connection or insight to tackle a play; he sees no point in just putting on another *Hamlet*.

When staging new scripts, Chaikin has worked closely with the writers, and his rehearsal process has sometimes edged toward ensemble creation. When he directed van Itallie's *Interview* in *America Hurrah*, he eliminated and shortened transitions between segments, called for rewriting of several monologues, and made basic changes in staging – including the use of "phrases" to create many individuals in a crowd and the direct address of some speeches to the audience. Van Itallie incorporated these revisions into the published script. Codirecting *Viet Rock* with Peter Feldman, he gave it an angrier bite than Megan Terry had conceived. These changes were made, atypically, without the playwright's participation, and she later restored her original version. He worked closely with Adrienne Kennedy on her very personal, autobiographical *A Movie Star Has to Star in Black and White*, condensing, tightening dialogue, and clarifying some of the more inaccessible sections.

On occasion, Chaikin has brought this approach to classical texts as well. One example is his treatment of *The Dybbuk*. He felt that S. Ansky's play, the best-known work of the Yiddish stage, was a kind of theatrical and personal legacy, and on some levels it captivated him. He loved the mythic dimensions of the play's world, where, as he told the New York cast, "the dead aren't relegated to some [cemetery] plot on Long Island, but intermingle with the living all over town – and inside people." He was excited, too, by the extremity of human experience in the story: "These people go to the limit

A washerwoman, on the subway, tells her story in *Interview* from *America Hurrah* (*left to right top:* Conrad Fowkes and Cynthia Harris, as a subway ad; *middle:* Bill Macy and Henry Calvert; *bottom:* Ronnie Gilbert, as the washerwoman, Joyce Aaron, and James Barbosa), at the Pocket Theater, New York, 1966. Photograph by Niblock/Bough.

of what you can think. They keep trying to go to the border and to hang out there and see what it's possible to say there."

Still, he felt that *The Dybbuk* was structurally clumsy and in certain ways outdated. It had been written in the shadow of pogroms, "when people thought that was the worst thing that could happen to Jews – and now we're doing it after World War II"; he felt that a post-Holocaust perspective had to be incorporated. He wanted, also, to put the sexism and materialism of the play's *stetl* world into sharper relief.

So he kept the basic shape and content of the original story: A passionate young Hasidic scholar, prevented from being with his

A scene from *The Dybbuk* at the New York Shakespeare Festival Public Theater, 1977. Channon (Bruce Myers) explains the lure of the mystical Cabala to a worried fellow scholar (Bernard Duffy) in the synagogue. Photograph by Inge Morath/Magnum.

love, dies with dangerous, mystical Cabala teachings on his lips, and then enters the young woman on her wedding day as a *dybbuk*, a spirit taking refuge in a living body. But Chaikin and Mira Rafalowicz reworked nearly every scene, in some cases adding or eliminating entire episodes and characters. The opening segment in the synagogue now stressed the banishment of women to the upper gallery, away from the holy objects. Gossip about the impending nuptials, the dressing of the bride, and the marriage celebration itself were full of references to wealth and poverty. Ansky's messenger became an itinerant storyteller, creating a mystical backdrop for the action.

Although most of the writing of this new version took place outside rehearsals, some sections were developed by the company. For example, the actors improvised to create the wedding celebration and various mourning rites. Even scenes that were written without the actors' participation were revised on the basis of rehearsal experiences. Finally, Chaikin's *Dybbuk* was a hybrid of Ansky's play, new work by him and Rafalowicz, and ensemble creation.

In general, though, Chaikin believes that classics should be staged as written, not modernized or "improved." Although he breaks this rule as often as he observes it (his *Antigone* was a new, somewhat altered version; his *Electra*, starting out from the Sophocles original, became a totally new play), he feels that a classical work should not be used casually as a jumping-off place for what amounts to a piece of one's own. Chaikin says he prefers either to enter and fully respect the world of someone else's script or to create a new work from scratch. If he has directed relatively few preexisting plays (as opposed to his own ensemble creations), it is because, in fact – like the writers who have collaborated with him – he feels constrained by the requirement to be creative within a framework not really his own. But he feels that directors of other people's plays *should* be constrained in this way.

Chaikin's directorial stamp in these cases is subtle. He does nothing like the total revampings of Grotowski's early theater or even the cultural transposings of Brook's Shakespeare productions. Rather than impose a concept, he tries instead to grasp very precisely what each moment is about, how the various moments relate to each other thematically and rhythmically, and how best to transmit those findings to an audience. He works, in a sense, like a musical conductor as much as like a traditional theater director.

This approach to scripts can be seen clearly in Chaikin's work with *Endgame*, the play to which he has returned most often. Chaikin's initial attraction to Beckett was

that he was a living writer who had written in a language for the theater that seemed to me of a *special* kind of power, shifting words in such a way that the words would then be heard differently, felt differently. Contexts were destroyed at the end of a thought; he destroyed certain things and recovered other things in language. It was very exciting to me, and I just wanted to be in his world. I was just very exhilarated by Beckett at the time.

What struck Chaikin was not only Beckett's innovative use of form but also his confrontation with extremes of the human condition, his refusal of spurious hopes or any "substitute religion, some other realm that one can look to because this one isn't enough." Chaikin feels now that Beckett has "written more articulately for the stage than any writer since Shakespeare."

But each time Chaikin has become immersed in Beckett's work, he has come to feel drained by it – and then angry at having been lured into a world that saps rather than restores energy. He has said during these periods that he "hate[s] Beckett." Then, always, he has come back.

Chaikin as Hamm and Peter Maloney as Clov in the Open Theater production of *Endgame*, directed by Roberta Sklar, New York, 1969. Photograph by Ken Sklar. Print courtesy of Roberta Sklar.

Chaikin's first interest in Beckett was as a performer: "I was very drawn to him as an actor because of something about the music and the rhythms of it and the broken thoughts – not to speak of the *cry* in it." Knowing that Beckett had heard about the Open Theater's work, Chaikin contacted him several times, asking for suggestions about what to perform. Beckett's replies were cordial but unhelpful, and Chaikin decided in 1969 to play Hamm in *Endgame*. Roberta Sklar directed the production, which Chaikin later recalled as "the second time in my life I felt very glad to be acting" (the other time was when he played Galy Gay at the Living Theater). Still, he was not satisfied with his performance and said that he would like to act in the play again one day "to find some of the things which I missed in the Open Theater production, to hit some of the notes which I missed in that particular score."

When Chaikin returned to the work in 1977, it was as a director. He had been invited to give a class at Princeton University by allowing students to observe a production in process from start to finish. He chose *Endgame* for this project, partly because its small cast meant that he could keep within his budget without using student actors.*

He saw the script as a complex score with precise shapes and dynamics:

Beckett speaks to you so much through the music of it. I find this even in his novels, certainly in his poetry, even in his essay on Proust. The music and the thought are not separated. I didn't use musical terms too much, because I felt it's not music, but one has to use musical terms because occasionally it's just a more direct way of speaking to say "this sort of crescendoes" than to say "this develops and so the momentum picks up between them."

He worked with great attention to detail, searching for exact meanings and rhythms. Daniel Seltzer, who headed the Princeton theater program and played Hamm, recalled:

All of the rehearsals were very nuanced rehearsals. He would spend four hours on six lines. I don't think that's an exaggeration. It didn't happen all the time, but at least we would spend five hours on two pages. And there would be a lot of stopping and starting and stopping and starting.

The key to *Endgame*, Chaikin felt, was Beckett's notion of *playing* or playacting: finding a routine to get through a bit of time, returning to having nothing to do, finding another way to play out the next moment, and so forth. This constant improvising of roles for oneself, Chaikin told the actors, is an extreme version of something people do in real life:

You run into a friend, and you say, "that's a great shirt, it's a terrific shirt," and he says, "Gee, you really like this shirt?" And then the friend's voice drops and he says, "My friend is in the hospital" and your voice drops to match it and you ask, "Will he be all right?" Then the voice goes up again, and he says, "Do you know where the nearest uptown subway is?"

---

*Chaikin avoids working with student actors because he dislikes "the sense that the person doesn't have the breadth of experience of something that they're playing." His cast at Princeton consisted of Daniel Seltzer (Hamm), Chris McCann (Clov), Charles Stanley (Nagg), and Shami Chaikin (Nell).

In *Endgame,* the shifting among various presentations of the self is raised to the level of conscious theatrical role playing. Chaikin pointed out the many direct stage references planted in the script: "An aside, ape! . . . I'm warming up for my last soliloquy"; "This is what we call making an exit"; "What is there to keep me here?" – "The dialogue." In addition, there are subtler allusions: "Since that's the way we're playing . . . let's play it that way"; "Me – to play" (Hamm's first words, which he later repeats twice more). At the front of his script, Seltzer noted their idea: "While you wait, you ENGAGE with life, discarding, *desiring,* and yet living in the eternal impossibilities of the present. (Drama is [the] perfect vehicle.)"

The basic form of the play, Chaikin told the actors, was vaudeville. The variety-show format connected all the sections; the characters were, on some level, performers adopting different roles to entertain the audience (and themselves). Chaikin also saw the stamp of burlesque routines on many of the bits: Clov's "I'm back with the glass" (or steps or biscuit or insecticide); Clov's war with a flea; Hamm's "little turn" around the room, and the fine adjustments to re-place him perfectly center; Hamm's mid-routine asides to the audience – "This is deadly."

As rehearsals progressed, Chaikin came to feel that a way into the routines was through an approach similar to his work with "modes," and he developed several new adaptations of Open Theater exercises to work on the play. A few were nonverbal improvisations: Without using Beckett's text, Seltzer or Chris McCann (Clov) would begin to speak in a particular sound and rhythm, the other would try to match the dynamic, and they would do a scene together. Mostly, though, Chaikin felt that the modes should be discovered *"through* and *by* the *words."* So one of the actors (usually Seltzer, since Hamm initiated most of the routines) would derive a sound and rhythm from the text, and then the other would try to meet it, using his character's lines.

It was difficult and uneven going. Steven Gomer, Chaikin's assistant director, recalls that it took several weeks to discover the idea of modes in the play, and then there was no time to crystallize specific solutions for most sections. And while the work was intensely personal, requiring the actors to locate private associations, it also, Chaikin insisted, had to derive directly from the text and transmit well to the audience.

The company did find a number of modes that seemed precise and clear. For example, the dialogue

HAMM: Nature has forgotten us.
CLOV: There's no more nature.
HAMM: No more nature! You exaggerate.
CLOV: In the vicinity.

became "A public forum: Topic: *Nature.*" The little exchange

HAMM: Why don't you kill me?
CLOV: I don't know the combination of the cupboard.

became a movie murder mystery. When Hamm was recalling
Mother Pegg, "She was bonny once, like a flower of the field. And a
great one for the men!" Seltzer took on the air of an old Irish gossip;
his speech pattern, he claimed, was "a parody of a very old professor emeritus at Princeton, who talks that way." The several times
that Hamm says, "We're getting on," Chaikin felt, should all be in
the same mode, a message to the audience: "I know it's difficult
going, but don't worry, it's moving along." For Hamm's long story,
about a man coming to beg food for his boy, Seltzer analyzed the
narrative into four distinct voices recounting and commenting on
the tale.

Chaikin and the actors tried to realize not only what each mode
was, but where and how it came up and disappeared: who started
it, at what point the other picked it up, who dropped it. They
examined the moments when one character hesitated to join in,
such as

HAMM: I've got on with my story. (*Pause.*) I've got on with it well. (*Pause.*
   Irritably.) Ask me where I've got to.
CLOV: O, by the way, your story?

They focused on Hamm and Clov's competitiveness, who won each
routine, each round. Chaikin pointed out not only the places where
characters claimed their triumph, such as

CLOV: Do you believe in the life to come?
HAMM: Mine was always that.
   (*Exit Clov.*)
Got him that time!

but also the unstated victories and defeats, such as Clov's announcement that there was no more painkiller.

Chaikin felt strongly that the actors must steer away from a kind
of "Chekhovian" dimension to the characters; the modes, he said,
should be *played at* rather than *filled.* On one hand, this would short-
circuit really moribund despair in the places where wretchedness
could break through the vaudeville. On the other, it would create a

Chaikin working with Daniel Seltzer and Chris McCann on "filled" versus "unfilled" modes in *Endgame*. Photograph by Gomer/Heller Productions.

deep, awful alienation. And he felt that the modes, like variety acts, should not carry over into one another: "Once something's finished, it never happened," and the characters must start over in a new routine. He spoke often about the moments of mode shifts, which often were indicated in the script as pauses. Seltzer noted, "Remember that the pauses . . . are ERASURES between the modes, may be pauses, but of quite varying lengths. Erasures = drops (of body, of persona), blanks." Some of these blanks were to be split-second. At one point in his script, for example, Seltzer wrote, "Don't PAUSE; rather *re-align.* A new channel."

Still, according to Gomer, this notion of playing at, rather than inhabiting, and then erasing modes remained a hazy idea that the company never totally incorporated:

Although we were stressing, "It shouldn't be filled, it shouldn't be filled," a lot of it *was* filled. A lot of times when Joe would ask for unfilled, Dan would fill it and Joe would like it. The show worked partly because the idea of unfilled only partly worked.

Seltzer said at the time that the concept of "erasures" was very clear and helpful as an idea, but tricky to realize in performance.

While he did not want real emotions in the modes, Chaikin did want real presence: "When something is brought up (verbalized), then that's what it's about." The actors were to *play* the routines, not *refer* to them. And they were constantly to be aware of the spectator's reactions and needs, to share *Endgame*'s music, phrasing, playfulness with them:

The big extremes in terms of what you feel from the audience are you feel a silence or you feel a laugh – but obviously there are many many more things and more interesting and complex things between the absolute silence and the laugh. But the breathing with the audience is a very important matter. And the laughter is a breathing.

Chaikin continually stressed that the play must not become morose or static. It is true, he said, that Beckett undercuts the comedy – with Nell's "Nothing is funnier than unhappiness," with Hamm and Clov's amusement at the most dreadful things (such as someone being offered a job as gardener in their dead, ash-heap world). Still, Chaikin told the actors and designers, the play was filled with humor, and he wanted the show to be as funny as possible.

It also was critical, he said, to keep the action "eventful." For example, while Hamm's opening speech is about the oppressive prospect of endless successions of moments to be filled, "it has to also have a forward pulse." He told McCann at one point, "Try to find a kind of 'tallerness' [at the end] – like leaving. I'm trying to think what would be the clearest image of a kind of being there and leaving. I think it's a kind of tallness." And Seltzer noted in his script: "To 'wind down,' to *play* 'the end,' is a great trap, a danger to this play. This sort of pessimism is too weak for Beckett, and, ultimately, BORING for an audience."

Fundamentally, Chaikin's intention was simply to be faithful to Beckett:

My attraction to doing *Endgame* is to do the play, to make it visible, to embody it as clearly as possible. Which doesn't mean that I don't have interpretations on the way, but it's not to do a treatment of it or a number on it or use it as a sort of trampoline to do something I have in mind with it. I wanted to do the *play*.

He made no alterations in the dialogue and no cuts.

He did, of course, make choices about emphasis. For example, he decided not to underscore the chess analogy. The company considered the correspondences between the play's action and chess moves, and Seltzer made notes about common elements of thwarting and complicity, but that dimension of the play remained subsidiary. "Of the dozen possible predominant interpretations," Chaikin explained, "I go by what's active and what's lively and what's theatrical and what's interesting. And that was not so much. I think that is already implied in the title, and that's enough." Chaikin's major interpretation was to go with the play's potential for humor.

And he did depart from a few of Beckett's stage directions:

Serving the play and a kind of loyalty that I felt to the play doesn't mean that I don't feel I can breathe in it and see something one way as opposed to another. Or that I have to go to Beckett's log to see what he meant by something or other. I feel intimate enough with it so that I can make judgments about it . . .

We made small changes from things he suggested, and I think they were for the better. I don't feel apologetic about them at all. I feel that in spirit and in the scope of the play, we were faithful.

He did not, for example, adhere to Beckett's description of Hamm and Clov's faces as "very red." It seemed too mysterious:

Beckett does get very obscure, more than meets the eye. If one delves into the text, there are associations and extremely private things he has, even with his family. That's been revealed in that biography by Deirdre Bair. I figured that if something were just so obscure that it didn't have thought or visceral clarity, then we didn't have to use it – unless it seemed like something that was good to use anyway, and that was one that didn't.

If the audience began to worry about not understanding the play, he felt, not only would they be distracted from the experience, but the work would take on an unpleasant ponderousness.

Jeremy Lebensohn's bare-bones set – wooden doorframe, two windows hung in space, a garbage bin for Nagg and Nell – also deviated from Beckett's description. It lacked a framed picture facing the wall; Chaikin felt that was too facile a joke. And, at Chaikin's request, it included a step under Clov's kitchen door in order to make the comings and goings more pronounced and expand Clov's options for routines.

Chaikin's largest departure, though, came from concern for the performers' comfort rather than from artistic considerations. The actors playing Nagg and Nell would not be able to get in and out of their ashcans during the play unless the cans were consolidated into a single, shared trashbin downstage. Chaikin did not think this arrangement ideal (in fact, he would have preferred to have them not only separate but upstage, although Beckett wanted them front left); but he used it because he was unwilling to have the actors trapped for the entire show.

Despite Chaikin's attempts to emphasize the humor and eventfulness of the play, as rehearsals progressed Beckett's enervated, de-
pressive world began to exhaust him. He became more and more
mired in *Endgame*'s material and found he could not let it flow. He
would stop the actors every few seconds. After six weeks of rehearsals, there had not been a single runthrough. Even when everyone
felt the need to see larger shapes and relationships, even when they
had agreed to go through the play from start to finish, Chaikin could
not stop interrupting. He told the actors at one point to ignore his
comments and keep going, but they could not really do that – and if
they managed to, he would eventually ask them to stop. "One
time," Gomer recalls, "I thought Dan was going to kill him."

Finally, Chaikin reached the point where he could no longer deal
with the play. Eleven days before the first performance, he decided
to stay away and direct by proxy for a while. He and Gomer discussed the work daily, and Gomer worked with the company. Chaikin did not actually come back to Princeton until the dress rehearsal.
In this way, the show came together, though at the price of the
actors feeling underrehearsed, insecure, and in Seltzer's words, "a
little deserted."*

It was, in fact, a lively and a rather warm *Endgame*. The enter-
tainer's conviviality that Seltzer brought to the routines colored the
show's whole mood. His tyranny seemed avuncular and pathetic as
well as sinister. McCann developed a kind of jerky, syncopated
movement style that peppered the physical stasis created by the
other characters. The overall effect was like people dancing a jig,
even though the ground had fallen away underneath.

Endgame ran at Princeton's little Theatre Intime for three weeks in
April 1977. There was no advertising outside the immediate area, and
the New York press was not invited. Word began to spread about the
production as it was closing. By then, Chaikin had second thoughts
about having kept so quiet about the show. On the one hand, he was
"glad that it was finished." He was fed up with Beckett and not at all
sure he wanted to promote *Endgame*'s sensibility. And he was feeling
his usual ambivalence about opening work up to the public: "Part of
me doesn't want anyone to see anything; I like to do it and then it
should just obliterate." Still, on the other hand, he wished that the
show had been available to a wider audience.

*Even at the time, though, Seltzer said that he "knew why he [Chaikin] had to go."
He added that Chaikin was "a towering kind of genius, a real perceptive giant," and
that "this in some ways makes his rehearsal techniques idiosyncratic."

Chaikin decided to revive his *Endgame* in New York the following season, only to be prevented by illness. Eventually, it was set for the Manhattan Theatre Club's 1979–80 subscription series. Seltzer again played Hamm, but the other roles were recast.* Gomer served as assistant director again and actually ran many of the work sessions, since an extension of Chaikin's run of *Tongues* and *Savage/Love* created an unforeseen schedule conflict.

For the first several weeks, Chaikin held rehearsals in his Greenwich Village apartment, a more convenient commute for everyone than the Upper East Side Manhattan Theatre Club. They worked with a ladder borrowed from the building maintenance staff and newspapers taped on a wall to represent windows. Rehearsals were extremely smooth and productive. Seltzer and Chaikin had already built a basic vocabulary for working with the material, and Michael Gross, the new Clov, was able to pick it up quickly. Although they once again worked very precisely with details, they began having runthroughs early on.

In large measure, Chaikin continued the approach he had found in Princeton, working with the different modes that Hamm and Clov (and Nagg and Nell) assume. Sections that had not really gelled in the earlier production became better defined. For example, in the little exchange about whether Clov's flea has been exterminated,

CLOV: Looks like it.
  Unless he's laying doggo.
HAMM: Laying! Lying you mean. Unless he's *lying* doggo.
CLOV: Ah? One says lying? One doesn't say laying?

the characters were, in Chaikin's words, "two scholars discussing a fine point of grammar." Hamm's line after he has been enjoined from taking his painkiller too soon after his tonic – "In the morning they brace you up and in the evening they calm you down. Unless it's the other way round." – became a routine that Seltzer noted as "Ah, these hospitals!"

The central mode still was vaudeville. For Chaikin, "One of the primary realities [in the play] is the vaudeville team, keeping the audience *amused* in this play about inertia and despair and deadendedness." He told the company, "If there's one main guideline for the style, it would have to be vaudeville – if one had to stay with only one, which one doesn't." Again, they tried to spot and work

---

*Michael Gross played Clov, James Barbosa (who had been Nagg to Chaikin's Hamm in the Open Theater production) played Nagg, and Joan MacIntosh played Nell.

Hamm (Daniel Seltzer) and Clov (Michael Gross) are again a vaudeville team in the Manhattan Theatre Club production of *Endgame*, New York, 1979. Photograph by Nathaniel Tileston.

up the play's many little entertainment bits: Clov's sight gags with ladder, telescope, and dog; Hamm's straight-man asides; the cross-talk patter between them.

Chaikin tried to clarify his notion of erasures. He told the company in an early rehearsal: "What's going on from point to point is that you don't know what to do. And then somebody starts something and then there's that for whatever its duration is. And then again you don't know what to do." These pauses, he explained, had to do not with pacing but with shape, in the sense of musical phrasing: "One thing ends, and another can begin." As an actor reached the end of a routine one time, Chaikin called out: "Drop it. There's nothing. It can be just an instant, but for that instant there's nothing." In the New York rehearsals, he often used the word "seam" rather than "pause" for the place where one thing ended and another began.

Again, Chaikin recalls, the concept of erasures was easier for the company to grasp intellectually than to embody:

In terms of the actors, it was very difficult to describe this thing. There's a thing that Beckett says, I think in *Waiting for Godot*, "Let us persevere in what we have resolved, before we forget." I mentioned that in rehearsals and said that in a way you can think about that as something that happens to Beckett's characters. They start doing something and they just forget it in midstream. And so we'll take these points where it's like an erase. Something is brought up and it's sort of erased, or it's dropped.

At a dress rehearsal, he told the actors, "You must let go of the last mode, give a reality to finishing it – drop – and find the impulse for the new one; then launch it."

The New York rehearsals did not only follow paths struck at Princeton. "The thing about the play's density and intricacy," Chaikin says, "is that it really does yield, again and again, things you don't expect. It really keeps being discoverable."

The biggest change for the New York production was allowing some modes to be emotionally filled. At an early rehearsal, he told Gross, "In a lot of what Clov does, there can be a joke, but the joke doesn't cancel out the other thing." Chaikin was willing now to give place to the "Chekhovian" dimension – even to let it break through the playfulness. Many of Hamm's moments in particular were changed. Chaikin told Seltzer, "Take the line, 'To think perhaps it won't all have been for nothing,' and experience what it would be to feel that – rather than undercutting it immediately. For that moment, there's a kind of meaning." Hamm's question, "Is she [Mother Pegg] buried?" – which in Princeton had been, in Gomer's words, "sort of like 'would you go get something at the store?" – became a kind of bereavement. Other spots that Seltzer now made more real than routine were "Do you not think this has gone on long enough?" "If you must hit me, hit me with the axe," and "One day you'll be blind, like me." The group understood this time, Gomer says, that in Beckett it was perfectly coherent to have "a joke, pure joke, then in the next beat go into a heavy profound thing, then into another joke." They were no longer "afraid of the emotion."

Chaikin talked about a kind of receptiveness, an openness of looking, that would arise in the midst of the characters' closedness: "There's no wonder; they know everything; there's no more this, no

Nagg (James Barbosa) and Nell (Joan MacIntosh) reminisce about the past in *Endgame* at the Manhattan Theatre Club, New York, 1979. Photograph by Nathaniel Tileston.

more that. And then something new comes up, and you *explore* it." Seltzer noted in his script, "A big trap in this play: to think the characters have lost the art of *wonder*. Remember always: speaking/ words are *EVENTFUL*." A sense of awe and bewilderment now seasoned the play in spots: at the moments when Hamm asks "What's happening?"; at Clov's "Why?" questions ("Why this farce day after day?" "There's one thing I'll never understand. Why I always obey you"). The show became warmer, more alive.

Allowing emotion into some modes helped to solve questions about Nagg and Nell. In Princeton they had gotten very little attention in rehearsals, and, according to Gomer, "No one had any idea what Nagg and Nell were about." Now much of their talk could really be about longing for the past, delicacy, manners.

More important, Chaikin now admitted a more human plane of interaction between Hamm and Clov, beneath and sometimes cutting through their playacting:

They *are* people too, and they are people most vividly at those moments that have to do with, "Well, I'll leave you." "I'll leave you" is one of the, quote, routines of the play, and also one of the most human, directly related-to-relationship things in the play. It's both.

They're comics, the two actors, they're competitive actors. But that doesn't at all rule out the way in which the play gives expression to things to do with relationships, like partings. It's the main thing going on in the play between the two of them, that they're going to part, from the moment they meet practically. That's what's so rich about it, that it's on different levels at once, and it asks to be seen in those ways and played in those ways.

Hamm's curse, for example, that one day Clov too will be blind and immobile, was seen now as something that "could only be found in a deep relationship." Chaikin tempered his notion of erasures enough to allow for motivation. For example, Hamm's question, "Do you remember when you came here?" was not only the beginning of a new routine but also an attempt to keep Clov from leaving after the viciousness of the curse.

The possibility of ongoing feelings – and, the fact that Chaikin was doing runthroughs – made him more concerned than before with the overall contours of the play. Certain moments, he said, were "like roadsigns for curves"; until you reach the turn, it is not there, but once you have passed it, your direction is altered. Hamm's description of the madman who looked out at fields of corn and saw only ashes was an example of such a pivot. Even during Princeton rehearsals, Chaikin had referred to Hamm's "I was never there . . . Absent, always" as the play's "recognition scene." Now that recognition did not disappear when the next routine began. Chaikin also spoke to the actors about building the play's sense of time, of the passing of each event. Most of Hamm's monologues, he said, were *about* time.

Chaikin focused particularly on how this play about the end of everything moved to its own conclusion. He told the actors, "when there's no more painkiller, you both understand that it's almost the end of the play. Without the painkiller as bait, it's finishing." But drawing to a close could not mean winding down. Rather, it meant accelerating the process of discarding. *Endgame*, on one level, was about the accumulation of "no mores" – no more sugarplums, living creatures outside, light, tide, coffins. Even at Princeton, Seltzer had noted: "Major activity of the play: to DISCARD: not about death, but state of no connection taken to the point of fantasia." Now in New York casting off became the force that drove the play to its finish. Chaikin spoke of Hamm collecting all his possessions – the gaff and the dog – in order to throw them off, to release himself from them. Seltzer's notes at Hamm's final words – "to speak no more . . . You . . . remain" – were about a final discarding: "There'll be no more speech. If I can hold my peace and sit quiet, it will be all over with sound and motion – all over and done with."

Although he was giving more voice to the pain, Chaikin remained

Hamm prepares to fling away the dog as he accelerates his process of discarding. Manhattan Theatre Club, New York, 1979. Photograph by Nathaniel Tileston.

determined not to surrender to morbidity. He felt that the enormous sadness in *Endgame* should mostly come up through the humor, and the hugest meanings through the silliest, and most trivial images. Seltzer noted at various points: "Don't play 'Significance,' " and "NEVER, in Beckett, play 'the void,' " and "It's a rip-off intellectually to pretend that after vaudeville, 'we're getting serious.' *Keep* the tone of play and discovery. Not sad. Let the final speech spin off . . . don't hold on to it ceremoniously." Chaikin told the actors that they had "an obligation to every moment to entertain the audience": "If you get comfortably slow, it is completely compatible with the material, but that's not the best way to do it." Any time he had to choose between humor and weight, he still went with the play's comedy. Indeed, he said toward the end of the run,

If I could find ways to make it still much funnier, I would. If I could find funnier objects, props, I would. If I could find that certain routines between them could be funnier, certain timings, the banter, I would certainly do it. There wouldn't be any question to it. I might even do it to the point that the

Clov launches the play with a lively flourish as he uncovers Hamm.
Manhattan Theatre Club, New York, 1979. Photograph by Sylvia Plachy.

pithiness of the despair was less. That the despair was more the reference and less embodied.

Chaikin wanted liveliness now in the play's physical design as well. The lighting, by Beverly Emmons, who had done the Princeton production too, was warm and even showy. Three overhead racks with colored gels ran parallel to the stage front, visible to the audience, giving a presentational theatricality to the overall picture. Sally Jacobs's set was wide and shallow like a vaudeville stage. Against sand-colored walls, Clov's kitchen door (upstage right) and a radiator and pipes were institutional green; two translucent windows had green panes and tan curtains. A double trashbin for Nagg and Nell sat upstage left. And the costumes were designed, as at Princeton, by Mary Brecht. Hamm wore layers of dirty, tattered elegance – a crumpled brocade dressing gown over clerical-looking undergar-

Hamm and Clov in a moment of active waiting for the game to be over.
Manhattan Theatre Club, New York, 1979. Photograph by Nathaniel
Tileston.

ments. Clov sported a ratty brown sweater, more hole than sweater,
and baggy pants, tucked into floppy old black boots. Nagg and Nell
wore plain, old-fashioned white nightdresses.

In performance, Seltzer again brought a strange congeniality to
Hamm's selfishness, giving him a twinkle and even a kind of robust-

ness. Gross's Clov, tall and angular in contrast to the lump shape of the seated Hamm, was a live cartoon, hovering, puttering, and pacing. Nagg and Nell, ageless and skittish, added an out-of-place innocence that threw Hamm and Clov's world into relief.

Preparing the show for several Paris performances after the New York run, Chaikin once again went into rehearsals (mostly because he had to work in a new Clov, since Gross had a prior commitment). He kept nudging the actors toward humor and humanity. And he made several changes in the set and lights. He asked Jacobs to get rid of the radiator and pipes, which were not called for in the script and about which, in fact, he had been dubious from the start: "I think it grounded it too much in a basement. It might also be a tower that he was looking out of, if not an ark, or this or that. I think it a little bit limited the playfulness of visual imagination." There was also the ashcan question:

In terms of the sightlines, the only way we could put Nagg and Nell upstage, which we both wanted, was to put them together. There wasn't enough room otherwise. And I really had persuaded Sally that I don't think the bins have to be garbage cans. The academic that says they have to be a single kind of garbage can or it's incorrect is ridiculous. But what I do think was wrong was that it looked like they could touch too easily, inside. I never meant that to be the case at all. They were supposed to be isolated. All his characters are isolated. We didn't want it to appear as though they were in a bicycle built for two. I think unintentionally that was implied.

Chaikin had come to feel, too, that the lighting made Hamm and Clov's room too hospitable:

I kept saying to Beverly and to Sally that I didn't want to go with the visual grimness. I didn't want it to be altogether cold. I don't regret that, but I think that the lights were *too* warm. I liked the flashiness of the lights, the fact that the ceiling was made up of different colors. I wish the ceiling could stay that way but not so much warm the stage, not make the air on the stage that color. But Beverly pointed out that if the skin of the actors was to be warm at all, if it was to look as if the actors had blood in them, it had to be. But the wall *shouldn't* be. The lighting thing was not resolved when we opened.

Preparing for Paris, Chaikin and Emmons went over the problems again, and Emmons went to Paris to make the changes.

Both the New York and the Paris productions were lauded by the critics.* Mel Gussow wrote in the *New York Times* that the show was

*There was some strong dissent. John Simon, in *New York* magazine, assailed Chaikin's unfaithfulness to the script. And the *Daily News*'s Douglas Watt found the production "dull."

an "authoritative production," with "prodigious" acting. Emory Lewis, in the *Bergen Record*, called it "brilliant," "a revelation," and said that Chaikin had "rescued the play's Irish wit from the pedants." Erika Munk's *Village Voice* review praised the show's clarity and its tempering of despair:

This is the most lucid *Endgame* imaginable, but each move is played to draw from the clawing, inhuman text (Beckett's adjectives) a measure of compassion larger than seemed possible . . .
    Chaikin's achievement isn't to make the play's wit and lyricism apparent – that would be easy – but to make us comprehend, even feel warmly towards, its bile and self-pitying melancholy.

In Paris, *Le Monde* gave front-page space to Mathilde La Bardonnie's rave: "Everyone who still has faith in the theater, who still believes in the delight that good actors can provide, absolutely must go . . . to see *Endgame*"; Chaikin, she wrote, rather than staying on the play's surface, had "penetrated deep enough to find the laugh, the brutal burst of laughter" at its root.
    Chaikin was pleased, of course, that the reviews showed an understanding of his intentions. But he regretted that, as always, good reviews made the audiences too deferential.

When Chaikin, who had not gone to Paris with the show, arrived three weeks after it closed to perform *Tongues* and *Savage/Love*, he found a message from Beckett suggesting that they meet, if Chaikin was interested. They got together at a café and talked for an hour and a half about music, theater, life in Paris, life in New York, and Chaikin's *Endgame*.
    Beckett had not seen the production – he never goes to the theater, he said – but had gotten a very detailed description and was enthusiastic. He was especially pleased with what he had heard about Seltzer's Hamm, and had sent him a note.* He talked too about what he had heard of Chaikin's work as an actor, and gave him some material that he thought Chaikin might like to perform.
    Chaikin was both moved and disturbed by the contact. "At one point, when we were talking on the phone, he said, 'I would be happy if we could get together.' And I thought, 'He uses words like "happy"! This person who writes those plays about how everything's all washed up and who uses language so precisely can still talk like that.' " His impression of Beckett was one of pain and kindness:

*It probably arrived the day after Seltzer's death.

Something is crushed in him. He is deeply wounded. But what he writes out of is the other part of himself. He is a reporter about living as a fragment.

And he can still be nice. I have the feeling that he doesn't make gestures. He has to be too economical about what he gives out to make gestures. But he has the care to be nice.

This meeting briefly revived the unsteadiness that Chaikin had in fact experienced again directing *Endgame* for New York and Paris: "I was feeling that I was getting like a piece of fabric, at the end where it gets raveled. I felt personally precarious. I felt that I couldn't stand it in rehearsals anymore." The need to work with a new Clov had nearly pushed him beyond his threshold:

There is a budget of time that one gives to something. I didn't know I'd go back into rehearsals with a new actor. That was the point at which I thought: "I don't want to go back into this fucking thing. I don't want it. It has sapped me in a way. It's usurped something." The thing that repels me about this play is that it deactivates. It takes energy away. I think there is something wrong with that.

What had kept Chaikin from utterly turning against Beckett's work was remembering its effect on him as a spectator seeing a play just once:

When I went to see [Andrei Serban's production of] *Happy Days*, I thought, "it's so wonderful, so eloquent." I said to myself, "This guy has the courage to speak about and theatricalize the border of what's tolerable to exist with. Since he's able to complete the play and get to the next scene, his inertia is not so great that it's in fact arresting him, paralyzing him. Here he is recording this thing."

But when I'm working on a Beckett play, I do feel it's just too much day after day. It's just too much.

Finally, Chaikin's love for Beckett keeps him coming back. Shortly after the *Endgame* production left for Paris, he said: "I can't stand him now. I never want to do anything by him again." A few days later, it was: "I don't want to do anything right now. I don't want to direct *Happy Days* especially; I don't want to do *Endgame* again; I don't want to do *Krapp's Last Tape* as either an actor or director. As you know, I was working on *Stories and Texts for Nothing*, and there is some stuff in that that I was really drawn to." And, about two minutes later:

He's my favorite living writer for the theater. I don't know if "favorite" is right; he's the one I esteem the most. Whenever I get over this production, I'd like at some point again to look into *Texts for Nothing*. I'd like to find a way maybe to perform it, because it's really like a song, haunting, just marvelous!

7   Afterword

> Theater is prehistoric. And it includes in it the most astonishing thoughts and the most frightening. It embodies and enacts those things which one can think and even some things that one can barely think. The history of theater is as astonishing as any legacy that we have.
>
>   – Chaikin, Aug. 8, 1980

Chaikin's work connects, finally, with the most primitive, ancient traditions of theater, with dramatic enactment as a way of giving voice to basic forces that bind human communities. More narrowly, his work is a chapter in several intersecting modern histories: the rebellion against science's denial of the irrational; the movement of theater beyond naturalism; the relationship between the stage and media; and the rollercoaster development of postwar American culture.

The charge of the sixties, which helped to launch Chaikin's work, is largely spent now in theater as in the rest of American society. And most of the individual cast that made up the stage vanguard then has backed either into obscurity or into the mainstream – which looks very different as a result. Indeed, much American theater carries some stamp of that period of revolution. Artists' refusal to accept the tyranny of the commercial box office has been answered by a diversified nonprofit base that apparently has survived even recession economics. If political theater that tackles issues of national and international scope has retrenched, the noncommercial stage has remained a prime forum for gay, feminist, and ethnic activist groups. Even Broadway has swung open a bit (as it periodically does): Amid revivals of *Peter Pan* and *Mame*, it has seen, for example, the homosexual *Bent*, the (albeit tame) political themes of *Evita*, and several powerful works by South African playwright Athol Fugard.

Equally important has been the theater's artistic broadening. The contemporary stage is rich with an unprecedented variety of forms and with the search for ways to expand expression even further. The focus (and fashion) in theater experiment has changed, of course, over two decades. The humanistic, politically committed, actor-centered avant-garde that dominated the sixties and early sev-

208

enties has largely taken the background to high-tech and dispassion-ate postmodernism. But, in fact, explorations of all sorts have con-tinued, and there has been a chain reaction of inspiration. Innova-tors have continued to emerge, breaking boundaries, finding new forms, reassessing and realigning values.

Moreover, amid the various pyrotechnics and blazes, a few sus-tained energies have carried through. And even with his career still in process and the results of his influence still developing, even though the subtlety of his work makes his contributions difficult to pinpoint and his avoidance of the mainstream sometimes makes them easy to miscredit, it is apparent that the most central, lasting, and nourishing energy has been Chaikin's.

Chaikin is one of very few artists from early off-off-Broadway who is still working experimentally. Rather than playing out a one- or two-note inspiration, he has provided a continuing line of explora-tion; his research, though sometimes stumbling or turning in circles, has always finally been able to move on and grow to a next phase – "like snakeskins." While the climate of theater experiment has cer-tainly nurtured Chaikin's explorations, his work has been one of the major forces that have inspired others. If many of his approaches seem familiar now, it is precisely because they have become ab-sorbed into the fabric of modern theater.

Chaikin has helped to introduce not only an expanded vocabulary but, more important, a way of developing theater languages. Col-laborative creation is accepted as an alternative approach to making theater. Its fruits have appeared not only in venues like LaMama that generally welcome experimental work, but even on Broadway in such shows as Elizabeth Swados's *Runaways* and Michael Ben-nett's *A Chorus Line*. There is much wider understanding of the value of "presence." Indeed, one sees examples of the actors being acknowledged along with the characters in all kinds of theater these days, from Jerry Mayer's one-man shows and the Wooster Group's *Rhode Island Trilogy* to *Sweeney Todd*. Abstract musical or collage-like structures are appearing on the stage more often – in work by Mere-dith Monk, Robert Wilson, the Mabou Mines, and others – without the old dramaturgical framework of dreams.

Chaikin's work also has infiltrated actor training to the point where nearly every major American theater school, except the pri-vate salons of Method teachers, and many abroad, include some type of Chaikin exercises in their programs. Sometimes the work is only half understood; sometimes, especially in the more conserva-tive places, it sneaks in through stage-movement classes, where it is

Chaikin, New York, 1983. Photograph by Eileen Blumenthal.

tolerated by the "real" acting teachers. But most recent veterans of American acting schools have done at least some variety of sound-and-movement or chord exercises. Even if the exposure goes no further, the result is a generation of performers with some notion that emotion memory and daydreaming are not the only routes into a character moment, that theater can explore and expand experience rather than just present what is already understood.

Chaikin's loyalty to off-off-Broadway, despite prominence and opportunities to "move up," has helped to keep that forum not merely a place where beginning artists can learn and showcase their craft, or where eccentrics can stage far-out ideas, but a laboratory where the most serious and far-reaching explorations go on. His insistence that theater artists have a responsibility for what their work promotes, through its content and its social context, led one *Village Voice* critic to call him "the conscience of us all." Backstage after a performance of *Tongues* and *Savage/Love*, Stella Adler said of Chaikin, "He's all that's left of purity in the world!"

Indeed, while Chaikin is not widely known among the theatergoing public, the seminal nature of his work has been recognized within the theater world. Writing about *Tongues* and *Savage/Love* in the Sunday *New York Times*, Mel Gussow recalled the Open Theater as "America's most celebrated performance group" and talked about its influence "on artists as wide-ranging as Robert Wilson, Andrei Serban, André Gregory, JoAnne Akalaitis, Lee Breuer, and Sam Shepard." Even Stanley Kauffmann, perhaps now the least sympathetic of major New York critics to Chaikin's work, has repeatedly acknowledged Chaikin's impact in his *New Republic* reviews. When the *Village Voice* gave its first "Lifetime Achievement" award for contribution to off- and off-off-Broadway theater, Chaikin was the judges' immediate and unanimous selection; he was, they said, the "only imaginable choice."

Chaikin's real importance, though, is not as a model that others have copied – though he certainly has been that – but as a subtler and deeper agent. He continues to search for the germs of living culture that can grow in and vitalize the theater, that can "turn the whole thing":

Theater's province in a way is not clear now. I think theater has a role to play, and it will have a role to play later that's even more definite and necessary than the one it has now. A little later theater will have a very, very precise voice of what it does that nothing else does.

Chronology

Chaikin's practice of showing performance pieces in progress and opening plays "as furtively as possible" sometimes makes citation of the first performance a bit tricky. *The Serpent*, for example, was initially presented in public on March 8, 1968, at Colgate College, as a work in progress, then was done for friends at the Pocket Theater in New York on April 18; its May 2 performance in Rome was treated by the press as an opening; back from Europe in the fall, *The Serpent* was shown at Vassar College in early December, then reworked before its "first" American performances in January. *The Mutation Show*'s delivery into the world was even more complicated. I have handled such cases here by noting only the major points when a piece was offered to the public in a given shape.

Although I have generally recorded the length of each show's run, these figures should not be taken as indexes of a show's critical or box office success. Usually in Chaikin's noncommercial venues the number of performances is set in advance. Thus, for example, *Antigone* did its full seven-week run at the Public Theater in 1982 despite largely unfavorable press, while *Tongues*, which was very enthusiastically received by critics and audiences, played at the Magic Theater in 1978 for only the prearranged five days (though it was later revived elsewhere).

1955–8

Chaikin moves to New York City. He takes acting classes with several prominent Method teachers, including Herbert Berghof, William Hickey, Mira Rostova, and Nola Chilton.

In 1957 he helps to form the Harlequin Players and directs its first production, a double bill of Sean O'Casey's *Bedtime Story* (in which Chaikin also plays John Jo Mulligan) and Edna St. Vincent Millay's *Aria da Capo* (in which Chaikin plays Corydon); performances are in a third-floor loft of the Alhambra Hall on New York's run-down Lower East Side. This first presentation of Chaikin's work as a director receives high critical praise, as do his performances. The company, however, disbands after less than two seasons.

Meanwhile, Chaikin is getting other acting jobs in summer stock

212

and off-Broadway. Among his roles are Robert in Alfred Hayes's *The Girl on the Via Flaminia* (Hudson Guild Theater, New York City, October 1957); Mr. Atkins in Howard Richardson and William Berney's *Dark of the Moon* (Carnegie Hall Playhouse, New York City, opening February 1958); and Ben Whitledge in Ira Levin's *No Time for Sergeants* (Gretna Playhouse, Mt. Gretna, July 1958).

1959–SPRING 1960

In the spring of 1959, Chaikin joins the Living Theater. He is cast as a replacement, playing the Boyfriend of Serafina and the Real Estate Agent in William Carlos Williams's *Many Loves*. He also portrays Ephron in Paul Goodman's *The Cave at Machpelah* (opening June 30, 1959) and Mangini, a small part, in Pirandello's *Tonight We Improvise* (opening November 6, 1959). Meanwhile, he understudies the role of Leach, the lead, in Jack Gelber's *The Connection* (opening July 15, 1959). When the actor playing Leach leaves to make a film, Chaikin takes over the role.

1960–1

Chaikin leaves the Living Theater in July 1960 to open on July 11 at the Gate Theater in a triple bill of one acts: e. e. cummings's *Santa Claus*, in which he plays Santa; Yeats's *Calvary*, in which he plays Lazarus; and de Ghelderode's *Escurial*, in which he performs the lead, the Jester. That program is not a critical success, and after its eleven-day run, Chaikin returns to the Living Theater. His new roles with the company that season are as the sailor, C. Maynes, in Brecht's *In the Jungle of the Cities* (opening December 20), and as the Count in two staged readings of Pirandello's *Mountain Giants* (April 3 and 10). Chaikin tours Europe with the Living Theater in June 1961.

1961–2

Chaikin continues acting at the Living Theater. During April and May he again tours Europe with the company.

1962–3

The Living Theater's *Man Is Man*, directed by Julian Beck, opens on September 18, with Chaikin playing Galy Gay. This experience, he later says, changes his aspirations from fame and fortune to more serious artistic and political goals. It also brings Chaikin his first major critical acclaim. He gets a *Village Voice* Obie award for the performance.

He is also cast in the company's production of Kenneth Brown's *The Brig* (opening May 15), playing with Gloria Foster in a love-scene coda following each brig act; these scenes are dropped from the play during previews, largely at Chaikin's suggestion.

Chaikin starts an acting workshop within the Living Theater, but it is short-lived. By early February, he is meeting informally with actors (mainly not from the Living Theater) and other stage artists to explore nonnaturalistic approaches to acting. Within weeks he becomes the key force in the group, which meets regularly – and names itself the Open Theater.

1963–4

During his Open Theater workshop's first full season, Chaikin begins various lines of exploration, including ensemble exercises, "insides," "circles," transformations, and rudimentary "on/off" and "expecting" investigations.

The company gives its first public performances, distinct from open demonstrations in its loft. A show of "Improvisations performed by actors and dancers" on December 13 at Jean Erdman's Theater of the Dance is followed three days later by a performance at the Sheridan Square Playhouse. That program consists of "A Ritual Hello" (a demonstration of the group's warm-up); an "Odets" "inside/outside" improvisation; two "perfect people" pieces; a transformation improvisation built around an airplane crash; a dream "conductor"; and a short play, *Eat at Joe's*, by Open Theater playwright Megan Terry. The second production, performed twice in mid-April at the Martinique Theater, consists of the opening warm-up; an on/off improvisation, a combined "perfect people"/dream "conductor" piece; the laughing "Contest"; "Picnic in Spring"; Brecht's *Clown Play*; a short work by van Itallie based on a recent New York City murder; a demonstration of formal storytelling; and a singing-styles transformation.

Meanwhile, the Living Theater is closed in October by the Internal Revenue Service for nonpayment of taxes. Chaikin performs elsewhere during the season. In February he plays Clarence in the premiere production of Terrence McNally's *And Things That Go Bump in the Night* at the Guthrie Theater in Minneapolis. Later he plays the

Detective in *Victims of Duty* (and the second furniture mover in *The New Tenant*) on a Ionesco double bill that opens May 24 at the Writers Stage Company.

1964–5

Chaikin continues his Open Theater explorations from the previous season and expands them into other areas, including "worlds."

The Open Theater performs eight programs on Monday nights at the Sheridan Square Playhouse, the first on October 12, then more or less biweekly from February through May. Chaikin directs virtually all of the (rehearsed) improvisations: the opening warm-up; singing-styles transformations; an open transformation (demonstrating the exercise); a dream "conductor"; two "unnoticed action" improvisations; new versions of the previous season's "Airplane," "Odets" and "Contest" pieces; a Rip van Winkle "worlds" improvisation; a "Trial" in which spatial areas determine roles; and a dream improvisation about an abortion.

The Open Theater's performance season also includes nearly a dozen short plays, mainly by company playwrights, but Chaikin's involvement in these is slight: He directs two short plays by van Itallie, *The First Fool* and *The Hunter and the Bird*; he also stages Maria Irene Fornes's *Successful Life of Three* and codirects Terry's *Calm Down Mother* early in the season, but both of these are redone by Richard Gilman for later programs. He performs in Terry's *Keep Tightly Closed in a Cool Dry Place*.

Chaikin continues to perform outside the Open Theater as well. He plays the Clown in Arthur Kopit's *Sing to Me Through Open Windows* at the Players Theater (opening March 15); he plays the title role in a reading of the Brecht/Marlowe *Edward II* at the Theater for Ideas (April 22–3); and he plays the Coolie in Brecht's *The Exception and the Rule*, at the Greenwich Mews Theater (opening May 20). He receives a second Obie for his performances in *The Exception and the Rule* and the previous season's *Victims of Duty*.

1965–6

Chaikin by now is concentrating his Open Theater workshop explorations less on theater games and trust exercises, more on his own ensemble studies (jamming, conductors) and on attempts to express extreme, or at least hidden, conditions, often locating them somatically. In fact, though, an Open Theater performance commitment of one week each month at LaMama channels much energy away from the laboratory studies.

Chaikin has relatively little to do with the LaMama performances: He directs the first program (opening October 27), comprised of improvisations, and does not participate again until the final program (opening April 27), for which he directs Brecht's *Clown Play*. He and Peter Feldman direct *Viet Rock* for its LaMama opening (May 21). Despite the production's critical success, Terry decides a week after opening to redirect the play herself.

During the summer, Chaikin works in London with Peter Brook and the Royal Shakespeare Company on *US (Tell Me Lies)*; he meets Grotowski, who is also participating on the project.

1966–7

Chaikin directs *Interview* in *America Hurrah* off-Broadway, (opening November 7 at the Pocket Theater). Despite some strain from the involvement of workshop members in two commercial productions – the successful *America Hurrah* and the restaged *Viet Rock*, now receiving poor notices at the Martinique – he continues his explorations, including elaborate "expecting" studies and work on excommunication rites.

During the winter, Chaikin's ensemble gives several performances of short, mostly improvisational pieces; although the work is largely based on Chaikin's explorations, he is only peripherally involved in staging and assembling these public showings. The majority of the productions are benefits for political causes and politically oriented arts organizations: For example, the company performs on December 8 for a "SANE" antinuclear benefit at Madison Square Garden in New York (Chaikin directs a piece called "Firebomb" for this event), and on January 30 and February 3 as part of the Angry Artists Against the War in Vietnam effort.

The Open Theater gets an Obie award "for maintaining a laboratory where a company of actors, directors, and playwrights confront the limits of contemporary theatre experience."

1967–8

Chaikin plays Julius Orlovsky in Robert Frank's film *Me and My Brother*.

Chaikin's workshop, devoted for the first time to creating a full-length performance piece, continues other explorations as well. His demonstration in October of Chinese theater technique marks the beginning of intensive work at distilling theater forms. The group also focuses more than ever before on physical work, perhaps inspired by a two-day visit from Grotowski and Ryszard Cieslak in December.

During the winter and spring, Chaikin's ensemble does several performances, mostly benefits like those of the previous season: For example, the company performs on January 12 and 13 for the Angry Artists cause, and on March 30 and 31 in the First American Radical Theater Festival. Three performances (February 5 at the Pocket Theater; February 19 at the Village Gate; and February 25 at St. Clements Church) are fundraisers for the company's planned summer tour.

Chaikin's main project for the season is the creation, with his workshop, of a full-length performance piece based on biblical stories. *The Serpent* opens on May 2 at the Teatro delli Arti, Teatro Club, Rome. Chaikin's ensemble then tours Italy, Germany, Switzerland, and Denmark with *The Serpent* and a program called *Masks*, a potpourri of songs, short plays, and Open Theater–created improvisations. *The Clown Play*, now codirected by Chaikin and Rhea Gaisner, is a staple of *Masks'* varying program, and his staging of *Interview* is performed a few times. Apart from this, Chaikin is little involved in *Masks*. Although the program is more representative than *The Serpent* of the Open Theater's first five years of work – and is the last showcase, apart from a few benefits, that this early work is to have – his interest now is in creating more developed, full-length performance works and in continuing his laboratory explorations.

1968–9

Chaikin resumes workshop activity in New York in early October. His explorations focus on language more than ever before, and he works a great deal with storytelling, not only using words but also expanding and compressing beyond the verbal.

In November the company participates in Michelangelo Antonioni's film *Zabriskie Point*.

In mid-December Chaikin begins to rework *The Serpent* with his ensemble. They give public performances of it in their loft starting in January and at a few colleges in New York State in the spring. They also perform *The Serpent* and some short pieces, mostly from *Masks*, for political benefits.

During the fall, also, Chaikin embarks with his ensemble on a new collaborative piece, this time about China. They draw on myths, fantasies, clichés, and facts about China, seeking images to express the richness and mystery of the culture. The exploration does not take, though, and they abandon it at the end of January. Chaikin then suggests a different theme: death and dying. This work will lead to *Terminal*. Roberta Sklar codirects the piece, and Susan Yankowitz contributes the text.

Chaikin also begins rehearsing the role of Hamm in a production of *Endgame* directed by Sklar.

During the summer Chaikin participates, by Grotowski's invitation, in a seminar at the Eugenio Barba theater laboratory in Denmark.

The Serpent wins an Obie award, and Chaikin and the Open Theater get a Vernon Rice Award for "outstanding contributions" to the theater. He also is awarded a Guggenheim Fellowship.

1969–70

For the first time since the start of the Open Theater, Chaikin's energy is channeled more into performances than workshops for an entire season.

Terminal opens on November 17 at the Théâtre Alhambra in Bordeaux, beginning the Open Theater's second European tour. The company performs through early January in France, Switzerland, Germany, and Holland, with *The Serpent, Terminal, Endgame* (opening November 26 at Cité Universitaire, Paris), and a production of *Ubu Cocu* directed by Peter Feldman. Back in New York, the players perform *The Serpent* and *Terminal* in their loft. They also take *Terminal* to several area colleges, mostly in New York State. That spring, they perform *Terminal* and *Endgame* at benefits and in prisons, beginning a commitment to prison performances that will continue through the end of the Open Theater. In late May the company undertakes a three-week series of performances at Washington Square Methodist Church in New York City.

The Serpent gets a Brandeis University Creative Arts Award.

That summer, ten actors and Sklar work with Luciano Berio in Santa Fe on his *Opera*, based largely on *Terminal*. Chaikin is not involved.

1970–1

By Chaikin's decision, the Open Theater is reduced in the fall to only his workshop, and that is pared down to six actors. He continues his explorations, focusing again on storytelling and on distilling forms.

The new, smaller company reworks *Terminal,* but drops the rest of the Open Theater's repertoire. In October the ensemble begins developing a new play, on the theme of change. It creates this piece without the close collaboration of a writer; Sklar codirects.

The Open Theater performs *Terminal* in colleges and prisons in the Northeast, touring through part of February and most of March, and at several political benefits. After a break, work resumes in mid-July to prepare *Terminal* and *Mutations* for the company's third foreign tour, with performances starting on August 6. This trip takes them to Algeria (where *Mutations* gets its first public showing as a work in progress on August 7, at the Théâtre National Algérian), Israel, Iran, and Yugoslavia. Chaikin, who for political reasons had strongly opposed participation in the shah's Shiraz Festival, does not accompany the actors to Iran. He rejoins them during the second week of September in Belgrade, where *Mutations* receives first prize in the Belgrade International Theater Festival.

1971−2

Returning to New York in September, Chaikin and the Open Theater rework *Mutations* into *The Mutation Show.* From mid-November through the end of April, the company performs *Terminal* and *The Mutation Show* in its New York loft at the Space for Innovative Development, a converted church on West Thirty-sixth Street, and at colleges and prisons throughout the United States and Canada, ending with a week of performances at the Tombs, the Men's House of Detention in New York City.

Between the out-of-town tours, which last from a few days to three weeks each, Chaikin holds workshops, focusing in particular on classical material, especially from Shakespeare and Greek tragedy. After the Tombs performances at the end of April, the company breaks for seven months.

The Mutation Show receives an Obie as "Best Theater Piece of 1971−1972." The Open Theater gets the New England Theater Conference's major annual award "for outstanding creative achievement in the American theatre." And Chaikin is granted an honorary doctorate from Drake University.

1972−3

After several informal meetings during the fall, Chaikin's workshop resumes its activities in December. The group continues to explore classical material including works by Ibsen and Chekhov.

Chaikin begins a new ensemble piece about levels of sleep and levels of awareness. It is understood that he means this to be the Open Theater's final major work before disbanding. Again the group does not collaborate closely with a single writer, but several playwrights, including van Itallie, Terry, and Sam Shepard contribute, and Mira Rafalowicz assists Chaikin as dramaturge.

The untitled work in progress is first shown publicly in New York on March 16, at the Space for Innovative Development, and then runs alternately with *The Mutation Show* through April 13. The company undertakes its fourth overseas tour from May 18 through June 30, performing the three works from its repertory in Zurich; in London, where it has a three-week run at the Round House Theatre; and in several Dutch cities. (*Nightwalk's* first performance as a titled work is at the Zurich Theatre 11, on May 24.)

Meanwhile, back home, Chaikin is given a Drama Desk award for his direction of *The Mutation Show*.

1973-4

The Open Theater gives its final performances, playing *Terminal*, *The Mutation Show*, and *Nightwalk* at the Theatre at St. Clements in New York City from September 8 through October 13, then touring to colleges in the United States and Canada from October 15 through December 1. The company's final performance is of *Nightwalk* at the University of California, Santa Barbara, on December 1.

Back in New York, with the Open Theater officially disbanded, Chaikin and several of the actors continue to meet regularly through the winter to work on classical material.

In the spring, Chaikin begins his first post–Open Theater project, a new version of the Electra story. Playwright Robert Montgomery writes the text, collaborating closely with Chaikin and the three actors (Shami Chaikin and Paul Zimet, both longtime Open Theater members, and Michele Collison, a member of Peter Brook's company). *Electra* is performed in late May; first it has a week of invitational showings at the Public Theater, then, starting May 27, a week of public performances at St. Clements.

1974-5

In the fall, Chaikin runs a weekly six-hour session in Kristin Linklator's new Working Theater, an organization aimed mainly at training theater teachers; he hopes to develop an ongoing laboratory without the pressure of heading a company himself. He concentrates largely on classical material. He become critically ill, however, and on October 18 undergoes open-heart surgery. When he is able, he completes his season commitment to the project, but does not continue his involvement beyond that.

Meanwhile, by early January, he is in rehearsal with *The Sea Gull*, directing van Itallie's new version. The production, which uses no Open Theater actors except Tina Shepard (as Nina), opens at the Manhattan Theatre Club on January 29 for a six-week run.

Chaikin then joins with the Theatre of Latin America to create a "documentary musical" about the overthrow of the Allende government. *Chile, Chile*, directed by Chaikin, plays at Washington Square Methodist Church in late May.

During this period, Chaikin also begins work with van Itallie and Richard Peaslee on a new collaborative piece. About half the actors in the project are former Open Theater members, and most of the others are from Chaikin's *Sea Gull*. The idea for the proposed play is to use traditional fable elements to express modern aspirations and fears. Preparation of this *Fable* continues during the summer at the Lenox Arts Center in Lenox, Massachusetts, where there are public previews of it in August.

Chaikin gets his second Guggenheim Fellowship.

1975–6

Chile, Chile is revived for two performances at St. Clements on September 26 and 27.

A Fable Telling about a Journey is performed at the Exchange Theater in the Westbeth artists' housing complex in New York City for five weeks starting October 21.

The Montgomery/Chaikin *Electra* is revived shortly afterward, with Tina Shepard replacing Collison; following a week of performances at the Exchange Theater in January, it goes on a national tour.

Chaikin arranges a production of *Woyzeck*; he plays the title role, and Leonardo Shapiro directs. *Woyzeck* plays at the Public Theater for a month, starting March 24, then at the Holland Festival in June.

1976–7

On October 11, Chaikin starts rehearsals at the Public Theater for Adrienne Kennedy's *A Movie Star Has to Star in Black and White*, the only new script he has ever directed that was not connected to one of his laboratories. The show is performed during the weekend of November 9–12 in the Public's workshop series; there is no advertising and the press is not invited.

Chaikin sets up the Winter Project as an open-ended theater workshop intended to be ongoing. He begins with approximately twenty actors, musicians, writers, and directors and a dramaturge; nearly all are people with whom he has collaborated before. They explore a variety of questions, especially how one can give voice to extreme passion. Chaikin also returns to his long-term concern with creating mourning rituals. The Winter Project does not show its work publicly this first season.

In the late winter Chaikin begins *Endgame* rehearsals at Princeton University, with a class of theater students observing his directing process. The show plays for three weeks, starting May 4, at the Theatre Intime; only local press is notified.

Chaikin receives the first "Lifetime Achievement" Obie award, for his contribution to off- and off-off-Broadway theater.

1977–8

In November Chaikin begins rehearsals at the Public Theater for *The Dybbuk*. Although Chaikin becomes critically ill with a heart infection in the final week before performances and feels that he has not finished the show, it opens to the public on schedule, on December 16, and plays for six weeks; Chaikin sends directing notes to the company from his hospital bed, based on audio tape recordings that are made for him.

When he can resume activity, Chaikin embarks on a second season with his Winter Project. They explore basic elements of theater, especially music and the actor–audience relationship. "Interviews" are used as a tool for "expecting" and for exploring characters and conditions. Much of the work uses preexisting texts, including poems and letters as well as speeches from plays. Since public performances are a condition of the Project's grants, limited audiences are admitted to observe a few rehearsed sessions during final weeks; the press is not invited.

In May Chaikin goes to San Francisco to create a performance piece with Sam Shepard. They co-write and codirect a monologue for Chaikin; Shepard composes and performs the instrumental accompaniment. *Tongues* plays at the Magic Theater in San Francisco for five nights, starting June 5.

On July 20, shortly after his return from California, Chaikin undergoes his second open-heart operation.

1978–9

In the fall Chaikin runs a workshop at the Center for Theater Practice, an organization established by Françoise Kourilsky; Meredith Monk also participates. Chaikin hopes, again, to find an administrative framework for his laboratory. And, again, his involvement lasts just one season.

In January Chaikin reconvenes the Winter Project, reduced now by funding cuts to a dozen people. Much of the work now involves interviews and refining domestic scenarios into tiny nuggets. Since the group is obliged to create a performance piece, its energy is geared in that direction. *Re-Arrangements,* mostly about the ways people emotionally connect with or protect themselves from each other, plays March 9–25 at LaMama.

In June Chaikin redirects *The Dybbuk* with Israeli actors at the Habimah Theater in Tel Aviv; at his insistence, and over strenuous administrative opposition, the cast includes an Arab performer as the (Jewish) bridegroom.

At the beginning of August, shortly after his return to the United States, Chaikin goes to San Francisco to create another piece with Shepard, this time about love. *Savage/Love* plays, with *Tongues,* at the Eureka Theater, September 6–9. The production gets a Bay Area Theater Critics Circle Award for "New Directions in Theater."

1979–80

Chaikin performs *Tongues* and *Savage/Love* (under the title *Tongues)* at the Public Theater, with Robert Woodruff directing. Its original engagement, as a workshop production from November 7 through November 26, is extended through January 21.

Meanwhile Chaikin goes into rehearsals and production directing *Endgame.* It opens on January 13 at the Manhattan Theatre Club, and plays for a month, then moves to the American Center in Paris in late February for a short run.

During March Chaikin performs *Tongues* in Paris, Rome, and Milan.

In May, shortly after his return from Europe, Chaikin begins the Winter Project's fourth season. The company is now reduced by funding limitations to five actors (Ronnie Gilbert, Will Patton, Atsumi Sakato, Tina Shepard, and Paul Zimet) and three musicians (Peter Golub, Skip LaPlante, and Harry Mann). Working closely with dramaturge Rafalowicz, assistant director Steven Reisner, costume designer Mary Brecht, and set designer Jun Maeda (all of whom had also collaborated on *Re-Arrangements)*, they create the Winter Project's first major performance piece, on the theme of home and homelessness. *Tourists and Refugees* plays at LaMama from July 9 through August 3.

1980–1

During October and November Chaikin tours with *Tongues* on the West Coast, playing at the Mark Taper Forum Laboratory and at colleges and universities from southern California to British Columbia.

Chaikin and director Steve Kent create *Texts,* a one-actor stage adaptation of Beckett's *Texts for Nothing* and *How It Is.* They begin rehearsals at the Public Theater in late January, and Chaikin performs the piece for three weeks starting March 3.

The Winter Project also reconvenes in March (with a few personnel changes, including the addition of former Open Theater actor Raymond Barry). It creates *Tourists and Refugees No. 2,* on the same theme as the prior year's piece, but with a wholly new structure and about half new material. *Tourists and Refugees No. 2* plays at LaMama from April 29 through May 24.

Starting June 12, Chaikin performs *Texts* for three weeks in London at the Riverside Studios, and in Paris at the American Center.

When he returns, Chaikin prepares *Tourists and Refugees No. 2* for performances at the International Theater Festival in Caracas in July. He does not accompany the actors to Venezuela.

1981–2

For the Winter Project's sixth season, Chaikin again focuses on death and mourning. He wants to create a piece that takes place in the final moments of a person's life. Chaikin is both director and chief writer for this ensemble creation, in which Gloria Foster portrays the dying woman. *Trespassing* opens February 24 and plays at LaMama for four weeks.

Chaikin continues his study of mourning with a production of *Antigone,* which begins rehearsals at the Public Theater in mid-March. Using a new translation by John Chioles, he and Rafalowicz alter the text to emphasize the elements of mourning and political tyranny. Sally Jacobs designs the set. *Antigone* opens on April 16 and runs for seven weeks.

In early June Chaikin goes to Tel Aviv to create a political piece with a group of Jewish and Palestinian actors, the first such collaboration done in the country. Work continues during the Israeli invasion of Lebanon, and *The Other*'s initial performances are part of the First Festival of Jewish Theater at the beginning of July. The show resumes its run after the festival at the Neve Tzedek Theater Center, then tours through other parts of Israel.

1982–3

From the fall through February Chaikin develops and directs a series of four half-hour radio theater programs for satellite distribution. *Night Voices*, about the moment of falling asleep, features Chaikin and other Winter Project members as performers.

Chaikin divides the Winter Project's season into two parts. He preserves the first, which runs from mid-December to mid-February, as a workshop. During the next three weeks he creates a chamber piece with three performers. *Lies and Secrets* opens on March 9 and plays at LaMama for two weeks, then goes to London in May for a run at the Riverside Studios.

Chaikin disbands the Winter Project.

1983–4

Chaikin performs the title role in Chekhov's *Uncle Vanya*, directed by Andrei Serban; the show runs from September 1 through October 2 at LaMama.

He works with Sam Shepard from mid-January through mid-February at the American Repertory Theater in Cambridge, Mass.; they begin a new piece, about a captured angel, and plan to resume this work when their schedules permit. In late February, he goes to Israel for several weeks to work with a group of Jewish and Palestinian actors on a performance piece. Then, in mid-April, he goes to direct *Waiting For Godot* at the Stratford Festival Theater in Ontario, Canada; but he quits almost immediately because of a dispute over casting the show.

On May 7, Chaikin undergoes his third open heart operation. In connection with the surgery, he suffers a stroke, from which, as of late summer, he is continuing to recover.

Notes

Each note opens with the first four words of the paragraph for which it provides sources. Notes that deal with a continuous discussion covering more than one paragraph are identified. Where a workshop, rehearsal, lecture, or social meeting rather than a written source is cited in these notes or is mentioned in the text without a source citation, it should be assumed that I was present.

All interviews and conversations cited are mine with Chaikin and took place in New York, unless otherwise noted. Since I interviewed Chaikin more than a dozen times over nine years and some of his views changed during that period, I have included dates with all Chaikin interview citations. Also, I have distinguished between these formal, taped interviews and casual conversations, of which we have had several hundred; although Chaikin has agreed to my use here of any off-the-record remarks I had noted, the reader should understand that certain comments – about his family, for example – would not have been made intentionally for publication. For interviews with people other than Chaikin, the date (or dates, for several-session meetings) are given only at the first mention.

All published and manuscript sources are identified in these notes fully at the first reference only; published sources and published and unpublished dissertations are also listed in the bibliography. The Chaikin Papers (CP), Open Theater Papers (OTP), and van Itallie Papers (VIP) are all housed at the Kent State University Libraries, Kent, Ohio. Documents in private hands are identified by the abbreviation PC (private collection) and the owner's name; much of this material probably will wend its way, in time, to the Kent State collections as well.

1. OVERVIEW

["To express the extreme"] Talk to actors, Center for Theater Practice, New York, N.Y., Oct. 1, 1978.

[Perhaps the strongest single] Antonin Artaud, *The Theater and Its Double* (New York: Grove Press, 1958), p. 82.

[Indeed, a great deal] The description of Chaikin's childhood here and through the paragraph beginning [Chaikin became expert, during] is from conversations, 1977–82 (quotations from Dec. 16, 1979, and July 25, 1980).

[Meanwhile, Chaikin helped form] Chaikin's Scrapbook, Chaikin Papers, Kent State University Libraries, Kent, Ohio (hereafter abbreviated CP). Footnote: Chaikin's Scrapbook, CP.

[Despite his involvement with] "I thought . . .": interview, Aug. 8, 1980; "to be important": Ettore Sottsass and Fernanda Pivano, interview with Chaikin, May 12, 1968, Rome, pt. 2, p. 12, Open Theater Papers, Kent State University Libraries, Kent, Ohio (hereafter abbreviated OTP); "He was very concerned . . .": interview with Fred Katz, April 20, 1975.

226

[In 1959 Chaikin auditioned] "unrelieved dread": Alice Kellman, "Joseph Chaikin," *Drama Review*, 20, no. 3 (1976): 19; "I felt . . . ," "This time . . .": Saul Gottlieb, "*America Hurrah:* The Open Theater Emerges," copy of 37-page typescript, pp. 5–6, OTP.

[Chaikin was a principal] Chaikin's Scrapbook, CP; Chaikin, Open Theater Notebook, 1964–5, CP; Chaikin, *The Presence of the Actor* (New York: Atheneum, 1972), p. 49.

[In 1962 the Living] Interview, Aug. 8, 1980.

[But as Chaikin got] "I got offers . . .": interview, Aug. 8, 1980; "There I was . . . ," "started cutting out . . .": Robert Pasolli, *A Book On the Open Theatre* (New York: Avon Books, 1970), p. xiv; "knowing that . . .": Chaikin, *Presence*, p. 51.

[Until that time, Chaikin] Chaikin, *Presence*, pp. 51–2.

¡Chaikin's aspirations began to] "might really . . . confused": Chaikin, *Presence*, p. 51; "Perhaps if I . . .": Chaikin, Open Theater Notebook, 1963–4, CP.

[It was within the] "no one had . . . ," "working out . . .": Sottsass and Pivano, interview with Chaikin, pp. 5–6, 2, OTP; "You never knew . . .": Elenore Lester, "He Doesn't Aim to Please," *New York Times*, Dec. 25, 1966, sec. 2, p. 1.

[About this time, in] Conversation, Aug. 3, 1977; Sottsass and Pivano, interview with Chaikin, p. 2, OTP.

[In its earliest days] Among the earliest members were Valerie Belden, Isabelle Blau, Paul Boesing, Michael Bradford, Mimi Cozzens, Ron Faber, Peter Feldman, Sharon Gans, Jordan Hott, Lynn Kevin, Geraldine Lust, Catherine Mandas, Murray Paskin, Gerome Ragni (who first conceived *Hair* for the Open Theater), Gordon Rogoff, Arthur Sainer, David Spielberg, Megan Terry, Sharon Thie, Lois Unger, Barbara Vann, Sydney Shubert Walter, Lee Worley, and Ira Zuckerman; after a few months, Rogoff introduced Jean-Claude van Itallie to the group. There are (brief) descriptions of the Open Theater's first weeks in Arthur Sainer, *The Radical Theatre Notebook* (New York: Avon Books, 1975), pp. 18–19; Chaikin, *Presence*, pp. 52-4; van Itallie, "Playwright at Work: Off Off-Broadway," *Tulane Drama Review*, 10 (Summer 1966):154. The Open Theater's work is described in detail in Eileen Blumenthal, "The Open Theater," Ph.D. diss., Yale University, 1977.

[The dominance of Chaikin's] "People were into . . . creeds": interview with Barbara Vann and James Barbosa, Jan. 25 and Feb. 28, 1975; "implied a susceptibility . . . process": Chaikin, *Presence*, pp. 53-4.

[This openness was not] *Open Theater's interests:* The early Open Theater's *non-catholicity* of interests can be seen from [Pasolli], notes from interview with Peter Feldman, Sept. 12, 1967, OTP; "to find ways . . .": Chaikin, "The Open Theater [questions by Richard Schechner]," *Tulane Drama Review*, 9, no. 2 (1964):191; "aesthetic intention . . . possesses": Michael Smith, "The Good Scene: Off Off-Broadway," *Tulane Drama Review*, 10 (Summer 1966):167.

[For the first seven] Interview with Vann and Barbosa; interview with Tina Shepard, Mar. 4, 1975; interview with Shami Chaikin, June 8, 1975; interview with Joyce Aaron, May 19, 1975; Shami Chaikin, "Open Theater 1973," 1-page typescript, OTP; Mel Gussow, "Experimental Open Theater Carrying On," *New York Times*, Apr. 27, 1971, p. 51. The dynamic of Chaikin's more recent workshops, which I have seen, very much corresponds to these descriptions.

[Chaikin invented literally thousands] Richard Toscan, "Joseph Chaikin: Closing the Open Theatre," *Theatre Quarterly*, 4 (Nov. 1974–Jan. 1975):38.

[In some ways, this] "Joe would offer . . .": Michael Smith, "Theatre Journal," *Village Voice*, Oct. 18, 1973, p. 71; "a musical world . . .": Gordon Rogoff recalled this earlier comment in conversation, Jan. 28, 1983.

[Actors in the ensemble] "I don't like . . .": conversation, Aug. 6, 1980; "I always feel . . .": Chaikin, *Presence*, p. 86.

[For a while, Chaikin] "people quit . . .": Toscan, "Joseph Chaikin," p. 42, "The time at work . . .": Ellen Maddow, *Nightwalk* Notebook, Jan. 12, 1973, personal collection (hereafter abbreviated PC)–Maddow; "Everything has opened . . .": Peter Maloney, diary, Oct. 24, 1967, PC–Maloney.

[Apart from Chaikin's workshop] "a peripheral . . .": [Pasolli], notes, OTP.

[Many short-term projects were] The description of Open Theater performances, 1963–7, in the next several paragraphs is from programs and notes by Chaikin and van Itallie in OTP and in the van Itallie Papers, Kent State University Libraries, Kent, Ohio (hereafter abbreviated VIP). Technically, *America Hurrah* was not an Open Theater production. But it was directed by Chaikin and Levy, got half its cast from the Open Theater, and, according to van Itallie, was "helped immeasurably by the presence of the Open Theater actors and directors who had worked together with the playwright for many years."

[But for all its *and* From the fall of] Interview, Apr. 20, 1975; interview with Tina Shepard; interview with Vann and Barbosa; Roberta Mohan, interview with Tina Shepard, Apr. 18, 1973, Kent, Ohio, OTP; Barbosa to Chaikin, Jan. 22, 1970, CP; Chaikin to Maloney, Jan. 16, 1970, PC–Maloney; Erika Munk, "Working in a Collective–Interviews with Susan Yankowitz and Roberta Sklar," *Performance*, 1 (Dec. 1971):87–8; Chaikin, *Presence*, pp. 79 ("in a concentrated . . ."), 156–7. Chaikin recalls the fierce sense of betrayal in the group when tensions began to rupture it: "We wanted to have a total, absolutely Utopian community . . . The internal hemorrhaging that was going on at the point when dissonance began in the group and people started to hate each other was very violent. Because it was the violence of this community." Interview, Apr. 20, 1975.

[But Chaikin thought that] "like a clearing . . .": Chaikin, Notebook, 1963–4, p. 96, CP; the annual debate about moving on: conversation with Vann, Dec. 1, 1983, Kent, Ohio; *Chaikin's uneasiness with the big budget:* conversations, 1974–7. Footnote: Open Theater financial records, OTP.

[Chaikin saw the Open] "stuck . . .": Toscan, "Joseph Chaikin," p. 37; "go on . . . ," "After you go . . .": Michael Feingold, interview with Chaikin, Sept. 15, 1974, PC–Feingold; "embalmed as . . .": Paul Zimet, *Nightwalk* notebook, PC–Zimet.

[Chaikin was also feeling] "There is a feeling . . .": Pasolli, *Open Theatre*, p. 10; "The O.T. . . . ": Worley to Chaikin, Aug. 21, 1968, CP.

[In retrospect, Chaikin feels] Interview, Apr. 20, 1975.

[In any case, by] Conversations, 1975–7.

[At the same time] Figures on funding were provided by the various foundations and government commissions.

[For a while after] Conversations, 1977–80; Kellman, "Joseph Chaikin," p. 20 ("a great sense . . .").

[Not until the final] Interview, Apr. 4, 1978.

2. AN OPEN THEORY

[Chaikin's theories about theater] "Principles . . .": OTP; "a silly idea": conversation, 1980.

[Theater's function, Chaikin says] "You don't have . . .": interview, July 12, 1979, Westhampton Beach, N.Y.; "celebration": Chaikin, "Open Theater," p. 196.

[Beyond this, he believes] "a real momentum . . . ," "I feel that theater . . . ," "to try to see . . .": interview, Apr. 4, 1978; "It's true . . .": conversation, Apr. 1978; "give expression . . .": interview, Aug. 8, 1980.

[Theater, in fact, can] Feingold, interview with Chaikin, PC–Feingold.

["Everything we do," Chaikin] Chaikin, "The Context of Performance," in *Actors on Acting*, ed. Toby Cole and Helen Krich Chinoy (New York: Crown, 1970), p. 669.

[Part of any play's] "very essential heart . . . some form or other": Toscan, "Joseph Chaikin," p. 38, "sense of being alive . . . ," "appreciation of being": Richard Schechner, "An Interview with Joseph Chaikin," *Drama Review*, 13, no. 3 (1969):144; "confrontation . . .": Pasolli, *Open Theatre*, p. 83.

[For Chaikin, this reminder] "People don't know . . .": Chaikin, Notebook, 1963–4, CP; "I think that people . . .": Sottsass and Pivano, interview with Chaikin, pp. 10–11, OTP.

[Moreover, actors' presentation of] Chaikin, *Presence*, p. 128; "All entertainment . . .": Chaikin, "Context of Performance," p. 666.

[For a time, he] Chaikin "Fragments," ed. Kelly Morris, *Drama Review*, 13, no. 3 (1969):146.

[Although the Open Theater] "very gifted . . . oriented": Gussow, "Carrying On"; "a lot . . . ," "dedicated . . .": Robert Pasolli, "The Man-Not-in-the-Street on stage Off-Broadway," *Village Voice*, Nov. 3, 1966, p. 26; "a certain kind . . .": Michael Thomas, "Off Broadway," *Plays and Players*, Mar. 1967, p. 61; "to understand . . .": Chaikin, "Open Theater," p. 194.

[By late 1967, though] "There is no need . . .": Chaikin, *Presence*, p. 119; "rightness": Chaikin, "What the Actor Does," *Performance* 1 (Mar.–Apr. 1973):59; "missionary thing": Feingold, interview with Chaikin, p. 31, PC–Feingold; "for the enemy . . .": Sainer, *Notebook*, p. 6; "One of the major . . .": Chaikin, "The Presence of the Actor," typescript draft, pp. 165–6, CP.

[Still, Chaikin has never] "There's too much . . .": conversation, Feb. 1979.

[In fact, Chaikin has] "Only for political . . .": conversation, Apr. 1982; "to make trouble . . .": conversation, Jan. 29, 1979; "We used to say . . .": telephone conversation, Aug. 6, 1980.

[Chaikin's mistrust of conventional] "As [a person] says . . .": Chaikin, *Presence*, pp. 72–73; "We don't say . . .": Toscan, "Joseph Chaikin," p. 38.

[After several years of] "Only words . . .": Chaikin, *Presence*, p. 131; "one has to . . .": Toscan, "Joseph Chaikin," p. 38; "to see each play . . .": John Lahr, "The Open Theater's Serpent," in Lahr, *Up against the Fourth Wall* (New York: Grove Press, 1970), p. 173.

[Actors must learn also] "The spoken . . .": Chaikin, *Presence*, pp. 131–2; "Sometimes words . . .": quoted in Zimet, *Nightwalk* Notebook, Jan. 10, 1973, PC–Zimet.

[In any case, theater] Toscan, "Joseph Chaikin," p. 37.

[Chaikin's research is not] Chaikin, "What the Actor Does," p. 58.

[For a while, Chaikin] *Chaikin's developing views about character:* Naseem Khan, "The Home of Experience," *Time Out*, June 1–7, 1973, p. 17; "Chayevsky . . .": Pasolli, "Man-Not-in-the-Street," p. 26; conversations, 1975.

[Chaikin's rejection of naturalism] "over coffee . . .": Chaikin, *Presence*, p. 85; "Just as good manners . . .": Chaikin, "Fragments," p. 145; "I think one . . .": Schechner, "Interview," p. 144.

[Chaikin wants the theater] "We want to develop . . .": Thomas, "Off Broadway," p. 61; "Where does . . .": Chaikin, "What the Actor Does," p. 58; "There are zones . . .": Chaikin, *Presence*, p. 25; "the actor can . . .": Toscan, "Joseph Chaikin," p. 37.

[It is important, moreover] "need an identity . . .": Chaikin, *Nightwalk* Notebook I, PC–Chaikin; "When a piece . . ." (Paul Zimet's wording of Chaikin's note), "Joe's politics . . .": Zimet, *Nightwalk* Notebook, Mar. 29, 1973, PC–Zimet.

[Rejecting realism, Chaikin has] In "The Presence of the Actor as Kinetic Melody: A Study of Joseph Chaikin's Open Theater through the Philosophy of Maurice Merleau-Ponty," Ph.D. diss., University of Missouri–Columbia, 1977, Erlene Laney Hendrix discusses at length the implications of the affinity that Chaikin's theater has with music.

[Chaikin's hobby and his] Visit, Columbia Presbyterian Hospital, New York, Jan. 12, 1978.

[Chaikin wants to explore] "exists not just . . .": Chaikin, *Presence*, p. 25; "Susanne Langer . . . ," "All the ingredients . . .": Chaikin, *Serpent* Notebook, CP.

[Theater, Chaikin feels, should] "most developed . . .": Hendrix, "Presence," p. 141.

[Chaikin also draws on] "overtones . . . pitch": Sainer, *Notebook*, p. 3; "a shape . . .": interview, Oct. 30, 1979.

[Chaikin feels that all] Chaikin, *Presence*, p. 128.

[Another way to transcend] Chaikin, *Presence*, p. 152.

[He feels that comedy] "makes anything tolerable": [Chaikin], "Language," type-script notes, apparently for a talk to the Open Theater actors, CP; "more power-ful . . .": quoted (or paraphrased) in Zimet, *Nightwalk* notebook, PC–Zimet; "It is felt . . .": Chaikin, "Fragments," p. 146.

[While experimenting with various] Chaikin, "Open Theater," p. 194.

[Beyond this, though, Chaikin] Chaikin, *Presence*, p. 64.

[As he has worked] "certain things . . .": Pasolli, *Open Theatre*, p. 118; "the task . . . changing it": interview, Apr. 20, 1975; "so very . . . ," "almost like . . .": Toscan, "Joseph Chaikin," p. 40; *improvised sections of later performance pieces:* conversation, 1975.

[Still, even within the] Interview, Sept. 27, 1975.

[Like most more traditional] *actors gaining broad life experiences:* Chaikin, *Presence*, pp. 58–9; "prepared responses": Chaikin, loose handwritten notes, CP; "screening out . . .": Chaikin, "Context of Performance," p. 664.

[But, unlike most more] Chaikin, "Notes on Character . . . and the Setup," *Performance*, 1 (Dec. 1971):80–1.

[Partly because he feels] "a kind of . . . ," "You shouldn't . . . ," "people who . . . ," "usually when . . .": interview, Apr. 20, 1975; "to give form . . .": Chaikin, "Character," p. 77.

[Since the basic value] Chaikin, *Presence*, p. 20.

[All actors can and] "a consciousness . . .": Chaikin, notes for actors rehearsing for performance at the Martinique Theater, 1964, typescript, VIP; "The basic starting . . .": Chaikin, *Presence*, p. 65.

[This sort of double] "Moment to moment . . .": Erika Munk, "The Actor's Involvement: Notes on Brecht – An Interview with Joseph Chaikin," *Drama Review*, 12, no. 2 (1968):149; "like a double . . .": Chaikin, *Presence*, p. 16.

[While Chaikin's engagement with] Munk, "Actor's Involvement," p. 149.

[At the same time] Interview, Aug. 6, 1980.

[So, unlike Brecht, Chaikin] "reflect . . . mediate it": Zimet, *Nightwalk* Notebook, PC–Zimet; "The most important . . .": Muriel Sharon, "Notes from the Open Theater," carbon of 3-page typescript, p. 2, accompanying letter dated July 18, 1966, OTP; "understanding . . .": Chaikin, Notebook, 1964–65, CP.

[Chaikin accepts the incompatibility] Interview, Sept. 27, 1975.

[Virtually all of the] Chaikin, "Open Theater," p. 194.

[But actors must, then] Chaikin, "What the Actor Does," p. 57.

[Emotion memory, in any] "Feeling is . . .": Chaikin, "What the Actor Does," pp. 57–8; "The Method actor . . .": Chaikin, "Presence" typescript draft, p. 22, CP; "To make a fight . . .": Chaikin, Notebook, 1964–5, CP; "An actor who is pumping . . .": Chaikin, *Nightwalk* Notebook II, PC–Chaikin.

[The Method can seduce] "I really can't . . .": interview, Sept. 27, 1975; "completely locked . . .": Chaikin, "Open Theater," p. 192; "leaves no room . . .": Zimet, *Terminal* Notebook, PC–Zimet (quoting from Chaikin's talk to the company before a performance in Bordeaux); "Traditionally . . .": Chaikin, *Presence*, pp. 2–3 (from a talk Chaikin gave to the company at the Open Theater's first meeting in the fall of 1969, transcribed by Maloney, PC–Maloney).

[Chaikin's final objection to] Chaikin, "What the Actor Does," p. 57.

[Chaikin believes that the] "All one's past . . . ," "In America . . .": Chaikin, *Presence*, p. 15.

[Chaikin is particularly concerned] "a kind of upbeat": *Sea Gull* rehearsal, Manhattan Theatre Club, Dec. 30, 1974.

[This approach to internal] Tina Shepard, *Nightwalk* Notebook, PC–Shepard (Shepard's wording of Chaikin's comment).

[Still, Chaikin does not] Talk to actors, Center for Theater Practice, Oct. 1, 1978.

[Chaikin once said, "The] "The single . . .": Chaikin, statement on the Open Theater, 1-page typescript from mid-1960s, OTP; "the only way": interview, Sept. 27, 1975.

[Although he cares very] "task group": Chaikin, *Presence,* p. 87; "If all we . . .": Chaikin, *Presence,* p. 83 (from Chaikin's talk to company, fall 1969, PC–Maloney).

[Chaikin became interested in] Sottsass and Pivano, interview with Chaikin, pp. 5–6, OTP.

[Chaikin is much more] "exclusionist . . . world," "to see where . . ." (referring of course, to the Open Theater): Pasolli, *Open Theatre,* pp. 32, 68; "You don't . . .": Pasolli, "Man-Not-in-the-Street," p. 29.

[The nature of Chaikin's] "Going from . . . ," "people will . . .": Chaikin, Notebook, 1963–4, pp. 64, 96, CP; "Be prepared . . .": Chaikin, Notebook, 1964–5, p. 33, CP; "Even though . . .": Chaikin's talk to company, fall 1969, p. 3, PC–Maloney.

[Actors, he said, must] "temptation . . .": Hendrix, "Presence," p. 196; "There are often . . ." (Zimet's wording of Chaikin's remarks to the Open Theater): Zimet, "Audience," 20-page typescript essay, pp. 15–16, PC–Zimet.

[Chaikin dislikes the changes] "Utopian . . . ," "Performing is sharing . . .": Chaikin, *Presence,* pp. 106, 103; "When we got . . .": interview, Apr. 20, 1975.

[Chaikin does not expect] "telegraphing . . .": conversation, ca. 1978; "in Madison . . .": conversation, Oct. 1979.

[In fact, he is] "There will be . . .": Toscan, "Joseph Chaikin," pp. 40–1; "if you're going . . .": Sainer, *Notebook,* p. 3.

[But, in contrast to] "I would say . . .": interview, Feb. 17, 1980; "It's very important . . .": Toscan, "Joseph Chaikin," p. 41.

[Since he recognizes the] "culture-vulture . . .": Brenda Smiley, "101 Open! UBU-DICK ENDGAMES NOW!" from unidentified newspaper, n.d., PC–Maloney; *theater for The Dybbuk:* conversation, fall 1977; interview, Nov. 8, 1977; *Manhattan Theatre Club audiences:* conversation, Dec. 1979.

[Chaikin's interest in audiences] Paine Knickerbocker, " 'America Hurrah': Search for Adaptability and Seductiveness," *San Francisco Examiner and Chronicle,* May 14, 1967, p. 3.

[Real-life interactions involve not] Interview, Sept. 27, 1975.

[Chaikin believes that the] "The audience . . .": Chaikin, speech given at a university, [winter or spring 1968?], recorded by Maloney, PC–Maloney; "In attributing . . .": Chaikin, "Context of Performance," p. 665.

[Whoever the spectators are] Andrzej Bonarski, interview for *Dialog* (Poland), June 1975, PC–Chaikin. An edited version of this interview appeared in *Performing Arts Journal,* 1, no. 3 (1977).

[Most of the tacks] *Chaikin's (limited) interest in Happenings and environmental theater:* conversation, 1980; "arbitrary experiment": Toscan, "Joseph Chaikin," p. 42; "You can be touched . . .": interview, Aug. 8, 1980.

[The audience must be] "When not . . .": paraphrased in Zimet, *Nightwalk* Notebook, Mar. 12, 1973, PC–Zimet.

[For Chaikin, the political] *Open Theater political-economic policies:* Open Theater Minutes, OTP.

[Chaikin is repelled by] "reinforc[ing] . . .": Chaikin, "Character," p. 78; "It is necessary . . .": Chaikin, *Presence*, p. 56; "I think that it's . . .": interview, Aug. 8, 1980.

[In the early years] "wanted very much . . . ," "There was nothing left . . .": interview, April 20, 1975; "invested . . .": Toscan, "Joseph Chaikin," p. 37; "a status . . .": Feingold, interview with Chaikin, p. 30, PC–Feingold.

[He found that acclaim] "a kind . . .'success' ": Chaikin, *Presence*, p. 106; "to never doing . . .": Feingold, interview with Chaikin, p. 24, PC–Feingold; "It's so precious . . .": interview, Nov. 8, 1977.

[Remaining in noncommercial theater] *militancy of a convert:* Pasolli, *Open Theatre*, p. xv (Chaikin himself uses such language); "being a little . . .": interview, Sept. 27, 1975; "doing it like . . .": Sottsass and Pivano, interview with Chaikin, pt. 2, p. 12, OTP; *success creating opportunities:* interview, Sept. 17, 1974; "being well-known . . . to me": Peter Maloney, "A Talk with Joe Chaikin," *Changes*, no. 77, Oct. 1972, p. 12.

[Chaikin has always thought] "The critic digests . . .": Chaikin, "Presence" typescript draft, p. 6, CP; "the whole quality . . .": van Itallie, 13-page typescript notes for a lecture, Storrs, Conn., Mar. 1969, pt. 1, p. 6, VIP; "respectful": conversation, Nov. 1979; "become birdlike": Zimet, 2-page manuscript notes for "Audience" essay, PC–Zimet.

[While Chaikin always has] "We don't invite . . .": Toscan, "Joseph Chaikin," p. 43.

[Lately, he has even] Bill Eddy, "Four Directors on Criticism," *Drama Review*, 18, no. 3 (1974):29; conversation, 1980.

[Chaikin described himself once] "neurotically suspicious . . .": Gottlieb, "America Hurrah," p. 36, OTP; "no money": Chaikin, Notebook, 1963–4, p. 52, CP; "The danger . . .": Open Theater Minutes, Nov. 27, 1968, CP (Chaikin made similar comments at other meetings during this period).

[Chaikin felt also that] Conversation, Dec. 23, 1975.

[Since disbanding the Open] "One of the things . . .": interview, July 12, 1979.

[Finally, a key aspect] "intolerable," "its whole . . . ," "what becomes alive . . . ," "Growth means . . .": Feingold, interview with Chaikin, pp. 27, 5, 31, PC–Feingold; "After each . . .": Chaikin, *Presence*, p. 83.

[In his Open Theater] "to go where . . .": Chaikin, Notebook, 1963–4, p. 68, CP; "go beyond the safe . . .": Chaikin, "Open Theater," p. 196; "We worked . . .": Feingold, interview with Chaikin, pp. 24–5, PC–Feingold.

[Breakthroughs, ironically, are one] "when you make . . .": Chaikin recalled this earlier remark in a telephone conversation, Feb. 7, 1984; "Just as . . .": Chaikin, "Presence" typescript draft, p. 170, CP; "Within one group . . .": Chaikin, *Presence*, p. 152.

3. THE WORKSHOP INVESTIGATIONS

[At a Winter Project *and* A few Project members] Winter Project workshop, 1978.

[The focus of Chaikin's] Conversation, Apr. 1978.

[The structure of these] Chaikin, "Open Theater," p. 196.

[In part, Chaikin's stimulation] "When questions . . . ," "to enter . . .": Chaikin, *Presence*, pp. 64, 134; "Forming an exercise . . .": Chaikin, "Character," p. 79.

[In the early years] Interview, Sept. 27, 1975.

[Unlike much of the] "The theater . . .": Chaikin, statement on the Open Theater, OTP.

[But while the Open] Chaikin, "Context of Performance," p. 666; Chaikin, "Fragments," p. 146; Chaikin, loose *Nightwalk* notes, PC–Chaikin; Chaikin, *Nightwalk* Notebook II ("When a painter . . .").

[By the end of] "recipes": Chaikin, "Character," p. 80; conversation, 1975; *exercises ad hoc:* talk to actors, Center for Theater Practice, Oct. 1, 1978; "every work . . .": Chaikin, "Character," p. 79; "simply imitate . . .": Chaikin, "Context of Performance," p. 667.

[Indeed, over the years] Interview, Sept. 27, 1975.

[Chaikin's fundamental interest has] "in some way . . . nobody's home": interview, Sept. 27, 1975; "awareness . . . feeling for space": Susan Pomeroy, "[Exercises of] the Open Theater," notes "compiled from conversations with Joe, 1966–67," copy of 6-page typescript, p. 1, OTP. The "on–off" work is also mentioned in Sottsass and Pivano, interview with Chaikin, p. 6, OTP; Chaikin, Notebook, 1963–4, pp. 11, 15A, OTP; Chaikin, *Serpent* Notebook, OTP; Chaikin, loose notes, OTP; van Itallie, "The Open Theater," in International Theater Institute, *Theater 2: American Theater, 68–69* (New York: Scribner, 1970), p. 84; van Itallie, "After Joe's workshop, Feb. 21, 1964," 2-page typescript notes, VIP; interview with Aaron; interview, Sept. 27, 1975; Sharon, "Notes from the Open Theater," p. 3, OTP.

[Extending this study of] "If you suddenly . . .": interview, Sept. 17, 1974.

[Part of the present] *adaptations of Spolin "games":* Pasolli, *Open Theatre*, pp. 16–20 (although Pasolli's descriptions tend to simplify Chaikin's exercises into recipes, they provide valuable information); Pomeroy, "[Exercises]," pp. 1–2, OTP; Susan Pomeroy, notes for "[Exercises of] the Open Theater," copy of 7-page typescript, OTP; Chaikin, Notebook, 1968, OTP; van Itallie, "Workshop, Feb. 21, 1964," VIP; van Itallie, "Open Theater," p. 84; "initially freeing": Chaikin, "Context of Performance," p. 668.

[In the mid-sixties, the] *trust exercises:* Pomeroy, "[Exercises]," OTP; Pomeroy, notes, OTP; interview, Sept. 27, 1975.

[The ensemble exercises that] *chords:* Pasolli, *Open Theatre*, pp. 32–3 ("I stand . . ."); Maloney, Diary, Nov. 17, 1967, PC–Maloney; Pomeroy, "[Exercises]," p. 2, OTP; interview with Shami Chaikin.

[In "breathing and talking] *Open Theatre*, Pasolli, pp. 24, 113; Pomeroy, "[Exercises]," p. 1, OTP; interview with Aaron.

[The most subtle, and *and* More complex exercises involved] *"conductors":* Pasolli, *Open Theatre*, pp. 26–31; Chaikin, Notebook, 1963–4, p. 5A, OTP; Pomeroy, "[Exercises]," p. 3, OTP; Pomeroy, notes, OTP; Zimet, *Nightwalk* Notebook, PC–Zimet; interview, Sept. 27, 1975; interview with Aaron; interview, Sept. 27, 1975 ("starts to be . . . ," "a sort of staple").

[Usually, in performance, actors *and* Jamming was then extended] *"jamming":* Chaikin, *Presence*, pp. 116 ("One actor comes in . . .")–17; interview with Tina Shepard; Mohan, interview with Tina Shepard, OTP; interview with Vann and Barbosa.

[Chaikin felt that this] "rhythms, jamming . . .": Zimet, *Nightwalk* Notebook, Mar. 12, 1975, PC–Zimet; "very valuable . . . leave it alone": conversation and interview, Sept. 17, 1975 (the quotations actually refer to conductors, but Chaikin has said that jamming is valuable in the same way).

[Presence involves the audience's] "where any actor . . .": Chaikin, *Serpent* Notebook, OTP; *audience contact in* The Serpent *and* Terminal: conversation, 1975; "Each chooses . . .": Megan Terry, *Viet Rock, Tulane Drama Review*, 11, no. 1 (1966):104; "sentimentalized . . .": Toscan, "Joseph Chaikin," p. 42; "exploded into . . .": interview, Aug. 8, 1980.

[The studies that Chaikin] *dedications:* "The idea was . . .": Chaikin, *Presence*, pp. 141–42; "would call up . . .": Zimet, "Audience," p. 11, PC–Zimet.

[Having settled on a] "I've chosen . . . ," "you are calling . . .": Chaikin, *Presence*, pp. 143, 141; "a meeting place . . .": Zimet, "Audience," p. 11, PC–Zimet.

[During the Open Theater's] *expecting:* "trees . . . ," "play to . . . ," "pull away . . .": Chaikin, Notebook, 1963–4, pp. 75A, 5, OTP.

[In the fall of] Sharon, "Notes from the Open Theater," pp. 1–2, OTP.

[In the most rudimentary] Phyllis Jane Wagner, "Jean-Claude van Itallie: Political Playwright, *Serif,* 9 (Winter 1972): 37; Peter Feldman, "Joe, on EXPECTATIONS," copy of 2-page typescript, OTP; Feldman, "Post Stanislavskian Acting," copy of 8-page typescript, Apr. 1967, OTP; Pasolli, *Open Theatre*, pp. 84–6; interview with Aaron; interview with Paul Zimet and Ellen Maddow, June 5, 1976; van Itallie, "Open Theater," pp. 84–6; van Itallie, 7-page typescript notes for lecture, Pittsburgh, Pa., Mar. 1969, p. 7, VIP; Chaikin, speech [1968?], PC–Maloney.

[Chaikin also explored how] Chaikin, Notebook, 1968, CP.

[The Winter Project explored] "The basic equation . . .": Hendrix, "Presence," p. 200; *spectator-at-performance improvisations:* Winter Project Workshops, 1976–9.

[An offshoot of this] Winter Project workshops, 1976–9.

[Chaikin has experimented with *and* In his work with *and* The performers were not] *storytelling:* Interview, Sept. 27, 1975 ("the dynamic . . . ," "The story can . . ."); interview with Shami Chaikin.

[Singing, like storytelling, involves] Zimet, *Nightwalk* Notebook, PC–Zimet (introducing the companies to types of vocal music; similar sessions took place in the Working Theater and the Winter Project); Kenneth Glickfeld, "Serpent Log," copy of 26-page typescript, Jan. 24, [1968], OTP ("in a direct . . ."); Chaikin, Notebook, 1963–4, p. 3, OTP; Chaikin, "To the Company," June 14, 1971, 2-page typescript, OTP; interview, Sept. 27, 1975; interview with Shami Chaikin; Zimet, *Terminal* Notebook, PC–Zimet.

[This work not only] Zimet, *Nightwalk* Notebook, PC–Zimet.

[Chaikin's singing exercises had] Jean Jacquot, "The Open Theater–The Serpent," in *Les voies de la création théâtrale,* vol. 1, ed. Jacquot (Paris: Editions du Centre National de la Recherche Scientifique, 1970), p. 286; Chaikin, *Serpent* Notebook, CP; interview with Tina Shepard ("you're not working . . ."); interview with Shami Chaikin.

[Toward the end of *and* Question-and-answer exchanges] Winter Project workshops, 1976–80; interview with Tina Shepard.

[Chaikin's work with interviews] "the precious . . .": Chaikin, *Presence*, p. 131; "something theatrical . . .": Chaikin, "Open Theater," p. 194.

[One of his first *and* Originally this exercise was *and* Applying this work to] *"sound and movement"*: Pasolli, *Open Theatre*, pp. 4–8; Pomeroy, "[Exercises]," p. 3, OTP; Pomeroy, notes, OTP; Chaikin, *Serpent* Notebook, CP; interview with Aaron; interview with Shami Chaikin; Maloney, Diary, Nov. 30, 1967, PC–Maloney.

[Chaikin also had actors] *"trying on" bodies*: Chaikin, Notebook, 1963–4, pp. 16, 18, CP; Maddow, *Nightwalk* Notebook, Oct. 11, [1972], PC–Maddow; Zimet, *Nightwalk* Notebook, PC–Zimet; *physical adjustments*: Pasolli, *Open Theatre*, pp. 3, 60; Pomeroy, notes, OTP.

[They also explored how] *"a trained liar"*: Chaikin, speech at New School for Social Research, New York, N.Y., Oct. 16, 1978; *"life masks" and face conversations*: Pasolli, *Open Theatre*, pp. 102–3; Pomeroy, notes, OTP; Zimet, *Nightwalk* Notebook, Jan. 22, Feb. 13, 1973, PC–Zimet; interview with Zimet and Maddow; van Itallie, "Thoughts on possibilities for Joe's workshop," 2-page typescript, Open Theater Notebook, VIP.

[One of Chaikin's priorities] Chaikin, "Open Theater," p. 194.

[In one series of *and* For Chaikin, the sometimes] *"perfect people"*: Pasolli, *Open Theatre*, pp. 37–8; Chaikin, Notebook, 1963–4, pp. 5, 6, 12 ("the stages . . ."), CP; Pomeroy, "[Exercises]," p. 3, OTP; van Itallie, "Perfect People" scripts, 7-page typescript, VIP; van Itallie, "The Inside of a Moment," typescript in van Itallie's Open Theater Notebook, VIP; van Itallie, "Joe Chaikin's group–Open Theatre–second notes," 1-page typescript, Open Theater Notebook, VIP; interview with Vann and Barbosa.

[Chaikin wants theater to] *"This challenge . . ."*: Chaikin, "Open Theater," p. 193; *"We're alone . . ."*: Chaikin, *Serpent* Notebook, CP.

[Some of the Open] *"jerky rhythm . . ."*: Pasolli, *Open Theatre*, p. 41.

[Another early Open Theater *and* In the basic exercise] *"insides"*: Pasolli, *Open Theatre*, pp. 14–15; Chaikin, Notebook, 1963-4, p. 74A, CP; Pomeroy, "[Exercises]," p. 4, OTP; Pomeroy, notes, OTP; van Itallie, "Inside," VIP; Sottsass and Pivano, interview with Chaikin, pt. 2, p. 3, CP; Glickfeld "Serpent Log," Feb. 11, [1968], OTP; interview with Aaron.

["Locked action" and "machine"] Interview with Vann and Barbosa.

[The early Open Theater *and* Sometimes the changes were] *"transformations"*: van Itallie, "Open Theater," p. 84; Pasolli, *Open Theatre*, pp. 20–2; Chaikin, Notebook, 1963–4, pp. 3, 15, 17, 66, CP; Wagner, "van Itallie," p. 37; Pomeroy, notes, OTP; Feldman, "Acting," p. 4, OTP; Gottlieb, *"America Hurrah,"* p. 12, OTP; [Pasolli], handwritten notes from Peter Feldman's Open Theater notes, OTP; van Itallie, "From discussion with Joe, June 1964," 1-page typescript, Open Theater notebook, VIP ("a fear . . . heights").

[To explore the complex] Interview, Apr. 20, 1975.

[He designated concentric circles *and* Chaikin came to use] Pasolli, *Open Theatre*, pp. 46, 43–5; Pomeroy, "[Exercises]," p. 5, OTP; Chaikin, Notebook, 1963–4, pp. 13, 15, 16, 18A, CP; Chaikin, Notebook, 1968, CP; van Itallie, "Workshop, Feb. 21, 1964," VIP; van Itallie, loose notes, VIP; interview, Apr. 20, 1975.

[Inspired by Büchner's *Woyzeck*] Pasolli, *Open Theatre*, pp. 72–4; Chaikin, Notebook, 1963–4, p. 3, CP; Chaikin, Notebook, 1964–5, p. 29, CP; Pomeroy, "[Exercises]," pp. 5–6, OTP; Pomeroy, notes, OTP.

[Instant scenes were an] Sharon, "Notes from the Open Theater," p. 2, OTP; *A Fable* workshop, 1975.

[An important inspiration came] The discussion of the Chinese theater demonstration here and through the paragraph beginning [In fact, although Chaikin] is from interview, Sept. 27, 1975 (all quotations); Maloney, Diary, Oct. 27, 1967, PC–Maloney; Glickfeld, "Serpent Log," Oct. 26, 1967, OTP; interview with Shami Chaikin; interview with Zimet and Maddow (on Sleeping Beauty).

[Highly distilled "phrases" and] Chaikin, *Presence*, pp. 113, 116; Pasolli, *Open Theatre*, pp. 90–1; Zimet, *Nightwalk* Notebook, PC–Zimet; interview, Sept. 27, 1975 ("we didn't . . ."); interview with Shami Chaikin.

[The economy of the] "If an emblematic . . .": Chaikin, *Presence*, p. 113.

[Another major input into *and* This work extended far *and* He began seeking emblems] *Rip van Winkle*, *"worlds,"* and *"modes"*: Chaikin, *Presence*, p. 128; Chaikin, "Presence" typescript draft, p. 140, CP ("couldn't put . . . ," "All we . . ."); Pasolli, *Open Theatre*, pp. 47–50; Chaikin, Notebook, 1964–5, pp. 3, 31, 55, CP; Glickfeld, "Serpent Log," Dec. 15, 1967, Jan. 24, Feb. 1, 18, 1968, OTP; Zimet, *Nightwalk* Notebook, PC–Zimet; Maddow, *Nightwalk* Notebook, PC–Maddow; interview with Aaron.

[Chaikin has explored both] "Make sound . . .": Zimet, *Terminal* Notebook, PC–Zimet; "shape of . . .": Zimet, *Nightwalk* Notebook, Dec. 11, 1972, PC–Zimet.

[Chaikin's more ongoing study *and* The Winter Project studied] Jacquot, "Open Theater," p. 286; Zimet, *Terminal* Notebook, PC–Zimet; interview with Zimet and Maddow; Winter Project workshops, 1976–9.

[Most important, though, music] "thought music": conversation, 1979; *instrumental/vocal sound pairings:* Winter Project workshops, 1979–81.

[Chaikin has even explored] *French horn experiment:* Winter Project workshop, May 21, 1980.

[Music also has provided] Interview, Aug. 8, 1980.

[The immersion of the] Winter Project workshop, July 1981.

[Part of Chaikin's interest] Interview, Apr. 4, 1978.

[Still, Chaikin's main engagement] "how we put . . .": Maloney, "Joe Chaikin," PC–Maloney; "breathing . . .": Chaikin, *Presence*, p. 131; *"words as code . . .":* Chaikin, letter to the Open Theater, 2-page typescript, June 14, 1971, OTP.

[He wanted to discover] "the intimate . . .": Chaikin, *Presence*, galley proofs, #50, CP; "The thing starts . . .": Maddow, *Nightwalk* Notebook, Oct. 16, 1972, PC–Maddow.

[Some of Chaikin's work] *Chaikin's involvement with sign language:* conversations, 1980; Chaikin, *Presence*, p. 131; *speech-sounds work:* Chaikin, *Presence*, pp. 129–32 ("a balancing . . . ," p. 131); Glickfeld, "Serpent Log," Nov. 13, 1967, OTP; Chaikin, *Serpent* Notebook, CP; interview with Zimet and Maddow.

[Although he has become] early Open Theater performance programs, OTP.

[During the first few] Chaikin, "Open Theater," p. 197.

[As Chaikin's interest in] *Open Theater scene-work meetings:* conversations with Tina Shepard and Chaikin, 1974–7.

[Often, though, since the] *excommunication rites:* Lester, "He Doesn't Aim to Please"; interview, Sept. 27, 1975 ("I thought . . . ," "to find the essential . . ."); Pasolli, "Man-Not-in-the-Street."

[A theme Chaikin has] *mourning explorations:* Interview, Apr. 4, 1978 ("The only persons . . ."); Chaikin, *Serpent* Notebook, CP; Zimet, loose notes on *The Serpent*, PC–Zimet; *The Serpent*, five handwritten suggested scenarios, apparently by company actors, OTP; *Dybbuk* rehearsals, Dec. 1980; Winter Project workshops, 1977.

[At the opposite end] Interview, Aug. 6, 1980.

4. EARLY COLLABORATIVE PLAY MAKING: *THE SERPENT*

[Twice while he was] *The Barrel* and *The Policeman* . . . scripts: PC–Chaikin.

[Although both of these] "so didn't . . .": interview, Sept. 27, 1975; "was no good": conversation, 1981.

[In the earliest weeks] Gottlieb, *"America Hurrah,"* pp. 11–13, OTP; Pasolli, *Open Theatre*, p. 50; Sottsass and Pivano, interview with Chaikin, pt. 2, p. 4, OTP; interview with Vann and Barbosa.

[The Open Theater's "insides"] Odets: van Itallie, "Variation on a Theme of Odets," typewritten, Open Theater Notebook, VIP ("a realistic . . . ," "bitter . . . precocious"); van Itallie, "Playwright," p. 155 ("The characters . . ."); Chaikin, Notebook, 1963–4, p. 92; interview with Jean-Claude van Itallie July 16, 1976, Charlemont, Mass.; interview with Vann and Barbosa; interview with Aaron.

[Another piece that van Itallie] *Picnic in Spring:* van Itallie, "Notes for Joe, March 5, 1964," 4-page typescript, Open Theater Notebook, VIP ("instant image . . . ," "Trees that were . . . ," "Where are you? . . . Never"); Chaikin, Martinique Notes, CP ("scene of lyrical . . . ," "to express . . ."); van Itallie, notes, Apr. 7, 1964, OTP; interview with van Itallie.

[The Open Theater also] There are complete programs and extensive notes for these performances in the OTP.

[A few pieces did] *Contest:* van Itallie, notes, Apr. 7, 1964, OTP ("What they want . . ."); Chaikin, Martinique notes, CP ("This scene is . . ."); Chaikin, Notebook, 1963–4, p. 3, CP; Chaikin, Notebook, 1964–5, pp. 19, 39, CP; Chaikin, loose notes, OTP; interview with van Itallie; interview with Vann and Barbosa. Footnote: Tina Shepard, *Mutation Show* Notebook, PC–Shepard; interview with Tina Shepard; conversations, 1975, July 1982.

[In October 1967, when] "wasn't really . . .": interview with Vann and Barbosa.

[The Open Theater's earlier] Interview, Apr. 20, 1975.

[The first issue was] Maloney, Diary, Nov. 4, 14, 1967, PC–Maloney; *The Open Theater–Europe 1968* [souvenir program] (New York, 1968), p. 7; interview, Apr. 20, 1975; Mohan, interview with Tina Shepard, pp. 3–4, OTP.

[The work began with] Maloney, Diary, Oct. 23, 1967, PC–Maloney; Pasolli, *Open Theatre*, pp. 110, 117; interview, Apr. 20, 1975.

[Chaikin wanted to explore] "vertical time": Lahr, "Open Theater," p. 167; "The inner . . .": Pasolli, *Open Theatre*, p. 106.

[His original intention was] Glickfeld, "Serpent Log," Oct. 17, 1967, OTP (first entry); Maloney, diary, Oct. 23, 1967, PC–Maloney; Mohan, interview with Tina Shepard, p. 2, OTP; interview, Apr. 20, 1975.

[To get perspective on] Lahr, "Open Theater," p. 168.

[The company was fascinated] Interview, Apr. 20, 1975.

[But the pull of] "The story . . .": Chaikin, *Serpent* Notebook, CP; "a veil of shame . . .": Chaikin, Notebook, 1963–4, p. 70, CP; "completely reunderstand . . .": Chaikin, *Presence*, p. 95; "to sense a connection . . .": Maloney, "An Actor's View, Part II: The Serpent," *Changes*, 3, no. 1 (June 1, 1971): 27.

[Still, the workshop's attitude] Chaikin, *Presence*, p. 95.

[The company read and *and* A number of scholars *and* Susan Sontag, a close] *research and speakers:* Zimet, *Serpent* notes, PC–Zimet (Campbell quotations); Eddy, "Four Directors," p. 29; Maloney, Diary, Oct. 27, Nov. 30, 1967, PC–Maloney; Maloney, "Actor's View, Part II"; Glickfeld, "Serpent Log," Nov. 6, 16, 1967, Jan. 12, 14, 1968, OTP; interview, Apr. 20, 1975.

[Most of the research] Chaikin, *Presence*, p. 102.

[Ultimately, all of the] "projecting . . .": Pasolli, *Open Theatre*, p. 116; "everyone has . . .": Khan, "Home of Experience," p. 16; "Where am I . . .": Chaikin, "A Note from the Director," p. 5, in *The Open Theater–Europe 1968*, OTP.

[Chaikin decided that the] "To understand . . .": Chaikin, loose notes, OTP; "may always . . .": Chaikin, "Context of Performance," p. 667; "a little bit . . .": Khan, "Home of Experience," p. 16; "the false garden . . .": Schechner, "Interview," p. 142 (also in Chaikin, *Presence*, p. 62); *-isms, round Eden:* Chaikin, *Serpent* Notebook, CP; *Osiris myth* (Zimet credits the idea to actress Jenn Ben-Yakov), "center from . . ." (Zimet credits this idea to actress Brenda Dixon): Zimet, *Serpent* notes, PC–Zimet.

[The best images of] "The stage . . .": Schechner, "Interview," p. 143 (also in Chaikin, *Presence*, pp. 162, 164, in slightly changed form); *Open Theater loft as "the void":* Maloney, "Actor's View, Part II."

[In one early session] "There is no sound . . .": Glickfeld, "Serpent Log," Oct. 19, [1967], OTP; "The notion . . .": Mohan, interview with Tina Shepard, p. 7, OTP.

[Looking for possible inhabitants] *Garden improvisations:* Glickfeld, "Serpent Log," Oct. 20, 23, 26, 30, Nov. 10, 20, [1967], OTP; Maloney, Diary, Nov. 21 [1967], PC–Maloney; Maloney, "The Making of *The Serpent*," in *The Open Theater–Europe 1968*, p. 12, OTP; Maloney, "Actor's View, Part II"; Wagner, "Van Itallie," p. 60 ("the gentle part," quoting van Itallie).

[Originally populated by most] Chaikin, *Serpent* Notebook, CP; interview, Apr. 20, 1975; interview with Zimet and Maddow; Schechner, "Interview," p. 143 (the "Ziz").

[In early improvisations, two] *Adam and Eve:* Glickfeld, "Serpent Log," Oct. 23, Nov. 21, 1967, OTP; Chaikin, *Serpent* Notebook, CP; Mohan, interview with Tina Shepard, p. 21, OTP.

[Having humans in the] *search for a writer:* Glickfeld, "Serpent Log," Oct. 10, Nov. 6, [1967], Jan. 28, 31 ("the chief . . ."), 1968, OTP; Maloney, Diary, Nov. 4, 14, 1967, PC–Maloney; Maloney, "The Making of *The Serpent*," p. 9, OTP; interview with van Itallie; van Itallie to Irving Wardle, Mar. 25, 1969, VIP; Wagner, "Van Itallie," p. 59; interview with Roberta Sklar, Feb. 11, 1981.

[The first verbal scene] Glickfeld, "Serpent Log," Nov. 28, Dec. 22, 1967, OTP; Maloney, Diary, Nov. 28, 1967, PC–Maloney; [van Itallie?], "Adam Meets Eve: On the Discovery of Language," copy of 1-page typescript, OTP; interview with van Itallie; interview, Apr. 20, 1975.

[Two crucial images that] Maloney, Diary, Nov. 14, 1967, PC–Maloney; Maloney, "The Making of *The Serpent*," p. 12, OTP; Chaikin, *Serpent* Notebook, CP.

[The Open Theater saw] "The serpent . . .": Chaikin, *Serpent* Notebook, CP.

[One day in the *and* Then someone tried putting *and* In early improvisations the] Glickfeld, "Serpent Log," Oct. 20, 23, Nov. 2, 20, 27, [1967], OTP; Mohan, interview with Tina Shepard, pp. 7, 9, OTP; Maloney, Diary, Nov. 13, 21 28, 1967, PC–Maloney; interview, Apr. 20, 1975 ("very beautiful," "They were charged . . ."); Mel Gussow, "A Bite into an Apple Long Ago," *New York Times*, June 2, 1970, p. 35 ("first the primordial . . .").

[The company viewed Eve's *and* Meanwhile, the playwrights wrote] *the temptation:* Interview with Zimet and Maddow; Maloney, Diary, Nov. 14, 21 ("the evil . . . ," "salesmanship"), 1967, PC–Maloney; Maloney, "The Making of *The Serpent*," p. 13, OTP; Chaikin, *Presence*, p. 98 ("The Serpent has . . ."); Glickfeld "Serpent Log," Nov. 14, 20, Dec. 12, 1967, OTP; Jacquot, "The Serpent," pp. 285, 190 (individualized Serpent voices); Zimet, *Serpent* notes, PC–Zimet ("Listen, listen" speech); van Itallie, temptation scene, dialogue with narrator, typewritten, OTP; Mohan, interview with Tina Shepard, p. 21, OTP; Schechner, "Interview," p. 142 ("What if . . . ," "He really doesn't . . . ," "she's doing . . .").

[Different actresses improvised biting] Glickfeld, "Serpent Log," Jan. 4, 1968, OTP; Mohan, interview with Tina Shepard, p. 8 ("We were improvising . . ."), OTP; Schechner, "Interview," p. 142.

[In performance, after biting] Glickfeld, "Serpent Log," Jan. 28, Feb. 17, 1968, OTP; interview, Apr. 29, 1975 ("It would be seeing . . .").

[In the later performances *and* This orgy of discovery] "Serpent" script for second performance in Rome, May 3, 1968, 3-page typescript, p. 3, OTP; *The Serpent*, a ceremony written by Jean-Claude van Itallie in collaboration with the Open Theater under the direction of Joseph Chaikin (New York: Atheneum, 1969; New York: Dramatists' Play Service, 1969) (unless otherwise indicated, all references to and quotations from the final version of *The Serpent* refer to this text); Mohan, interview with Tina Shepard, p. 22, OTP; Virginia Gerret, "The Audiences are 'With It' in US," *Canberra* (Australia) *Times*, June 25, 1969, p. 29 ("When one actress . . ."); Chaikin, *Presence*, p. 97 ("Once the actors . . ."); conversation, Dec. 30, 1974 ("It failed . . ."); interview, Apr. 20, 1975 ("Occasionally . . .").

[In any case, after] *consequences improvisations:* Glickfeld, "Serpent Log," Oct. 20, Nov. 2, 1967, Jan. 18, 1968, OTP; Rome "Serpent" script, p. 3, OTP; *nude workshops:* Maloney, Diary, Oct. 31, Nov. 3, 1967, PC–Maloney; Glickfeld, "Serpent Log," Nov. 2, 1967, OTP; Chaikin, *Presence*, p. 101; conversation, 1976.

[Then came the curses] The discussion of God improvisations here and through the paragraph beginning [Containing God's existence within] is from interview, Apr. 20, 1975 ("That was one . . . ," "a person lifting . . ."); Maloney, Diary, Oct. 27, Nov. 2, 21 ("Phil Harris . . ."), Dec. 1, 1967, PC–Maloney; Maloney, "The Making of *The Serpent*," pp. 13, 20 ("quaking sound"), OTP; Glickfeld, "Serpent Log," Oct. 20, 26, 30, Nov. 2, 17, 20, 27 ("should be . . . ," "if you don't know . . ."), Dec. 1, 1967, Jan. 25, 1968, OTP; "Description of Early Work on 'The Serpent,' " summary of work for writers, copy of 3-page typescript, pp. 2 ("demolish someone . . .")–3, OTP; Zimet, *Serpent* notes, PC–Zimet; Wagner, "Van Itallie," p. 60; Chaikin, "A Note from the Director," OTP ("man made God . . .").

[The company felt that] *the curses:* Feingold, interview with Chaikin, p. 20, PC–Feingold ("irreversibles"); Maloney, diary, Nov. 14, 1967, PC–Maloney; Mohan, interview with Tina Shepard, p. 22, OTP; interview with van Itallie.

[The workshop explored how *and* Chaikin considered trying these *and* According to Genesis, God] *"locked actions":* Zimet, *Serpent* notes, PC–Zimet; interview, Apr. 20, 1975 ("Because they were mythic . . . ," "to make it like snakes . . ."); Schechner, "Interview," p. 144 ("in a locked . . ."); Chaikin, *Serpent* notebook, CP; Glickfeld, "Serpent Log," Oct. 23, Nov. 20, 27, 1967, Jan. 4, 12, 14, 17, 1968, OTP; Rome "Serpent" script, p. 4, OTP ("Each other actor . . .").

[The workshop continued its *and* After various exercises and] *Cain and Abel:* Chaikin, *Serpent* Notebook, CP; Maloney, Diary, Nov. 17, 28, 1967, PC–Maloney; Glickfeld, "Serpent Log," Nov. 20, 1967, Jan. 21, 1968, OTP; interviews, Sept. 17, 1974 ("that killing him . . ."), April 20, 1975 ("The trigger . . ."); Mohan, interview with Tina Shepard, p. 23, OTP; Jacquot, "The Serpent," p. 299.

[The workshop developed several] Maloney, Diary, Nov. 30, Dec. 1, 1967, PC–Maloney; Glickfeld, "Serpent Log," Nov. 20, 28, Dec. 1, 7, 11, 1967, Jan. 5, 1968, OTP; Zimet, *Serpent* notes, PC–Zimet; interview, Apr. 20, 1975 ("When I did that . . .").

[The Cain–Abel variations] Interview, Apr. 20, 1975.

[In any case, the] "Its source . . .": Schechner, "Interview," p. 144.

[After this scene, in] Rome "Serpent" script, p. 5, OTP; Mohan, interview with Tina Shepard, p. 23, OTP.

[A narrator of some] Chaikin, *Serpent* Notebook, CP; Zimet, *Serpent* notes, PC–Zimet; Wagner, "Van Itallie," pp. 60, 63; Glickfeld, "Serpent Log," Jan. 12, 13, 28, OTP; Maloney, Diary, Dec. 8, 1967, PC–Maloney; interview with Aaron; interview with van Itallie; interview with Zimet and Maddow; Jacquot, "The Serpent," p. 298.

[These narrators also came] Maloney, Diary, Dec. 7, 8, 1967, PC–Maloney; Maloney, "Actor's View, Part II" (quoting the Bonhoeffer passage that is used in the *Serpent* text); Maloney, "The Making of *The Serpent,*" p. 25, OTP; Sottsass and Pivano, interview with Chaikin, p. 8, OTP.

[Chaikin thought that the *and* The chorus now conveyed] Chaikin, *Serpent* Notebook, CP; interview with Shami Chaikin ("Jean-Claude asked . . ."); interview with van Itallie; Mohan, interview with Tina Shepard, pp. 5, 8, OTP; Rome "Serpent" script, p. 6, OTP ("Adam" being drafted).

[In performance, the chorus] Interview with Aaron; interview with Shami Chaikin; interview, Apr. 20, 1975; Mohan, interview with Tina Shepard, pp. 20, 23, OTP; Oleg Kerensky, "Jean-Claude van Itallie in the Garden of Eden," *Times* (London) *Saturday Review,* July 20, 1968, p. 19 ("wordless . . .").

[The chorus became part] The discussion of "Begatting" here and through the paragraph beginning [Fearing that the "Begatting"] is from Glickfeld, "Serpent Log," Nov. 21, Dec. 14, 1967, Jan. 12, 1968, OTP; interview, Apr. 20, 1975 ("People were . . ."); Jacquot, "The Serpent," p. 301; Kevin Kelly, "Open Theater Disciplined, Gifted," *Boston Globe,* Jan. 19, 1969, pp. A24, A27; interview with Shami Chaikin; Zimet, *Serpent* notes, PC–Zimet; Maloney, Diary, Nov. 28, 1967, PC–Maloney ("After each couple . . ."); Maloney, "Actor's View, Part II" (on censorship worry).

[The Open Theater never] *fairy tale work:* Glickfeld, "Serpent Log," Dec. 18, 19, 1967, Jan. 12, 17, 28, Feb. 14, 1968, OTP; Chaikin, *Serpent* Notebook, CP ("the pursuit . . ."); interview, Apr. 20, 1975; *The Serpent,* seven type- and handwritten proposed scenarios, apparently by company actors, OTP; Zimet, *Serpent* notes, PC – Zimet; interview with Zimet and Maddow; interview with van Itallie.

[The company also thought] Chaikin, *Serpent* Notebook, OTP; interviews, Sept. 27, 1975 ("It was not interesting . . ."), Apr. 20, 1975; Glickfeld, "Serpent Log," Feb. 15, 1968, endnote, OTP; Zimet, *Serpent* notes, PC – Zimet.

[Another notion was to] Glickfeld, "Serpent Log," Nov. 14, 1967, OTP; Maloney, Diary, Nov. 14, 1967, PC – Maloney; early provisional outline for *The Serpent* (before May 1968), copy of 3-page typescript, OTP; *Serpent* scenarios, OTP; van Itallie, "The Riot-Demonstration," 1-page typescript, VIP.

[The story that did *and* Chaikin was not enthusiastic *and* The sequence, finally, not] *assassination segment:* Chaikin, Notebook, 1964–5, p. 9, CP; van Itallie, lecture, Storrs, Conn., Mar. 1969, VIP; interviews, Apr. 20, 1975, Sept. 27, 1975 ("It was primarily . . ."); Lahr, "Open Theater," p. 167 ("I think the Kennedy . . .").

[As the Open Theater] Maloney, "Actor's View, Part II."

[Another modern section, a *and* In performance, an actress] Interview, Apr. 20, 1975 ("wasn't played . . . ," "very important," "very organic . . ."); interview with van Itallie; Rome "Serpent" script, seq. 2, p. 6, OTP; Glickfeld, "Serpent Log," endnote, OTP; Zimet, *Serpent* notes, PC – Zimet.

[Although thematic connections among *and* The Serpent workshop began *and* The workshop considered a] *work on structure: Serpent* scenarios, OTP; "Plan" for *The Serpent,* Mar. 2, 1968, 1-page typescript, OTP; Glickfeld, "Serpent Log," Nov. 17, 1967, OTP; van Itallie to Wardle, Mar. 25, 1969 ("to put together . . ."), VIP; interview with van Itallie ("Every month . . ."); interview, Apr. 20, 1975; Zimet, *Serpent* notes, PC – Zimet.

[In fact, though, *The*] "We had escaped . . .": interview with van Itallie; *actors unsure of sequence:* Maloney, "Actor's View, Part II."

[Chaikin had felt all *and* But the piece needed] Chaikin *Serpent* notebook, CP; interview, Apr. 20, 1975 ("We needed the piece . . .").

[After experimenting with a *and* Periodically during the parade] Glickfeld, "Serpent Log," Feb. 7, 14, 1968, OTP; Mohan, interview with Tina Shepard, p. 20, OTP ("Each actor . . ."); interview, Apr. 20, 1975 ("full of a certain . . ."); Gussow, "A Bite"; Elliot Norton, "Elliot Norton Writes: Open Theater's Odd 'Serpent' Writhes and Wriggles at Loeb," *Boston Record-American,* Jan. 13, 1969, p. 30.

[The very end of *and* Sometimes this "invitation for] Rome "Serpent" script, p. 7, OTP; Chaikin, *Serpent* Notebook, CP ("tree of life"); Glickfeld, "Serpent Log," Feb. 22, 1968, OTP; Mohan, interview with Tina Shepard, p. 14, OTP ("ended with . . ."); Zimet, notes for an essay, 44-page typescript, pp. 17 ("invitation for . . . ," "all primed . . . them"), 19 ("the silence . . . ," "Often the audience . . ."), PC – Zimet; Jacquot, "The Serpent," pp. 300–1; interview, Apr. 20, 1975.

[The open ending was] Van Itallie and The Open Theater, *The Serpent,* p. 55 ("overtaken by . . ."); Mohan, interview with Tina Shepard, p. 23, OTP; Samuel Hirsch, "Open Theater's The Serpent a Fascinating Experience," *Boston Herald Traveler,* Jan. 13, 1969, p. 17; Lahr, "Open Theater," p. 67 ("The intention . . ."); interview, Apr. 20, 1975 ("a kind of present-day . . .").

[The play also was] Interview, Apr. 20, 1975.

[The Open Theater toured] Chaikin to Gwen Fabricant, May or June 1968, OTP ("constant trouble . . . completely stoned"); conversations with Maloney, May 1975, Dec. 1983; interview with Shami Chaikin; Mohan, interview with Tina Shepard, pp. 15, 16 ("We've learned . . ."), 18, 25, OTP; Pasolli, *Open Theatre*, pp. 121–2.

[When the Open Theater *and* Finally, though, he and *and The Serpent's* official American] *redoing The Serpent:* Open Theater Minutes, Dec. 13, 1968 ("I would really . . ."), Feb. 12, 1973, OTP; Chaikin, *Presence*, pp. 27 ("as though it were . . ."), 28 ("We started . . ."); interview Apr. 20, 1975; interview with van Itallie.

[In retrospect, Chaikin is] Interview, Apr. 20, 1975.

[The critics, on the] Kelly, "Open Theater," p. A24; Walter Kerr, "What If Cain Did Not Know *How* to Kill Abel?" *New York Times*, Feb. 9, 1969, pp. 1, 8 (reprinted with revisions in Kerr, *God on the Gymnasium Floor* [New York: Simon & Schuster, 1970]); Walter Kerr, "The Finest Company of Its Kind," *New York Times*, May 24, 1970, sec. 2, p. 3 (reprinted in Kerr, *Gymnasium Floor*); Walter Kerr, "A Critic Celebrates the Unpredictable," *New York Times*, July 3, 1983, sec. 2, p. 4; Gussow, "A Bite"; Catherine Hughes, "New York," *Plays and Players*, Aug. 1969, p. 65; Obie award, OTP.

5. THE GROWTH OF ENSEMBLE PLAYWRITING

[The thematic center has] Feingold, interview with Chaikin, pp. 1 ("live with it . . . ," "you find either . . . "), 2, PC–Feingold; Chaikin, *Presence*, p. 89 ("obsessed"); Sottsass and Pivano, interview with Chaikin, p. 12, OTP ("possess[ed]"); Schechner, "Interview," p. 146.

[During the early stages] "to hang around . . .": interview with Sklar.

[On one level, the] "In the beginning . . .": Mohan, interview with Tina Shepard, p. 3, OTP; "We don't necessarily . . .": interview with Tina Shepard.

[Naturally, each developing work] Zimet, *Nightwalk* Notebook, PC–Zimet; interview with Shami Chaikin.

[Still, all the way] Interview with Sklar.

[Gradually, for each play] "As you approach . . .": Mohan, interview with Tina Shepard, p. 3, OTP.

[As a general outline] Zimet, "Speech to Jewish Women's Group," 8-page typescript, p. 5, PC–Zimet ("all the friction . . ."); Maloney, Diary, Oct. 27, 31, Nov. 17, n.d. [early Nov.], 1967, PC–Maloney; Zimet, essay notes, p. 6, PC–Zimet ("the new members . . . appreciated"); Maloney, "An Actor's View, Part I: Lee," *Changes*, 2, no. 26 (May 15, 1971):29; interview with Aaron; interview with Shami Chaikin; interview with Peter Maloney, May 19, 1975; John Lahr, "Joseph Chaikin's Children," *New York Free Press*, Feb. 29, 1968, p. 6; conversations with Open Theater and Winter Project members, 1974–9.

[Some tensions have come] Zimet, essay notes, p. 3, PC–Zimet; Maddow, *Nightwalk* Notebook, Jan. 12 ("It's a fog . . ."), 21 ("I don't feel us . . ."), 1973, PC–Maddow. Footnote: Maddow, *Nightwalk* Notebook, Jan. 28 ("The fog . . ."), Feb. 19 ("The work seems . . ."), PC–Maddow.

[The pressure to produce] Interview, Apr. 20, 1975 ("Everybody played . . ."); Maddow, *Nightwalk* Notebook, Mar. 9, 1973, PC–Maddow; Chaikin, *Nightwalk* Notebook III, PC–Chaikin ("fair," "not based . . ."); conversation, 1979.

[Another problem for the] Zimet, essay notes, pp. 12–13, PC–Zimet.

[Playwrights have suffered similar] van Itallie to Wardle, Mar. 25, 1969, VIP ("two primary . . . uncomfortable"); Sainer, *Notebook,* pp. 148–9 ("as much a frustration . . . ," "If Joe or the actor . . ."); Sam Shepard to Chaikin, Jan. 18, 1973, PC–Chaikin ("vague . . . collaboration"); Munk, "Working," pp. 82–5.

[The playwrights' problems have *and* But the writers' position] Sainer, *Notebook,* pp. 4–5 ("When you work improvisationally . . ."), 150 ("ambiguous and insecure"); Chaikin, notes passed out to company on *Terminal* writers, copy of 1-page typescript, PC–Maloney ("Unless the writer . . ."); Munk, "Working," p. 82 ("neither an integral . . ."); interview with Susan Yankowitz, Mar. 11, Apr. 20 ("made to feel . . ."), 1975; interview, Apr. 20, 1975.

[A source of deep] The discussion of tensions over credit here and through the paragraph beginning [In any case, these] is from interview, Sept. 27, 1975 ("Someone would . . . ," "I've always found . . ."); interview with Maloney ("most words . . ."); van Itallie, lecture, Storrs, Conn., Mar. 1969 ("yet to be seen . . ."); interview with Sklar ("What goes on . . ."); interview with Shami Chaikin ("All of the things . . ."); Sainer, *Notebook,* pp. 147–9 ("My name does not . . . ," p. 149); interview with Yankowitz; van Itallie to Maloney, Aug. 12, 1968, PC–Maloney.

[In October 1970 Chaikin's] Charles Petzold, "Swiss Girl Finds U.S. Death Rites Odd," *Philadelphia Daily News,* Dec. 2, 1970, p. 39; Chaikin, *Presence,* p. 158 ("Dealing with human . . ."); Sklar, "The Mutation Show – Introduction and Synopsis," 2-page typescript, OTP; Tina Shepard, *Mutation* Notebook, PC–Shepard ("the legitimacy . . ."); "Joseph Chaikin and the Open Theater," typewritten press release, OTP ("multiple selves," "wrenched . . .").

[It was risky, thrilling] Gussow, "Carrying On" ("bring[ing] the group . . ."); Feingold, interview with Chaikin, p. 27, PC–Feingold ("I do think . . ."); interview with Tina Shepard.

[W. E. R. LaFarge *and* Chaikin felt, though, that] Interview, Apr. 20, 1975; interview with Sklar ("go through"); Chaikin, letter to the Open Theater, June 14, 1971, OTP; Open Theater Minutes, Oct. 4, 1971, OTP.

[One major source of] Tina Shepard, *Mutation* Notebook, PC–Shepard.

[They also, as before] Zimet, *Mutation* Notebook, PC–Zimet; Tina Shepard, *Mutation* Notebook, PC–Shepard; Interview with Tina Shepard.

[But the core of *and* This work led to] Tina Shepard, *Mutation* Notebook, PC–Shepard (list of selves); interview with Tina Shepard; Zimet, *Mutation* Notebook, PC–Zimet ("If you saw . . .").

[The actors improvised dozens] Interview with Tina Shepard. All quotations from *The Mutation Show,* unless otherwise credited, are from *Three Works by The Open Theater: Terminal* [small company version], *The Mutation Show, Nightwalk,* ed. Karen Malpede (New York: Drama Books Specialists/Publishers, 1974), and descriptions of nonverbal elements of the final version are from my own notes from performances.

[Chaikin wanted to parallel] Zimet, *Mutation* Notebook, PC–Zimet; Tina Shepard, *Mutation* Notebook, PC–Shepard; interview with Tina Shepard; interview with Zimet and Maddow; conversations, 1980.

[Chaikin thought that one] Zimet, *Nightwalk* Notebook, PC–Zimet ("the slaughtered . . ."); Zimet, *Mutation* Notebook, typewritten reading lists and machine copies of articles on wild and isolated children, OTP; interview with Tina Shepard.

[Various actors tried playing *and* At one point the *and* Some of the Kamala] Tina Shepard, *Terminal/Mutation Show* Notebook, Oct. 9, 1979, PC–Shepard ("You don't know . . ."); Zimet, *Mutation* Notebook, PC–Zimet (Kamala at different stages); interview with Tina Shepard; interview with Shami Chaikin.

[The company also read *and* All of the actors *and* Some improvisations explored Caspar] Zimet, *Mutation* Notebook, PC–Zimet ("the part . . . critical part"); interview with Tina Shepard; interview with Shami Chaikin.

[Like much of the] Interview with Sklar; Sklar, *Mutation Show* Notes, PC–Sklar; typewritten drafts of chants, OTP.

[Caspar's two scenes showed] *workshop sources for Caspar's journey:* Tina Shepard, *Mutation* Notebook, PC–Shepard; interview with Tina Shepard.

[The second Caspar segment *and* Over several weeks, this] Zimet, *Mutation* Notebook, PC–Zimet; Tina Shepard, *Mutation* Notebook, PC–Shepard; interview with Tina Shepard; interview with Sklar.

[The study became connected] Interview with Tina Shepard.

[Like the segment it] Interview with Sklar; Sklar, *Mutation* Notes, PC–Sklar ("The fluids . . .").

[The work on breaking] Tina Shepard, *Mutation* Notebook, PC–Shepard; interview with Tina Shepard ("we used to . . .").

[The more rewarding exploration] *gags:* Tina Shepard, *Mutation* Notebook, PC–Shepard; interview with Tina Shepard; interview with Zimet and Maddow.

[Along with the extreme] Tina Shepard, *Mutation* Notebook, PC–Shepard; Zimet, *Mutation* Notebook, PC–Zimet; Tina Shepard, *Terminal/Mutation* Notebook, PC–Shepard; interview with Tina Shepard.

[Exploring marriage traditions brought] Interview with Sklar; conversations, 1975–6.

[In any case, the] Interview with Tina Shepard ("Paul and I . . . ," "the sound . . .").

[The bridal pair was] *Mutation Show* sequences, handwritten and typewritten, OTP; Tina Shepard, *Mutation* Notebook, PC–Shepard; interview with Tina Shepard.

[The most striking of *and* In the final version *and* As the six stood] *"Human Gallery":* Tina Shepard, *Mutation* Notebook, PC–Shepard ("This is Fanny . . ."); interview with Tina Shepard; Zimet, *Mutation* Notebook, PC–Zimet (early photograph work).

[During the first weeks] The discussion of early structures here and through the paragraph beginning [Finally, though, none of] is from *Mutation Show* sequences, OTP; Sklar, "Mutation Show – Introduction," OTP; interview with Tina Shepard ("We were thinking . . ."); conversation, Jan. 23, 1983.

[To pull together the] The discussion of "testimonies" here and through the paragraph beginning [Some of the testimonies] is from Tina Shepard, *Mutation* Notebook, May 26, 1971, PC–Shepard ("declaration of . . ."); Zimet, *Mutation* Notebook, PC–Zimet; Zimet, *Nightwalk* Notebook, PC–Zimet; interview with Tina Shepard; interview with Sklar.

["The Mutants Give Testimony"] Tina Shepard, *Mutation* Notebook, PC–Shepard; Zimet, *Mutation* Notebook, PC–Zimet; interview with Tina Shepard ("The piece . . .").

[At the end of] "an ear-aching . . .": Bob Barber, " 'The Mutation Show' Presented at UCSB," *Santa Barbara News-Press,* Apr. 7, 1972, p. C15 (describing the scene in a performance of the later *Mutation Show*).

[Although *Mutations,* performed on] Mutations' *critical reception:* See the end of this section.

[One important change was *and* As *Mutations* metamorphosed into] *Mutation Show* sequences in OTP and Tina Shepard's *Mutation* Notebook, PC–Shepard; interview with Tina Shepard.

[One other important scene] Zimet, *Mutation* Notebook, PC–Zimet; interview with Sklar.

[Critical response to the] "will be every . . .": David Sterritt, "Open Theater: Collective 'Untitled,' " *Christian Science Monitor,* May 28, 1971, p. 15; *BITEF:* press release for *Mutation Show,* typewritten, OTP.

[Back in New York] Mel Gussow, "Open Theater Stages Splendid Mutation Show," "*New York Times,* Mar. 29, 1973, p. 40; Arthur Sainer, "Words from the West (2)," *Village Voice,* Apr. 27, 1972, p. 73; *Obie: Village Voice,* May 11, 1972.

[But Chaikin was less] "It had too few . . .": Interview, Aug. 8, 1980.

[Still, since *The Mutation*] Footnote: interview Sept. 17, 1974; conversation, fall 1975.

[The major exception to] All Chaikin quotations throughout the *Tongues* and *Savage/Love* section, unless otherwise credited, come from an interview on Oct. 30, 1979. All Sam Shepard quotations, unless otherwise credited, are from a telephone interview on Oct. 30, 1979 and a follow-up conversation a few days later. All quotations from the texts of *Tongues* and *Savage/Love* are from typewritten scripts, with handwritten musical and staging directions, provided by Chaikin; descriptions of nonverbal elements of the production are from this script and my own notes.

[The actual collaboration period] "Sam has an aversion . . .": Leah Frank, "Joseph Chaikin Stages Beckett's 'Comedy about Suffering,' " *New York Times,* Jan. 13, 1980, sec. 2, p. 23.

[One might have expected] "two primary . . .": van Itallie to Wardle, Mar. 25, 1969, VIP (describing collaborative playwriting).

[Chaikin and Shepard began] "thought music": See "Playing Music" in Chapter 3.

[Although they felt, in] "no urgency . . .": Sam Shepard, program note in Eureka Theater Summer Festival program for *Savage/Love,* 1979, PC–Chaikin.

[Before Chaikin had even] "I've been wondering . . .": Sam Shepard to Chaikin, July 2, 1979, PC–Chaikin.

[Because the work period] "On my way . . .": Frank, "Joseph Chaikin," p. 23.

[Instrumental music also became] "Both of . . .": Sam Shepard, program note, Eureka Festival Program, PC–Chaikin.

[After the initial performances] "too respectful": conversation, Nov. 1979; "not only an exquisite . . .": Mel Gussow, "Intimate Monologues That Speak to the Mind and Heart," *New York Times,* Dec. 9, 1979, sec. 2, p. 3; James Leverett, "Other Voices," *Soho Weekly News,* Nov. 22, 1979, p. 47.

[Finally, for all its] "from the person . . . better": interview, Nov. 8, 1977.

6. DIRECTING PLAYS: GOING FROM THE PART TO THE PERSON

[Chaikin told an interviewer] "I feel I've been misunderstood . . . ," "precious": Frank, "Joseph Chaikin," p. 23.

[When staging new scripts] *"Interview"*: interview with van Itallie; Pasolli, *Open Theatre*, p. 89; Jacquot, "The Serpent," p. 278; *America Hurrah*, by Jean-Claude van Itallie (New York: Dramatists Play Service, 1967), playwright's note, p. 10; Rhea Gaisner, "Jean-Claude van Itallie: Playwright of the Ensemble: Open Theater," *Serif*, 9 (Winter 1972):16–17. *Viet Rock:* Pasolli, *Open Theatre*, pp. 77–80; Phyllis Jane Wagner, "Megan Terry: Political Playwright," Ph.D. diss., University of Denver, 1972, pp. 103–7; Feingold, interview with Chaikin, p. 23, PC–Feingold. *Movie Star:* conversations and rehearsals, fall 1977.

[On occasion, Chaikin has] The discussion of *The Dybbuk* here and through the paragraph beginning [Although most of the] is from interviews, Nov. 8, 28 ("These people go . . ."), 1977; New York Shakespeare Festival rehearsals, fall 1977 ("the dead aren't . . . ," "when people thought . . .": first rehearsal).

[This approach to scripts] "that he was . . .": interview, Feb. 17, 1980; "substitute . . .": Frank, "Joseph Chaikin," p. 5; "written more articulately . . .": film of *Endgame* rehearsal, PC–Steven Gomer.

[But each time Chaikin] Conversations, Dec. 1979, Jan. 1980; interview, Feb. 17, 1980.

[Chaikin's first interest in] "I was very drawn . . .": interview, Feb. 17, 1980; *correspondence with Beckett:* interview, Feb. 17, 1980; conversations, 1970–82; several cards from Beckett, OTP and PC–Chaikin; "the second time . . .": Chaikin, *Presence*, p. 137; "to find some . . .": Maloney, "Joe Chaikin," PC–Maloney. The critical response to Chaikin's Hamm included the following descriptions: "a many-leveled, querulous character. . . . Bobbing his head and flexing his voice, he is like a man drowning and gasping for breath" (Mel Gussow, "Theater: Open 'Endgame,' " *New York Times*, May 6, 1970, p. 47); "an engaging presence, worldly, filled with self-disgust, and in the end touching" (Dick Brukenfeld, "Off-Off," *Village Voice*, Apr. 9, 1970, p. 51); "Joseph Chaikin, as the chairbound Hamm, throws an eerie light over the play like a revolving red light on a police car. He is sensual, domineering, crafty, and infinitely tender; he prattles and tells macabre stories and his dominion over the dwindling lives of his family is like the last hoarse gasp of King Lear over the strangled body of Cordelia" (Samuel Hirsch, "Samuel Beckett's 'Endgame' an Intellectual Charade in One Long Act," *Boston Hearld Traveler*, May 13, 1970, p. 22).

[When Chaikin returned to] Interview, Feb. 17, 1980. Footnote: interview, Feb. 17, 1980.

[He saw the script] "Beckett speaks . . .": interview, Feb. 17, 1980; "All of the rehearsals . . .": tape of discussion, Daniel Seltzer and Chaikin with students, Princeton, 1977, PC–Sara Laschever.

[The key to *Endgame* and The basic form of] Interview with Steven Gomer, Mar. 12 and Mar. 14, 1980 ("You run into . . ." [Gomer's wording of Chaikin's comment]); *notes on role playing in* Endgame: Seltzer, notes on working script of *Endgame*, PC–Seltzer estate.

[As rehearsals progressed, Chaikin *and* It was difficult and] Interview with Gomer; Seltzer, notes, PC–Seltzer estate ("*through* . . ."); interview, Feb. 17, 1980.

[The company did find] "Hamm: Nature has . . . Topic: *Nature*," *Hamm's long story: Seltzer, notes, PC–Seltzer estate; "Hamm: Why don't . . .": interview with Gomer; "She was bonny . . . talks that way," "We're getting on . . . moving along": tape, Seltzer and Chaikin, PC–Laschever.*

[Chaikin and the actors] Seltzer, notes, PC–Seltzer estate.

[Chaikin felt strongly that *and* Still, according to Gomer] *modes "unfilled":* Interview with Gomer ("although we were stressing . . ."); rehearsal, New York, Dec. 6, 1979 ("Chekhovian," "Once something's . . ."); Seltzer, notes, PC–Seltzer estate ("Remember . . . ," "Don't PAUSE . . ."); tape, Seltzer and Chaikin, PC–Laschever (Seltzer on difficulty of "erasures" in performance).

[While he did not] Seltzer, notes, PC–Seltzer estate ("When something is . . ."); tape, Seltzer and Chaikin, PC–Laschever ("The big extremes . . .").

[Chaikin continually stressed that] Interview, Feb. 17, 1980.

[It also was critical] *"eventfulness" of action:* Seltzer, notes, PC–Seltzer ("eventful," "To 'wind down' . . ."); tape, Seltzer and Chaikin, PC–Laschever ("Try to find . . ."); rehearsal, New York, Dec. 1979 ("it has to . . .").

[Fundamentally, Chaikin's intention was] Interview, Feb. 17, 1980.

[He did, of course *and* And he did depart] Interview, Feb. 17, 1980.

[Jeremy Lebensohn's bare-bones set *and* Chaikin's largest departure, though] Interview, Feb. 17, 1980; interview with Gomer.

[Despite Chaikin's attempts to *and* Finally, Chaikin reached the] *Chaikin's uneasiness and retreat:* interview, Feb. 17, 1980; interview with Gomer ("One time . . ."); tape, Seltzer and Chaikin, PC–Laschever ("a little deserted"). Footnote: tape, Seltzer and Chaikin, PC–Laschever.

[*Endgame* ran at Princeton's] Conversations, Apr. 1977; interview, Feb. 17, 1980 ("glad that . . . ," "Part of me . . .").

[In large measure, Chaikin *and* The central mode still] *Clov's flea,* "two scholars . . .": rehearsal, Dec. 6, 1979; "In the morning . . . hospitals": Seltzer, notes, PC–Seltzer estate; "One of the . . .": interview, Feb. 17, 1980; "If there's one . . .": rehearsal, Dec. 14, 1979.

[Chaikin tried to clarify *and* Again, Chaikin recalls, the] *"erasures,"* "What's going on . . . ," "Drop it . . .": rehearsal, Dec. 6, 1979; "One thing ends . . .": rehearsal, early Dec. 1979; "In terms of . . .": interview, Feb. 17, 1980; "You must let go . . .": Seltzer, notes, Dec. 29, 1979, PC–Seltzer estate.

[The New York rehearsals] Interview, Feb. 17, 1980.

[The biggest change for] *filled modes:* rehearsal, Dec. 6, 1979 ("In a lot . . . ," "Take the line . . ."); interview, Feb. 17, 1980 ("Chekhovian"); interview with Gomer ("sort of like . . . ," "a joke . . . ," "afraid of . . ."); Seltzer, notes, PC–Seltzer estate.

[Chaikin talked about a] Rehearsals, Dec. 1979 ("There's no . . . ," Dec. 6); Seltzer, notes, PC–Seltzer estate ("A big trap . . .").

[Allowing emotion into some] "No one . . .": interview with Gomer.

[More important, Chaikin now] "They *are* people . . .": interview, Feb. 17, 1980; "could only . . . ," "Do you remember . . ." as attempt to keep Clov from leaving: Seltzer, notes, PC–Seltzer estate.

[The possibility of ongoing] Rehearsals, Dec. 1979 ("like roadsigns . . . ," Dec. 6); interview with Gomer; Seltzer, notes, PC–Seltzer estate.

[Chaikin focused particularly on] *ending:* rehearsals, Dec. 1979 ("When there's no more . . . ," Dec. 14); Seltzer, notes, PC–Seltzer estate ("Major activity . . . ," "There'll be . . .").

[Although he was giving] Seltzer, notes, PC–Seltzer estate ("Don't play . . . ceremoniously"); rehearsal, Dec. 14, 1979 ("an obligation . . . ," "If you get . . ."); interview, Feb. 17, 1980 ("If I could find . . .").

[Preparing the show for *and* Chaikin had come to] Interview, Feb. 17, 1980.

[Both the New York] *reviews:* Mel Gussow, "The Stage: Chaikin Directs Beckett's 'Endgame,' " *New York Times,* Jan. 14, 1980, p. C12; Emory Lewis, "Bringing Out Humor in Beckett," *Bergen Record,* Jan. 14, 1980, p. A15; Erika Munk, "Seeing It Lit," *Village Voice,* Jan. 21, 1980, p. 85; Mathilde La Bardonnie, " 'Endgame' de Samuel Beckett: Quatre acteurs americains," *Le Monde,* Feb. 22, 1980, pp. 1, 22 (my translation). Footnote: John Simon, "Murder at the Manhattan," *New York,* Jan. 28, 1980, p. 58; Douglas Watt, "Endgame Dull Show," *Daily News,* Jan. 14, 1980, p. 25.

[Chaikin was pleased, of] Conversation, Jan. 1980.

[When Chaikin, who had *and* Beckett had not seen *and* Chaikin was both moved] *contact with Beckett in Paris:* conversation, Apr. 1980.

[This meeting briefly revived *and* What had kept Chaikin] Interview, Feb. 17, 1980.

[Finally, Chaikin's love for] "I can't stand . . .": conversation, Feb. 1980; "I don't want to do . . . ," "He's my favorite . . .": interview, Feb. 17, 1980.

7. AFTERWORD

["Theater is prehistoric. And"] Interview, Aug. 8, 1980.

[Chaikin's loyalty to off-off-Broadway] "the conscience . . .": Ross Wetzsteon, "Obies '77: Nobody Is Saying 'Theater Is Dead' Anymore," *Village Voice,* June 6, 1977, p. 89; "He's all . . .": Stella Adler, speaking to a companion in the green room on Nov. 26, 1979 (when asked if she might be quoted in a book about Chaikin, she replied "Absolutely," and repeated the remark).

[Indeed, while Chaikin is] Gussow, "Intimate Monologues"; Wetzsteon, "Obies '77" (*"Lifetime Achievement" award*). Kauffmann's review of *A Chorus Line* talked about that musical's debt to Open Theater methods of creation and, specifically, to the themes and forms of *The Mutation Show;* writing about very different material, the Fugard-Kani-Ntshona South African play *The Island,* Kauffmann noted that it was "reminiscent of the work that the Open Theater has done under Joseph Chaikin." Kauffmann's reviews are reprinted in Kauffmann, *Persons of the Drama* (New York: Harper & Row, 1976), pp. 268, 209.

[Chaikin's real importance, though] "Theater's province . . .": interview, Aug. 8, 1980.

Bibliography

This listing includes all published works cited in the Notes and selected others.

FILMS AND VIDEOTAPES (IN CHRONOLOGICAL ORDER)

The Serpent. Educational Broadcasting Corporation Film for Public Television, 1969. Distributed by Arthur Cantor, Inc., New York, N.Y.

The Serpent. Videotape for NOS Television, Hilversum, Holland, 1970.

Terminal. CBS *Camera Three* videotape, 1970. Distributed by New York State Education Dept., Albany, N.Y.

The Mutation Show. CBS *Camera Three* videotape, 1973. Distributed by New York State Education Dept., Albany, N.Y.

Nightwalk. CBS *Camera Three* videotape, 1973. Distributed by New York State Education Dept., Albany, N.Y.

The Dybbuk. Videotape of performance at New York Shakespeare Festival Public Theater, 1978. Theater on Film and Tape Collection, New York Public Library at Lincoln Center, New York, N.Y.

Tongues and *Savage/Love*. Videotape of performance at New York Shakespeare Festival Public Theater, 1980. Theater on Film and Tape Collection, New York Public Library at Lincoln Center, New York, N.Y.

Endgame. Videotape of performance at Manhattan Theatre Club, 1980. Theater on Film and Tape Collection, New York Public Library at Lincoln Center, New York, N.Y.

Tongues and *Savage/Love*. Videotape (using extreme visual distortion techniques) by Shirley Clarke, 1982. Distributed by Women's Interart Center, New York, N.Y.

Joseph Chaikin: Going On. A film by Steven Gomer, 1983. Distributed by Films for the Humanities, Princeton, N.J.

Miscellaneous videotape footage, including scenes from *The Connection* and *Woyzeck* and interviews. Files of RTBS Television, Brussels, Belgium.

PUBLISHED SCRIPTS (IN CHRONOLOGICAL ORDER)

Viet Rock. By Megan Terry. *Tulane Drama Review*, 11, no. 1 (1966): 196–227. Reprinted in Terry, *Four Plays*. New York: Simon & Schuster, 1967.

America Hurrah. By Jean-Claude van Itallie. New York: Coward-McCann, 1966; New York: Dramatists' Play Service, 1967.

The Serpent. A ceremony written by Jean-Claude van Itallie in collaboration with the Open Theater under the direction of Joseph Chaikin. New York: Atheneum, 1969; New York: Dramatists' Play Service, 1969.

Terminal. A collective work created by the Open Theater ensemble, co-directed by Joseph Chaikin and Roberta Sklar, text by Susan Yankowitz [first, large-company version]. *Scripts*, 1 (Nov. 1971): 17–47.

Three Works by the Open Theater: Terminal [revised, small company version], *The Muta-*

tion Show, Nightwalk. Ed. Karen Malpede. New York: Drama Books Specialists/ Publishers, 1974.

Terminal [first version, with stage directions adapted for small company]. In *The Radical Theatre Notebook*, ed. Arthur Sainer, pp. 108–45. New York: Avon Books, 1975.

A Fable. A collaborative piece written by Jean-Claude van Itallie, originally created collaboratively with director Joseph Chaikin. New York: Dramatists' Play Service, 1976; *Performing Arts Journal* 1, no. 3 (1977):124–47.

Re-Arrangements. By the Winter Project. *Performing Arts Journal*, 4, no. 3 (1980):147–57.

Tongues and *Savage/Love*. By Sam Shepard and Joseph Chaikin. In Shepard, *Seven Plays*, pp. 301–37. New York: Bantam Books, 1981.

PUBLISHED COMMENTARY BY AND INTERVIEWS WITH CHAIKIN (IN CHRONOLOGICAL ORDER)

Chaikin, Joseph. "The Open Theatre [questions by Richard Schechner]." *Tulane Drama Review*, 9, no. 2 (1964):191–7.

Munk, Erika. "The Actor's Involvement: Notes on Brecht – An Interview with Joseph Chaikin." *Drama Review*, 12, no. 2 (1968):147–51.

Chaikin, Joseph. "Fragments." Ed. Kelly Morris. *Drama Review*, 13, no. 3 (1969):145–7.

"Flip Pages." *yale/theatre*, 2 (Spring 1969):53–84.

Schechner, Richard. "An Interview with Joseph Chaikin." *Drama Review*, 13, no. 3 (1969):141–44. Reprinted in James Schevill, *Breakout! In Search of New Theatrical Environments*, pp. 442–7. Chicago: Swallow Press, 1973.

Chaikin, Joseph. "The Context of Performance." In *Actors on Acting*, ed. Toby Cole and Helen Krich Chinoy, pp. 665–9. New York: Crown, 1970.

"Notes on Character . . . and the Setup." *Performance*, 1 (Dec. 1971):76–81.

The Presence of the Actor. New York: Atheneum, 1972.

Maloney, Peter. "A Talk with Joe Chaikin." *Changes*, 77, Oct. 1972, pp. 11–12.

Chaikin, Joseph. "What the Actor Does." *Performance*, 1, (Mar.–Apr. 1973):56–9.

Eddy, Bill. "Four Directors on Criticism." *Drama Review*, 18, no. 3 (1974):24–33.

Toscan, Richard. "Joseph Chaikin: Closing the Open Theatre." *Theatre Quarterly*, 4 (Nov. 1974–Jan. 1975):36–43.

Chaikin, Joseph. "Interview [questions by Andrzej Bonarski]." *Performing Arts Journal*, 1, no. 3 (1977):117–23.

Berson, Misha. "Imagining the Other: A Conversation with Joe Chaikin." *Theaterwork*, 3 (Mar.–Apr. 1983):27–32.

"Theater at War: Chaikin, American Rep Carry Peace and Art to a Mideast in Crisis." *Theatre Communications*, 5 (Apr. 1983):1–5.

Coco, William, ed. Statement by Chaikin in "The Open Theater [1963–1973] Looking Back," *Performing Arts Journal*, 7, no. 3 (1983):46–8.

PUBLISHED COMMENTARY BY AND INTERVIEWS WITH CHAIKIN'S COLLABORATORS

Coco, William, ed. "The Open Theater [1963–1973] Looking Back" [statements by Gordon Rogoff, Jean-Claude van Itallie, Joyce Aaron, Susan Yankowitz, Paul Zimet, Richard Gilman, and Joseph Chaikin], 7, no. 3 (1983):25–48.

Gaisner, Rhea. "Jean-Claude van Itallie: Playwright of the Ensemble: Open Theater."
    Serif, 9 (Winter 1972):14–17.
Maloney, Peter. "An Actor's View, Part I: Lee," *Changes,* 2, no. 26 (May 15, 1971):28–
    9. "An Actor's View, Part II: *The Serpent,*" *Changes,* 3, no. 1 (June 1, 1971):26–7.
    "The Making of *The Serpent*" In *The Open Theater–Europe 1968* [souvenir program],
    pp. 9–25. New York, 1968. Translated as "Nascita del Serpente." *Sipario* (Milan),
    1968.
    "The Open Theater: An Actor's View, Part III," *Changes,* 3, no. 2 (June 15,
    1971):20–1.
    "The Open Theater: The Mutation Show." *Changes,* no. 75, July 1972, p. 17.
Munk, Erika. "Working in a Collective–Interviews with Susan Yankowitz and Ro-
    berta Sklar." *Performance,* 1 (Dec. 1971):82–90.
Munk, Erika, and Mackay, Barbara. "The Open Theater (Interview with John Dillon,
    Tina Shepard, and Paul Zimet)." *Performance,* 1 (Apr. 1972):92–9.
Rafalowicz, Mira. In "Dramaturgs in America: Eleven Statements." *Theater,* 10 (Fall
    1978):27–8.
Ryan, Paul Ryder. "Terminal–An Interview with Roberta Sklar." *Drama Review,* 15,
    no. 32 (1971):149–57.
Sklar, Roberta. "Toward Creating a Women's Theatre." *Drama Review,* 24, no. 2
    (1980):23–40.
van Itallie, Jean-Claude. "Funerals, Celebrations and Novelty." In International
    Theater Institute, *Theater 4: The American Theater, 1970–1971,* pp. 98–100. New
    York: Scribner, 1972.
    "The Open Theater." In International Theater Institute, *Theater 2: American Theater,*
    68–69, pp. 82–87. New York: Scribner, 1970.
    "Playwright at Work: Off Off-Broadway." *Tulane Drama Review,* 10 (Summer
    1966):154–8.

PUBLISHED CRITICISM

Barber, Bob. " 'The Mutation Show' Presented at UCSB." *Santa Barbara News-Press,*
    Apr. 7, 1972, p. C15.
Billington, Michael. "Texts." *Guardian,* June 18, 1981, p. 11.
Blumenthal, Eileen. "Joseph Chaikin Enters the Mystical World of 'The Dybbuk.' "
    New York Times, Jan. 1, 1978, sec. 2, p. 3.
    "The Presence of the Character: The Robert Montgomery/Joseph Chaikin *Electra.*"
    yale/theatre, 6 (Fall 1974):98–108.
    "Something Old, Something New." *Village Voice,* May 6–12, 1981, p. 89.
Brukenfeld, Dick. "Off-Off," *Village Voice,* Apr. 9, 1970, p. 51.
Copeland, Roger. "Remembering The Real Open Theater," *New York Times,* Dec. 25,
    1983, sec. 2, p. 11.
Croyden, Margaret. "Burning Bridges Is Natural." *New York Times,* Mar. 29, 1970, sec.
    2, pp. 1, 5.
Feingold, Michael. "Chaikin's New Path." *Village Voice,* Mar. 9, 1982, p. 83.
    "Chekhov Gets the Bride." *Village Voice,* Feb. 10, 1975, pp. 75, 77.
    "A New Way of Making Theater–And It's Over." *New York Times,* Oct. 7, 1973,
    sec. 2, p. 3.
    "Still Going On." *Village Voice,* Mar. 11–17, 1981, p. 79.
Frank, Leah. "Joseph Chaikin Stages Beckett's 'Comedy about Suffering.' " *New York
    Times,* Jan. 13, 1980, sec. 2, pp. 5, 23.

Gerrett, Virginia. "The Audiences Are 'With It' in US." *Canberra* (Australia) *Times,* June 25, 1969, p. 29.

Giner, Oscar. "Mark Me: The Dybbuk." *Theater,* 9 (Spring 1978):149–51.

Gottlieb, Saul. "Ein neues amerikanisches Theater?" *Theater heute,* 8 (Sept. 1967):46–8.

Gussow, Mel. "A Bite into an Apple Long Ago." *New York Times,* June 2, 1970, p. 35.

"Chaikin of Open Theater Stages Remarkable 'Electra.' " *New York Times,* May 24, 1974, p. 22.

"Experimental Open Theater Carrying On." *New York Times,* Apr. 27, 1971, p. 51.

"Intimate Monologues That Speak to the Mind and Heart." *New York Times,* Dec. 9, 1979, sec. 2, p. 3.

"Open Theater Stages Splendid 'Mutation Show.' " *New York Times,* Mar. 29, 1973, p. 40.

"The Stage: Chaikin Directs Beckett's 'Endgame.' " *New York Times,* Jan. 14, 1980, p. C12.

"Stage: Joseph Chaikin's Beckett Solo." *New York Times,* Mar. 9, 1981, p. C12.

"Stage: Stunning Horror." *New York Times,* Apr. 15, 1970, p. 51.

"Theater: Open 'Endgame.' " *New York Times,* May 6, 1970, p. 47.

"Theater: A Shepard Joint Effort." *New York Times,* Nov. 16, 1979, p. C6.

Hirsch, Samuel. "Open Theater's The Serpent a Fascinating Experience." *Boston Herald Traveler,* Jan. 13, 1969, p. 17.

"Samuel Beckett's 'Endgame' an Intellectual Charade in One Long Act." *Boston Herald Traveler,* May 13, 1970, p. 22.

Hoffman, Ted. " 'Re-Arrangements': Vaudeville of the Soul-in-Angst." *Villager,* Mar. 27, 1979, p. 13.

Hughes, Catherine. "New York." *Plays and Players,* Aug. 1969, pp. 64–5.

"New York." *Plays and Players,* July 1970, p. 56.

Jacquot, Jean. "The Open Theater–The Serpent." In *Les voies de la création théâtrale,* vol. 1, ed. Jacquot, pp. 271–308. Paris: Editions du Centre National de la Recherche Scientifique, 1970.

Junker, Howard. "Group Theater." *Newsweek,* May 26, 1969, pp. 128, 133.

Kauffmann, Stanley. *Persons of the Drama.* New York: Harper & Row, 1976.

Kelley, Martin P. "A Search for New Theater." *Albany Times-Union,* Apr. 11, 1970, p. 6.

Kellman, Alice. "Joseph Chaikin." *Drama Review,* 20, no. 3 (1976):17–26.

Kelly, Kevin. "Open Theater Disciplined, Gifted." *Boston Globe,* Jan. 19, 1969, pp. A24, A27.

Kerensky, Oleg. "Jean-Claude van Itallie in the Garden of Eden." *Times* (London) *Saturday Review,* July 20, 1968, p. 19.

Kerr, Walter. "A Critic Celebrates the Unpredictable." *New York Times,* July 3, 1983, sec. 2, pp. 1, 4.

"The Finest Company of Its Kind." *New York Times,* May 24, 1970, sec. 2, p. 3. Reprinted with revisions in Kerr, *God on the Gymnasium Floor,* pp. 21–4. New York: Simon & Schuster, 1970.

"What If Cain Did Not Know *How* to Kill Abel?" *New York Times,* Feb. 9, 1969, pp. 1, 8. Reprinted with revisions in Kerr, *God on the Gymnasium Floor,* pp. 24–7. New York: Simon & Schuster, 1970.

Khan, Naseem. "The Home of Experience." *Time Out,* June 1–7, 1973, pp. 16–17.

Kleb, William. "Theater in San Francisco: Shepard and Chaikin Speaking in *Tongues.*" *Theater,* 10 (Fall 1978):66–9.

Knickerbocker, Paine. " 'America Hurrah': Search for Adaptability and Seductiveness." *San Francisco Examiner and Chronicle,* May 14, 1967, p. 3.

Kolodin, Irving. "Music to My Ears: Berio's 'Opera' Loses, but Open Theater Wins." *Saturday Review,* Aug. 29, 1970, p. 8.

La Bardonnie, Mathilde. " 'Endgame,' de Samuel Beckett: Quatre acteurs ameri-
    cains." *Le Monde*, Feb. 22, 1980, pp. 1, 22.
Lahr, John. "The Open Theater's Serpent." In Lahr, *Up against the Fourth Wall*, pp.
    158–74. New York: Grove Press, 1970. Reprinted from *Evergreen Review*.
    Reviews of *Terminal* and *The Mutation Show*. In Lahr, *Astonish Me*, pp. 201–10. New
    York: Viking Press, 1973. Reprinted from *Village Voice*.
    "Theater: Joseph Chaikin's Children," *New York Free Press*, Feb. 29, 1968, p. 6.
Lester, Elenore. "He Doesn't Aim to Please." *New York Times*, Dec. 25, 1966, sec. 2,
    pp. 1, 3.
    "I Am the Audience in Action." *New York Times*, Mar. 7, 1976, sec. 2, pp. 5, 34.
Leverett, James. "Other Voices." *Soho Weekly News*, Nov. 22, 1979, pp. 47, 50.
Lewis, Emory. "Bringing Out Humor in Beckett." *Bergen Record*, Jan. 14, 1980, p. A15.
Loney, Glenn. "Joe Chaikin: Bringing It All Back Home." *Other Stages*, Apr. 23, 1981,
    pp. 1, 3–4.
Munk, Erika. "Exiles." *Village Voice*, July 16–22, 1980, p. 75.
    "Seeing It Lit." *Village Voice*, Jan. 21, 1980, p. 85.
Norton, Elliot. "Elliot Norton Writes: Open Theater's Odd 'Serpent' Writhes and
    Wriggles at Loeb." *Boston Record-American*, Jan. 13, 1969, p. 30.
Pasolli, Robert. *A Book on the Open Theatre*. New York: Avon Books, 1970.
    "The Man-Not-in-the-Street on Stage Off-Broadway." *Village Voice*, Nov. 3, 1966,
    pp. 24, 26, 29.
    "Theatre: The Open Theatre." *Village Voice*, May 20, 1965, p. 17.
Pegnato, Lisa J. "Breathing in a Different Zone: Joseph Chaikin." *Drama Review*, 25,
    no. 3 (1981):7–18.
Petzold, Charles. "Swiss Girl Finds U.S. Death Rites Odd." *Philadelphia Daily News*,
    Dec. 2, 1970, p. 39.
Rogoff, Gordon. "Questioning Love." *Village Voice*, Mar. 19, 1979, p. 85.
Sainer, Arthur. "Chile, Chile." *Village Voice*, Sept. 29, 1975, pp. 106–7.
    The Radical Theatre Notebook. New York: Avon Books, 1975.
    "Words from the West (2)." *Village Voice*, Apr. 27, 1972, p. 73.
Schevill, James. "The Open Theater: The Thinking Actor and the Working Play-
    wright; The Open theater and Terminal." In Schevill, *Breakout! In Search of New
    Theatrical Environments*, pp. 336–42. Chicago: Swallow Press, 1973.
Simon, John. "Murder at the Manhattan." *New York*, Jan. 28, 1980, p. 58.
Smith, Michael. "The Good Scene: Off Off-Broadway." *Tulane Drama Review*, 10
    (Summer 1966):159–76.
    "Theatre Journal." *Village Voice*, Oct. 18, 1973, p. 71.
Sterritt, David. "Open Theater: Collective 'Untitled.' " *Christian Science Monitor*, May
    28, 1971, p. 15.
Taylor, Karen Malpede. "The Open Theatre." In Taylor, *People's Theatre in Amerika*,
    pp. 234–50. New York: Drama Book Specialists/Publishers, 1972.
    "Two Kaspars – By Peter Handke and the Open Theater." *Performance*, 1 (May–June
    1973):29–37.
Thomas, Michael. "Off Broadway." *Plays and Players*, Mar. 1967, pp. 60–1, 63.
"Village Voice Off-Broadway Awards, Season 1966–1967." *Village Voice*, May 25,
    1967, p. 25.
"Village Voice Off-Broadway Awards, Season 1971–1972." *Village Voice*, May 11,
    1972, p. 66.
Wagner, Phyllis Jane. "Jean-Claude van Itallie: Political Playwright." *Serif*, 9 (Winter
    1972):19–74.
Watt, Douglas. " 'Endgame' Dull Show." *Daily News*, Jan. 14, 1980, p. 25.
Wetzsteon, Ross. "Obies '77: Nobody Is Saying 'Theater Is Dead' Anymore." *Village
    Voice*, June 6, 1977, p. 89.

UNPUBLISHED THESES

Blumenthal, Eileen. "The Open Theater." Ph.D. diss., Yale University, 1977.

Hendrix, Erlene Laney. "The Presence of the Actor as Kinetic Melody: A Study of Joseph Chaikin's Open Theater through the Philosophy of Maurice Merleau-Ponty." Ph.D. diss. University of Missouri–Columbia, 1977.

Mohan, Roberta N. "The Open Theater Production of *The Serpent: A Ceremony:* An Examination of Aesthetic Purpose and Creative Process." M.A. thesis, Kent State University, 1973.

Richter, George R., Jr. "Jean-Claude van Itallie, Improvisational Playwright: A Study of His Plays." M.A. thesis, University of Colorado, 1969.

Wagner, Phyllis Jane. "Megan Terry: Political Playwright." Ph.D. diss., University of Denver, 1972.

MANUSCRIPT COLLECTIONS

The Chaikin Papers (CP), Open Theater Papers (OTP), and van Itallie Papers (VIP) are housed at the Kent State University Libraries, Kent, Ohio.

Index

Aaron, Joyce, 31, 94, 107n, 127, 144, 186
actor, Chaikin as, 10–14, 18, 30, 32, 33,
    34, 176, 179, 189, 206, 212–15, 247
Adler, Stella, 211
"Airplane" improvisations, 214, 215
Akalaitis, JoAnne, 211
Algeria, performances in, 219
Alhambra Hall, 212
American Repertory Theater, 37, 225
Angry Artists Against the War in Viet-
    nam, 216, 217
Ansky, S., *The Dybbuk,* 30, 43, 60, 65,
    102, 185–7, 222, 223
Antonioni, Michelangelo, *Zabriskie Point,*
    217
Artaud, Antonin, 3, 4, 5, 27
Artservices, 29n
audience, 1, 15, 16, 38, 39–40, 42, 46,
    48, 50, 51–2, 57–62, 63, 76–9, 117–18,
    120, 127, 135, 136, 167–8, 184, 191–2,
    194, 206, 222

Barba, Eugenio, 23, 218
Barbosa, James, 18, 107n, 114, 132, 186,
    197n, 200
Barry, Raymond, 58, 88, 96, 107n, 114,
    123–4, 148n, 156–9, 162, 168, 224
Bartenieff, George, 27
Bay Area Theater Critics Circle award,
    223
Beaumont, Vivian, Theater, 60
Beauvoir, Simone de, 179
Beck, Julian, *see* Living Theater
Beckett, Samuel, 3, 100–1, 185, 206–7;
    Endgame, 18, 20, 30, 60, 100, 102, 179,
    188–207, 218, 222, 223, 247; *Stories
    and Texts for Nothing (Texts),* 30, 31,
    65n, 207, 224; *Waiting for Godot,* 225
Belden, Valerie, 227
Belgrade International Theater Festival
    award, 25, 170, 219
Ben-Yakov, Jenn, 107n, 239
Bennet, Michael, *A Chorus Line,* 209, 249
Bergen Record, 206
Berghof, Herbert, 10, 212
Berney, William, 213
Berio, Luciano, *Opera,* 218

Black Theater Workshop, 28
Blau, Isabelle, 227
body song exercises, 81
Boesing, Paul, 227
Bonhoeffer, Dietrich, 108–9, 126
Boston Globe, 139
Bradford, Michael, 227
Brandeis award, 25, 218
Bread and Puppet Theater, 28
breathing and talking together exercise,
    74
Brecht, Bertolt, 3, 17, 38, 39, 52–3, 91,
    100, 185; *Clown Play,* 214, 216, 217; *Ed-
    ward II,* 215; *The Exception and the Rule,*
    215; *In the Jungle of the Cities,* 11, 213;
    Man Is Man, 11–14, 189, 213–14
Brecht, Mary, 203, 224
Breuer, Lee, 211
Broadway, 3, 62–3, 117n, 208, 209; *see
    also* economics of theater
Brook, Peter, 4–5, 23, 29, 43, 49, 72, 92,
    117n, 188, 216, 220
Brown, Kenneth, *The Brig,* 4, 214
Büchner, Georg, *Woyzeck,* 30, 92, 101,
    221

Caffe Cino, 4
California, University of, at Santa Bar-
    bara, 220
Calvert, Henry, 186
Campbell, Joseph, 108, 111, 150, 160
Canada, performances in, 219, 220, 224,
    225
Caracas Theater Festival, 36, 98, 224
Carnegie Hall Playhouse, 213
Center for Theater Practice, 223
Chaikin, Shami, 88, 107n, 127, 129, 144,
    148n, 163, 167, 168, 169, 190n, 220
character, approaches to, 1, 16, 50–1,
    53–4
Chekhov, Anton, 89, 100–1, 219; *The Sea
    Gull,* 30, 31; *Uncle Vanya,* 30, 225
Chile, Chile, 221
Chilton, Nola, 10, 14, 74, 86, 212
China Project, 19, 217–18
Chinese theater, 92–4, 96, 101, 120, 153,
    217

Chioles, John, 224
chord exercise, 73, 105, 118, 210
Cieslak, Ryszard, 217
Cino, Joe, 4
circles exercises, 91–2, 103, 105–6, 120, 214
Civic Repertory Theater, 2
classical theater, 3, 30, 93, 100, 185, 188, 219, 220, 221; *see also individual playwrights*
Cocteau, Jean, 4
Colgate College, 212
Collison, Michele, 220
comedy, 48, 106, 128, 179, 195, 202–3
conductor exercises, 74–5, 90, 106, 214, 215
Contest, 106, 214, 215
Cooper, David, *The Death of the Family*, 150
Cooper, Patricia, 111–12, 115
Cozzens, Mimi, 227
criticism, 17, 63, 139, 169–70, 183–4, 205–6, 212, 214
cummings, e.e., *Santa Claus*, 213

Daily News, 205n
dance, 5, 48, 70, 76
death and mourning, themes of, 6, 20, 21, 36, 39, 82, 101–3, 122, 125–6, 134, 135, 136, 175–6, 185–7, 218, 222, 224
dedicating performances, 77
Denmark, performances in, 137, 217
Dixon, Brenda, iv, 107n, 239
Drake University, 8, 219
Drama Desk Award, 25, 220
dream exercises, 90, 106, 214, 215
Duffy, Bernard, 187

economics of theater, 1, 3, 15, 25, 28–9, 38, 49, 62–3, 64–5, 137, 208
Einstein, Albert, 109
Electra, 29, 65n, 170n, 188, 220, 221
Eliot, T. S., 100
El Teatro Campesino, 28
emblem exercises, 93–4, 120, 150, 165–6; *see also* phrase exercises
Emerson, Ralph Waldo, 5, 46
Emmons, Beverly, 183, 203, 205
England, performances in, 216, 220, 224, 225
ensemble playing, 14, 16, 56–7, 72–6, 214
environmental theater, 27, 61, 168
Eureka Theater, San Francisco, 183, 223
European performances, 137, 213, 218; *see also individual countries*

excommunication exercises, 101, 150, 216
exercises, 15, 191; *see also* workshops *and individual exercises*
expecting exercises, 77–8, 214, 216, 222
expressionism, 47, 90

Faber, Ron, 18, 107n, 114, 227
Fable [Telling about a Journey], A, 29, 107, 170n, 221
Fabricant, Gwen, 169
Federal Theater Project, 2
Feldman, Peter, 17, 18, 185, 216, 218, 227
Field, Crystal, 27
film, 40, 44, 47, 61, 216
Firebomb, 216
First American Radical Theater Festival, 217
Ford Foundation, 28
Foreman, Richard, 27
Fornes, Maria Irene, 17, 215
Foster, Gloria, 103, 214, 224
Fowkes, Conrad, 186
France, performances in, 183–4, 205–6, 218, 223, 224
Frank, Robert, *Me and My Brother*, 216
Freud, Sigmund, 150
Fugard, Athol, 249

Gabor, Nancy, 129
Gaisner, Rhea, 217
Gans, Sharon, 227
Gate Theater, 213
Gelber, Jack, *The Connection*, 4, 11, 213
Genet, Jean, 3, 100
Germany, performances in, 137, 217, 218
Ghelderode, Michel de, *Escurial*, 213
Gilbert, Ronnie, 31, 49, 80, 89, 94, 186, 223
Gilman, Richard, 64, 215
Ginzberg, Louis, *Legends of the Jews*, 109, 111, 112, 114, 120, 122
Golub, Peter, 224
Gomer, Steven, 191, 193, 196, 197, 199, 200
Goodman, Paul, 5, 109, 213
grants, 28–9 64–5; *see also* economics of theater *and individual sources of funding*
Graves, Robert, 108
Greenwich Mews Theater, 215
Gregory, André, 27, 211
Gretna Playhouse, Mt. Gretna, Penn., 213
Gross, Michael, 197–205
Grotowski, Jerzy, 4–5, 23, 43, 49, 69, 81, 96, 119, 188, 216, 217, 218

Group Theater, 2–3
Guggenheim Fellowship, 218, 221
Gussow, Mel, 139, 170, 184, 205–6, 211
Guthrie Theater, Minneapolis, Minn., 214

Habimah Theater, 30, 223
Handke, Peter, 152n, 168
Happenings, 4, 61, 117
Harlequin Players, 10, 212
Harris, Cynthia, 107n, 127, 144, 186
Harris, Philip, 107n, 119, 121, 130
Harvard University, 138–9
Hayes, Alfred, *The Girl on the Via Fla-minia*, 213
Haynes, Jayne, 107n
Hickey, William, 10, 212
Holland, performances in, 218, 220, 221
Hott, Jordan, 227
Hudson Guild Theater, 213
Hughes, Catherine, 139

Ibsen, Henrik, 219
improvisation, 14, 49, 93, 105, 117, 146, 215, 216; *see also individual exercises*
inside/outside exercises, 87, 91, 101, 105, 214
instant scenes exercises, 92, 106
interview exercises, 81–3, 150, 164, 222, 223
Ionesco, Eugène, 3, 100, 215
Iran, performances in, 219
Israel, performances in, 219, 223, 225
Italy, performances in, 137, 183, 212, 217, 223

Jackson, George, *Soledad Brother*, 150, 156–9
Jacobs, Sally, 203, 205, 225
jamming exercises, 75–6, 100, 112, 161, 165, 177, 215
Jarry, Alfred, 4, 18, 20, 218
Jewish heritage, 5, 36, 43
Judson Memorial Church, 4
Jung, Karl, 46, 108

Kass, Peter, 10
Kauffmann, Stanley, 211, 249
Kelly, Kevin, 139
Kennedy, Adrienne, *A Movie Star Has to Star in Black and White*, 30, 65n, 185, 221–2
Kent, Steve, 30, 224
Kerr, Walter, 139
Kevin, Lynn, 227
Kourilsky, Françoise, 223

LaBardonnie, Mathilde, 206
LaFarge, W. E. R., 149
Laing, R. D., 150
LaMama, 4, 18, 27, 36, 37, 65, 209, 216, 223, 224, 225
language, 15, 44, 47, 98–101
LaPlante, Skip, 177, 179–83, 224
Lebensohn, Jeremy, 195
Lee, Ralph, 88, 107n, 114, 123–4
Le Monde, Paris, 206
Lenox Arts Center, 221
levels of address, 60–1, 77
Leverett, James, 184
Levin, Ira, *No Time for Sergeants*, 10, 213
Levy, Jacques, 17, 131
Lewis, Emory, 206
Lies and Secrets, 37, 225
"Lifetime Achievement" award, *see* Obie award
Lillard, Tom, 20, 88, 96, 148n, 154–5, 161, 163, 167
Linklator, Kristin, 17, 220
Littlewood, Joan, 100
Living Theater, 4, 11–14, 28, 57, 73, 104, 117n, 189, 213–14
locked action exercises, 90, 120–1, 125, 135–6
London, Roy, 112, 119
Ludlam, Charles, 28
Lust, Geraldine, 227
Lyman, Dorothy, 107n, 130

Mabou Mines, 209; *see also individual artists*
McCann, Chris, 190–1, 193, 194, 196
MacGrath, Leueen, 31
machine exercises, 72, 90, 106
MacIntosh, Joan, 197n, 200
McNally, Terrence, *And Things That Go Bump in the Night*, 214
Macy, Bill, 186
Maddow, Ellen, 88, 161–3, 165
Madison Square Garden, 59, 216
Maeda, Jun, 224
Magic Theater, San Francisco, Calif., 212, 222
Malina, Judith, *see* Living Theater
Maloney, Peter, 107n, 114, 189
Mandas, Catherine, 227
Manhattan Project, 27
Manhattan Theatre Club, 27, 30, 60, 65, 197, 221, 223
Mann, Harry, 177, 179–83, 224
Mannino, Anthony, 10
Martinique Theater, 214, 216

Masks, 217
Mayer, Jerry, 209
Meadow, Lynne, *see* Manhattan Theatre Club
medical problems, 6, 8, 14, 29, 37, 47, 175–6, 179, 197, 221, 222, 223, 225
Medicine Show, 22
Method acting, 3, 15, 51, 53–4, 56, 59, 83, 209, 212
Mideast performances, 166, 219; *see also individual countries*
Mikulewicz, Bil, 169
Millay, Edna St. Vincent, *Aria da Capo,* 10, 212
"modes" exercises, 95–6, 191–4, 197–8
Monk, Meredith, 27, 209, 223
Montgomery, Robert, 29, 220, 221; *see also Electra*
mourning, theme of, *see* death and mourning, themes of
Munk, Erika, 206
music, 15, 46–8, 74, 76, 96–8, 119, 134, 135, 136, 148, 153, 155, 158, 161, 165, 167, 169, 172–3, 176–8, 179–83, 188, 190, 198, 222; *see also* singing exercises
musical theater, 3
Mutation Show, 22–3, 48, 75, 90, 98, 101, 147, 148–70, 175n, 212, 219–20, 249; breaking and gags, 158, 159–60, 161, 162, 166–7, 169; Caspar Hauser, 22–3, 152–3, 155–9, 160, 162, 164–5, 167–8, 169; healer, 151; human gallery, 162–5; Kamala, 23, 151–2, 153–5, 156, 158, 161, 162, 164–5, 167; mutant gallery, 150–1, 161, 164–5, 166–7; rules for the audience, 167–9; structure, 164–6, 166–9; wedding ceremony, 141, 160–2, 167
Myers, Bruce, 187
"My house is burning" exercise, 100, 152

National Endowment for the Arts, 28
naturalism, 1, 2–3, 4, 8, 15, 45–6, 47, 70, 83, 89, 90, 105, 208
Negro Ensemble Company, 28
Neighborhood Playhouse, 2
New England Theater Conference award, 219
New Lafayette Theater, 28
New Republic, 211, 249
New York Magazine, 205n
New York Shakespeare Festival Public Theatre, 30, 63n, 65, 138, 183, 212, 220, 221, 222, 223, 224

New York State Council on the Arts (and New York State Commission on the Arts), 28
New York Times, see Gussow, Mel; Kerr, Walter
Night Voices, 225
Nightwalk, 23–4, 26, 46, 64, 72, 76, 87, 94, 96, 98, 141, 143–4, 171, 220

Obie award, 12, 14, 25, 63, 170, 211, 214, 215, 216, 218, 219, 222
O'Casey, Sean, *Bedtime Story,* 10, 212
"Odets" inside/outside improvisations, 105, 214, 215
off-Broadway, 3, 10, 18, 27, 63, 138, 213, 216; *see also* economics of theater
off-off-Broadway, 1–4, 27–8, 211
on/off exercises, 71, 86, 214
Open Theater, 1, 14–30, 34, 38, 40, 42, 50, 51, 53, 56, 58, 60–6, 69–70, 71–103, 104–39, 189–90, 191, 197n, 211, 214–20; end of, 25–7, 141
Other, The, 36, 43, 106n, 225
Other Theater, 29

Papp, Joseph, 27, 65; *see also* New York Shakespeare Festival Public Theater
Paskin, Murray, 227
Patton, Will, 49, 84–5, 94, 223
Peaslee, Richard, 119n, 122, 221
"perfect people" exercises and improvisations, 87–9, 99, 106, 161, 214
performance art, 4
Performance Group, 117n; *see also* Richard Schechner
phrase exercises, 93, 120, 133, 150, 161, 185; *see also* emblem exercises
physical work, *see* somatic (outside-in) approaches
Picnic in Spring, 105–6, 214
Pirandello, Luigi, 213
Plays and Players, 139
playwright, Chaikin as, 104, 161
playwright, role of, 137, 140, 142, 145–8, 149, 170
Pocket Theater, 212, 215, 217
politics and theater, 3, 4, 5, 12, 26, 28, 29, 38, 39, 41–3, 44–6, 52, 59, 77, 208, 216, 219, 225
presence, 15, 23, 38, 39–40, 44, 48, 50, 51–3, 61, 67, 70, 71–83, 90, 116, 137, 166, 194, 209
Princeton University, 30, 190, 196, 201, 203, 222
prison performances, 23, 60, 62, 218, 219

Provincetown Players, 2
psychology, 1, 45; *see also* Method acting

Quena Company, 27

Racine, Jean, 4
Rafalowicz, Mira, 23, 30, 170, 187, 224–5
Ragni, Germone, 227
realism, *see* naturalism
Re-Arrangements, 34, 42, 65, 79, 82, 83, 94–5, 98, 144, 179, 223, 224
Reinhardt, Max, 8
Reisner, Steven, 224
Richardson, Howard, and William Berney, *Dark of the Moon*, 213
Rip Van Winkle exercises, 94–5, 96, 106, 215; *see also* "worlds" exercises
Riverside Studios, London, 37
Rockefeller Foundation, 28
Rogoff, Gordon, 64, 227
Rostova, Mira, 10, 212
Royal Shakespeare Company, *see* Brook, Peter

Sainer, Arthur, 170, 227
St. Clement's Church, 29, 217, 220, 221
St. Marks in the Bowery, 4
Sakato, Atsumi, 89, 223–4
SANE, 216
San Francisco Mime Troupe, 28
Santvoord, Peg, Foundation, 28
Savage/Love, 30, 64, 107, 172–3, 197, 206, 211, 223
Schechner, Richard, 27
Schindler, Ellen, 107n
Schmidman, JoAnn, 20, 88, 141, 148n, 163, 164, 169
Seka, Ron, 31
Seltzer, Daniel, 31, 102–3, 190–206
Serban, Andrei, 30, 207, 211, 225
Serpent, The, 19, 58, 63, 76–7, 90, 102, 103, 106–39, 145, 147, 164–5, 170, 212, 217–18; Adam and Eve, 111–12; autopsy, 133, 135; the "begatting," 128–9; Cain and Abel, 122–5; chorus of women, 125–8, 133, 135, 136; ending, 136; Garden of Eden, 109–11, 135; God's curses, 118–22, 133, 137, 165; Kennedy/King assassination, 129–33, 135, 152; opening procession, 135–6; snake, tree of life, and temptation, 112–16, 121–2, 126, 136, 137; workshop, 143, 144
Shakespeare, 8, 30, 100, 188, 219; *see also* classical theater

Shapiro, Leonardo, 30, 221
Shepard, Sam, 23, 30, 34, 37, 107, 145, 148, 171–84, 220, 225; *Icarus' Mother*, 171; *Nightwalk*, 171; *Savage/Love*, 172–3, 223 (*see also Savage/Love*); *Terminal*, 171; *Tongues*, 171–9, 222 (see also *Tongues*)
Shepard, Tina, 19, 20, 23, 24, 31, 55, 58, 68, 72, 84–5, 88, 89, 95, 103, 107n, 115, 116, 129, 140, 148n, 154–5, 160–1, 163, 221, 224
Sheridan Square Playhouse, 214, 215
Sherman, Margo Lee, 31
Shiraz Festival, 219
Shubert Foundation, 28
Simon, John, 205n
singing exercises, 80–1, 214, 215
Sklar, Roberta, 18, 23, 112, 134, 140, 142, 149–50, 154–5, 158, 160, 189, 218, 219
social masks, 8–10, 44, 87
social myths, 9, 44, 45
social responsibility of theater, 1, 41
Soho News, 184
somatic (outside-in) approaches, 16, 54–6, 67, 83–6, 215
Sontag, Susan, 109, 118–19
Sophocles, 101; *Antigone*, 30, 65n, 102, 188, 212, 224–5
sound and movement exercises, 83–6, 105, 210
sound summary exercises, 92
Space for Innovative Development, 23, 219, 220
Spielberg, David, 227
Spolin, Viola, 10, 72, 74, 90
Stanley, Charles, 102, 190n
Stewart, Ellen, *see* LaMama
Stoltenberg, John, 149
stop/start exercises, 92
storytelling exercises, 79–80, 86, 100, 214, 218
Stratford Festival Theater, Ontario, Canada, 225
Strindberg, August, 4
Swados, Elizabeth, *Runaways*, 209
Switzerland, performances in, 137, 217, 218, 220

Talking Band, 27
Taper Forum, Mark, Los Angeles, Calif., 224
Tavel, Ron, 28
television, 3, 11, 38, 40, 41, 59, 62, 87
Terminal, 20–2, 43, 50, 76, 82, 93, 101,

102, 117n, 145, 147, 164–5, 170, 171, 218–20
Terry, Megan, 17, 18, 23, 91, 100, 214, 215, 220, 227; *Keep Tightly Closed in a Cool Dry Place*, 18; *The Serpent*, 111, 116; *Viet Rock*, 18, 63, 76, 185, 216
Theater for Ideas, 215
Theatre for the New City, 27
Theatre of Latin America, 221
Thie, Sharon, 100, 227
Tongues, 30, 31, 34, 64, 65n, 98, 107, 171–9, 183–4, 197, 206, 211, 212, 222, 223, 224
Tourists and Refugees (and *Tourists and Refugees No. 2*), 35–6, 43, 48–9, 65n, 79, 80, 83, 85, 87, 89, 94, 97, 98, 224
Transcendentalism, 5
Transformation exercises, 18, 90–1, 106, 214, 215
Trespassing, 36, 65n, 97, 102–3, 224
"Trial" improvisations, 215
trust exercises, 73, 215

Unger, Lois, 227
unnoticed action exercises, 88–9, 215
US (*Tell Me Lies*), 216

van Itallie, Jean-Claude, 17, 23, 87, 88, 90–1, 100, 105–6, 145, 214, 215, 220; *America Hurrah*, 18, 23, 62–3, 107, 134, 165, 185–6, 216, 217; *A Fable Telling about a Journey*, 29; *The Sea Gull*, 221 (*see also* Chekhov, *The Sea Gull*); *The Serpent*, 19, 111, 116, 120, 125–7, 131–3, 134, 137, 138, 147
Vann, Barbara, 107n, 129, 227
Variation on a Clifford Odets Theme, see "Odets" inside/outside improvisations
Vassar College, 212
Venezuela, performances in, *see* Caracas Theater Festival
Vernon Rice Award, 25, 218

Vietnam war, 4, 41, 44, 216
Village Gate, 217
Village Voice, 211; *see also* Munk, Erika; Obie awards; Sainer, Arthur

Walden, Stanley, 119n, 131
Walter, Sydney Shubert, 227
Washington Square Methodist Church, 20, 218, 221
Washington Square Players, 2
Watt, Douglas, 205n
wattage exercises, 71
Westbeth Theater and [Westbeth] Exchange Theater, 30, 221
West Coast performances, 183–4, 224; *see also individual theaters*
Williams, William Carlos, 4, 11, 213
Wilson, Robert, 27, 209, 211
Winter project, 31–7, 43, 57, 67, 71, 79–85, 94, 96–8, 99, 102–3, 107, 142, 145, 148, 179, 182, 222–5
Woodruff, Robert, 173, 223
Wooster Group, *Rhode Island Trilogy*, 209
Working Theater, 101, 220–1
workshops, 14, 67–103, 214; *see also* Harlequin Players; Open Theater; Winter Project
"worlds" exercises, 94–6, 106, 110, 215
Worley, Lee, 17, 26, 86, 107, 127, 143, 227
Wright, Richard, *Black Boy*, 150, 160
Writers Stage Company, 215

Yankowitz, Susan, 20, 145–8, 218
Yeats, William Butler, *Calvary*, 213
Yugoslavia, performances in, 219

Zimet, Paul, 21, 23, 24, 30, 46, 58, 64, 80, 82, 88, 89, 94, 95, 107n, 129, 148n, 156–7, 160, 162–4, 169, 220, 224
Zuckerman, Ira, 227